WRITTEN PATHS TO HEALING

Education and Jungian Child Counseling

JOHN ALLAN
and
JUDI BERTOIA

Spring Publications, Inc.
Dallas, Texas

© 1992 by Spring Publications, Inc. All rights reserved
Published by Spring Publications, Inc.;
P.O. Box 222069; Dallas TX 75222
Printed in the United States of America on acidfree paper
Cover designed and produced by Margot McLean

Library of Congress Cataloging-in-Publication Data
Allan, John A. B. (John Alexander Bonnell), 1941–
Written paths to healing : education and Jungian child counseling
/ John Allan and Judi Bertoia.
p.   cm.
Includes bibliographical references.
ISBN 0–88214–350–6 (pbk.)
1. Composition (Language arts)—Therapeutic use.   2. English
language—Composition and exercises—Therapeutic use.   3. School
psychology.   4. Jung, C. G. (Carl Gustav), 1875–1961.   5. Children-
-Language.   I. Bertoia, Judi.   II. Title.
RJ505.C64A55   1992
618.92'89166–dc20   92–7531
                                                     CIP

Contents

PART IV: IMAGERY AND WRITING

List of Figures

List of Appendices

Acknowledgments

WE ARE INDEBTED to our colleagues and senior graduate students who have worked with us over the past ten years on many of the projects mentioned in this book. Our thanks go out to them and especially to Annette Carlson, Sandra Clark, Bev Gordon, Karen Green, Darlene Harris, Bob Hatton, Dean Smith, and Diane McRae. We are grateful to Robin Randel and Jim Smith who were especially encouraging during the early stages of much of this work. For their specific suggestions, we would also like to thank Suzanne Elliott for her ideas on letter writing, Linda Phillipson for her guidelines to writing fairy tales in the classroom, and Dorothy Watts for her guide to classroom cooperation.

We would like to express our appreciation to Gregg Furth whose teaching and insights were most valuable, especially for the symbolic material in fairy tales, and to Carol Martin for her work on serial storywriting.

Much of the material has been published in article format elsewhere. In one of the chapters, "Journal Writing as a Developmental Guidance Method," John Buttery was the first author. John, an inspirational former grade-seven teacher, devised very innovative and creative ways for using journal writing in language arts (see chapters one and three). In other chapters, Pat Dyck co-wrote "Improving School Climate" and "Vision Quest"; Eileen Anderson "Children and Their Crises"; Judith Nairne "Scapegoating"; Bonnie Field "The Inner Journey"; and Bill Brechin, "My Guardian Spirit."

Special thanks to Bay Gumboc and Lori Walker for the many hours of typing; Ed Montgomery for the fine photographic prints and Lyn Cowan and Mary Helen Sullivan for the editorial help. Also our appreciation to Dr. E. Edinger for permission to adapt his diagrams (figs. 1.1–1.8). For her patience in continuous proofreading, we thank Richelle Bertoia. Finally, we express our deep gratitude to all those students whose written and drawn material appears in these pages, for this is what gives life to the material. We especially want to thank Rebecca Ann Wojdak for permission to use her drawing on the front cover and Ramona Grewal for permission to use her drawing on the back cover.

Other acknowledgments include:

Journal Writing as a Developmental Guidance Method. Buttery, J., and Allan, J. (1981). *Canadian Counsellor* 15: 134–38. Copyright 1981 Canadian Journal of Counselling. Adapted with permission.

Improving School Climate through Cross Grade Interactions: An Example of Counselor–Teacher Collaboration. Allan, J., and Dyck, P. (1983). *Elementary School Guidance and Counseling.* Copyright 1983 American Association for Counseling and Development. Adapted with permission.

Children and Their Crises: A Classroom Guidance Approach. Allan J., and Anderson, E. (1986). *Elementary School Guidance and Counseling* 21: 143–49. Copyright 1986 American Association for Counseling and Development. Adapted with permission.

Resolution of Scapegoating through Classroom Discussions. Allan, J. (1981). *Elementary School Guidance and Counseling* 16: 121–32. Copyright 1981 American Association for Counseling and Development. Adapted with permission.

Transition: Childhood to Adolescence. Allan J., and Dyck, P. (1984). *Elementary School Guidance and Counseling* 18: 277–86. Copyright 1984 American Association for Counseling and Development. Adapted with permission.

My Guardian Spirit: A Guided Imagery Activity for Intermediate Students. Allan, J., and Brechin, W. (1988). *Holistic Education Review* 1 (3): 44–47. Copyright 1988 Holistic Education Review. Adapted with permission.

Part I

Rationale and Theory

Introduction

Jungian Approaches to School Counseling

In over twenty-five years of teaching and counseling in the schools and in child guidance clinics, we have found writing to be a very valuable therapeutic aid. We have seen many examples of how children and adolescents can transform some very negative emotions and painful experiences through the writing process. Not only are they able to bring about a change in their emotional well-being, but they often gain a new understanding of themselves and their world and are able to make substantive changes in their perceptions, cognitions, and behavior.

Over the years we have done many different types of writing projects with our students. This book is a collection of articles about these projects, each reflecting a different way of using writing in counseling and language development. These chapters are all based on activities that we have done in the school setting with students from kindergarten to grade twelve. Some involve working with students individually, some in special group counseling sessions, while many chapters are from writing sessions with regular students in the normal classroom setting. The activities involve journal writing, letter writing, dreams, fairy tales, problem-solving, sentence stems, and writing about issues such as crises, divorce, loss, approaching adolescence, leaving home, and scapegoating. In each of these situations we try to show how students heal themselves and to give examples from their work. Our tasks as counselors and teachers are to provide the environment ("the safe and protected place") and the structure (i.e., questions and open-ended formats) in which therapeutic writing can occur. Our experience is that, if we pick appropriate topics and formats, then usually most students are excited by the activities and begin writing quite quickly, producing some very meaningful work. We have titled the book *Written Paths to Healing* because we provided counselors, teachers, and students with diverse writing activities (or paths) which can lead to healing and to developing a rich reflective and interior life.

One purpose of this book is to show how we, as Jungian school counselors, use writing as a vehicle for self-growth. A central tenet in Jungian Psychology is the importance to an individual of maintaining a balance between inner and outer worlds—that is, the inner world of feelings, desires, and needs and the outer world of work, relationships, and community. Much of the curriculum in education has focused on memory and skill acquisition. To a great extent it has ignored the inner world of symbol, image, fantasy, and creativity. In this book we try to show ways of bringing together the inner and outer worlds in the life of the students while at school. We do this through various writing activities which provide students with a structure for commenting on their inner feelings, the demands of the outer world, and the struggle between the two realities.

It is the "struggle of opposites," between the desire to grow and the desire to regress, that is so central to Jung's ideas about growth and development. In order for transformation and development to occur, we must "work" with these utterly different impulses inside ourselves. That means we must look at and examine opposite and often painful experiences and emotions; we must safely "contain" the various impulses so they are not acted out in a destructive way to self or others. By doing this, an integration and transformation can occur which helps both inner and outer development. One safe place, or "temenos" as Jung called it, where conflicting thoughts, feelings, and actions can be safely expressed is on a piece of paper, in a journal or diary, or in a special notebook.

Overview of the Book

We have organized the material in this book under various themes. The first chapter explains key Jungian concepts and gives examples as they relate to the writing process. The first major section (Part II) consists of picture and writing journals, dream journals, and letter writing, and examples are given of programs for various age levels. Letter writing focuses on letters from the counselor to students, students to the counselor, letters to significant others, and the "unsent" letter.

Part III shows how classroom discussion activities on such important topics as crises, scapegoating, school social climate, and transition from childhood to adolescence can be enhanced by the writing process. The material presented here also shows how sentence stems and other brief written work can help children express their thoughts and feelings around such issues as divorce, loss, and classroom problems.

Part IV, Imagery and Writing, gives many examples of how guided imagery activities facilitate the deepening of the writing process and the connection between the conscious and unconscious mind. Topics are drawn from common archetypal themes that reside in the human psyche. These are the Journey, Fairy Tales, Healing, and the Guardian Spirit.

Chapter 1

JUNGIAN THEORY AND PRACTICE

IN THIS CHAPTER we wish to address some of the reasons why writing heals and why it is a valuable tool for teachers and counselors alike. As the theoretical basis of our work lies in the theory and practice of Analytical Psychology as developed by the Swiss psychotherapist C. G. Jung, we will start with an overview of some of his understandings on development and human nature. This will be followed by excerpts from students' writings which illustrate aspects of his theory.

Some Principles from Analytical Psychology

Archetypes. To Jung (1970), the development of the human psyche parallels that of the physical body: just as our bodies have evolved over three million years, so have our psyches. Just as the body developed survival mechanisms, so did the psyche develop ways of perceiving and responding that facilitate growth. He calls these innate mechanisms of perceiving and responding *archetypes.* The key or central organizing principle he called the "archetype of the Self." It is this component that strives to grow and to make or seek meaning out of our existence. It is the inherited part of the psyche that links body to psyche and instinct with image. To Jung the archetypal realm is not subservient to the biological drives, but rather the image guides the instinct toward satisfaction. The archetypal world manifests itself through fantasies and dreams and is recognizable "around the basic and universal experiences of life such as birth, marriage, motherhood, death and separation" (Samuels, Shorter, and Plaut, 1986, p. 26).

The archetype of the Self is essentially an innate, unconscious psychological structure that orchestrates psychological growth and development. At birth the ego, the center of consciousness in Jungian terms, is embedded in the archetypal unconscious matrix and is present in a weak and undifferentiated form (fig. 1.1). To Jungians, the

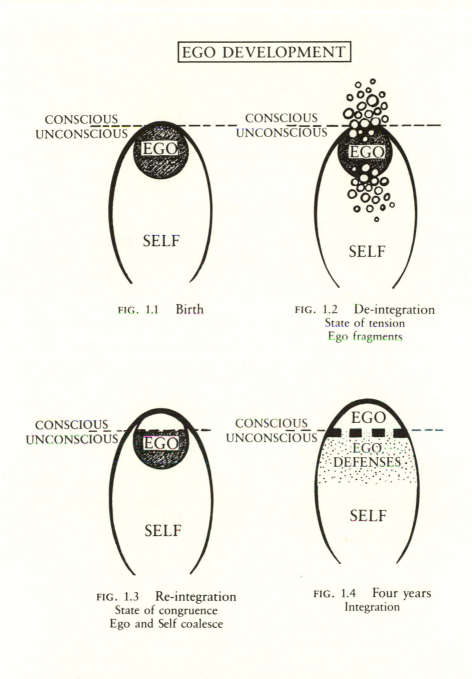

EGO DEVELOPMENT

CONSCIOUS
UNCONSCIOUS

EGO

SELF

FIG. 1.1   Birth

CONSCIOUS
UNCONSCIOUS

EGO

SELF

FIG. 1.2   De-integration
State of tension
Ego fragments

CONSCIOUS
UNCONSCIOUS

EGO

SELF

FIG. 1.3   Re-integration
State of congruence
Ego and Self coalesce

CONSCIOUS
UNCONSCIOUS

EGO

EGO
DEFENSES

SELF

FIG. 1.4   Four years
Integration

Figures 1.1–1.8 are adapted from E. Edinger, *Ego and Archetype* (Baltimore: Penguin Books, 1974), p. 5. By permission of Dr. E. Edinger.

ego slowly emerges out of the matrix of unconscious or archetypal life to establish its own existence and to allow the infant more conscious control over his or her actions.

The Ego. Fordham (1957), a London Jungian analyst, postulates that the ego is built up slowly by repeated processes of "de-integration and re-integration" in the first year of life. For example, frustration, pain, and hunger cause a breaking up of psychic structures, "de-integration" (fig. 1.2), whereas a good feed, pleasurable holding, and sleep restore psychic equilibrium, "re-integration" (fig. 1.3), and lay the foundation for healthy ego development.

The ego is a central tenet in Jungian psychology because ego, as a psychological structure, has the job of mediating between inner drives and the reality of the outer world. From a Jungian perspective, there is quite a sophisticated ego structure in place by one year. However, it is usually not until the third or fourth year of life (fig. 1.4) that more durable internal security is experienced which leads to independent functioning and more effective regulation of impulses (Kalff, 1980; Neumann, 1955). Though ego is the center of consciousness, there is always some overlap between the two zones (conscious and unconscious life), as aspects of ego are clearly seen to function during sleep and dream time.

In children's drawings and stories, the unconscious is often depicted as the sea and the ego as the land. When children are overwhelmed by strong emotions, the ego may be assigned to the image of a "log" or "boat" that is being battered or tossed around on the stormy sea. As the children begin to calm down and integrate painful emotions, "islands" appear in the stories and are often followed by themes that take place on "land." This can represent the developing and strengthening of ego functions. The students have become more "grounded."

Ego Defenses. In certain respects, the ego is a very fragile structure which in infancy and early childhood becomes threatened quite easily. In order to protect itself, it has at its disposal various defensive mechanisms. Some of these are biological, as in dorsal arching, tonic neck, and mass reflexes; whereas others are psychological, as in hallucinations, repression, projection, and in the splitting of "good" and "bad." As one can imagine, the process of "de-integration" mentioned above is not always followed with successful re-integration processes where calming, food, and pleasure are provided by caring adults.

When this negative pattern of "de-integration" occurs too frequently, anxiety is high, psychic energy goes into building up rigid defense mechanisms (such as denial, paranoia), and the individual learns to avoid pain through flight behaviors. Little energy then is left for growth, learning, and the development of ego. The pain, hurt, and aggression (both internal and external) are so great that ego cannot integrate or handle these powerful emotions and so must defend itself against them or be annihilated or overwhelmed.

In our school-aged children we commonly see two major patterns of defensive structures—either very rigid or seemingly non-existent. In the former, the barrier between the conscious (Ego) and the unconscious (Self) systems is very rigid and thick. These children tend to be very controlled, somewhat aloof or detached, and emotionally flat (fig. 1.5), though given to extreme outbursts of violence and temper when their defenses are threatened or disintegrate. However, with some other children it is as if they have no inner control and very poor defensive structure. These children tend to be hyperkinetic, impulsive, and undersocialized, and the boundary between the conscious and unconscious worlds is so thin that few impulses can be held in check (fig. 1.6). In contrast, the healthy coping child shows a wide range of emotion and demonstrates both appropriate control and flexibility; that is, the child is able to hold some emotions in check, express others, and also focus his or her attention on learning, friendships, and on successfully completing various academic and social tasks (fig. 1.7).

Ego–Self Axis. Healthy emotional development occurs when there is a good relationship and connection between the unconscious (Self) and the conscious (Ego) mind. This occurs when the child's ego can handle pain and pleasure appropriately, that is, by sobbing when hurt, by verbalizing feelings when angry, by turning to parents and teachers for help, and by taking in pleasure and experiencing love, affection, laughter, and humor. For healthy emotional development, ego (consciousness) needs to look at painful experiences, feel the pain, understand the situation, and then let go and move forward. Jung likens the development of ego, throughout life, to a heroic struggle. Every now and again the ego needs to be replenished. This replenishment can happen in many ways—through satisfying relationships, positive experiences, sleep and dreams, relaxation, and artistic and creative endeavors. In these experiences there is often an alignment of the Ego–Self axis, or a coming together of the conscious and unconscious life. This would be similar to a state of con-

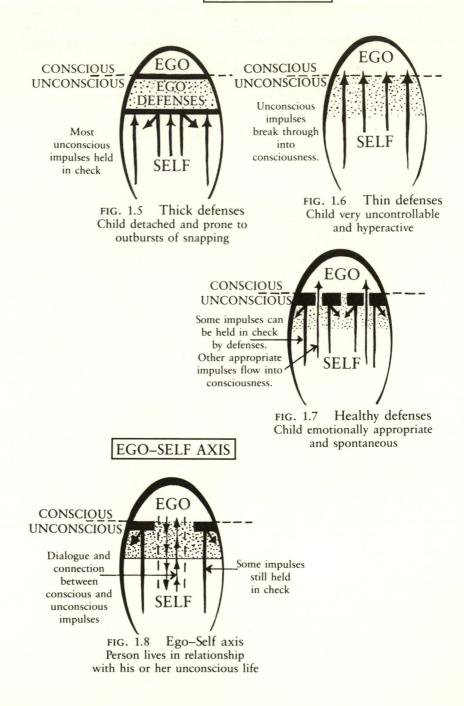

EGO DEFENSES

FIG. 1.5   Thick defenses
Child detached and prone to
outbursts of snapping

FIG. 1.6   Thin defenses
Child very uncontrollable
and hyperactive

FIG. 1.7   Healthy defenses
Child emotionally appropriate
and spontaneous

EGO–SELF AXIS

FIG. 1.8   Ego–Self axis
Person lives in relationship
with his or her unconscious life

gruence (Rogers, 1967). This connected flow between the conscious and unconscious life has been termed the Ego–Self axis (Edinger, 1973). This is very much an "on again–off again" experience throughout our lives. We will achieve this connection, lose it, and, if we take our interior life seriously, gain it, time and time again (fig. 1.8).

In our work, as exemplified in this book, we try to set up structures in the school system which facilitate ego development and improve the lines of communication between the conscious and unconscious worlds so that difficult emotions can be integrated into consciousness and pleasure, joy, relaxation, and creativity can come into play. For example, writing allows the ego to integrate and transform emotional pain, and the relaxation and imagery exercises allow for inner experiences of warmth, lightness, and creative play. Often the written work produced after such experiences brings forth in the child feelings of competency, success, and wonder. These experiences enable life to be lived at a greater depth and with more integration of a wide range of emotional experiences, thus building up a rich interior life. Here is an example of the establishment of the Ego–Self axis in an eight-year-old boy's story.

THE WHALE

Once upon a time there was a whale who loved to whistle. He didn't have any friends but humans. One night he heard the humans talking about the whale. They were saying that they would like some coral from underneath the sea, but nobody could go underneath. So they decided to go and ask the whale to go and get some. The next morning there was coral on the bay. The whale put the coral there for the humans. The humans danced with joy. They hugged the whale.

This spontaneous story from a boy who was just finishing treatment reflects his newly established Ego–Self axis. There is a beneficial connection between the humans (i.e., ego consciousness) and underneath the sea (i.e., the unconscious). The "whale," a Self symbol, is the intermediary who travels up and down the Ego–Self axis "listening" to consciousness and who brings the riches in the unconscious ("the coral") up into consciousness ("on the bay"), which results in much joyousness (dancing and hugging).

Drive. The central drive in Jung's thought is not sexual libido as stated in Freud's work but the desire to grow, unfold, relate, and

to establish a separate identity. He calls this the individuation process. The individuation process is to Jung (1964) the most central
drive in the human psyche. It will change its expression slightly according to the developmental task or stage of development of the
individual. This individuation process gains its energy or drive from
the "struggle of opposites" that occurs within us on a continuous
basis. To Jung, it is the ability to work with this "tension of opposites" that leads to the resolution of difficulties and the creation
of something new. Often characterized by a rhythm of chaos, struggle, and resolution, this process is one that repeats itself continuously
throughout our life cycle if we work on developing both our inner
and outer lives. To Jung, it is the act of doing, making, or symbolizing
inner impulses that facilitates both inner and outer growth and the
individuation process. Work, and especially "work on or with oneself," can bring about this change, growth, and maturity. Part of this
work is done by the ego as it strives to integrate and understand
painful feelings.

The Language of the Psyche. The first language of the infant is
essentially an auditory visual language. Though infants connect to
the outer world of caretakers by cries, utterances, and vocalizations,
they also take in the world visually, and what they see slowly becomes
imbued with emotion and ultimately with meaning. Structures within
the psyche help the infant organize perceptions and responses on
an unconscious basis. In childhood, meaning is often attached to
such primary emotions as love, joy, and pleasure and takes on the
characteristic of "the good," while anger, frustration, pain, fear
become characterized as "the bad." The young child tends to see and
incorporate the world in pictures, pictures characterized by emotion
or affect, which in turn tend to become images and symbols. This
visual language has primacy for the first year to year and a half of
life until verbal communication begins to develop and to gain ascend-
ancy over the visual mode as a cognitive processing structure. With
development, verbal language pushes visual language into second
place, just below the level of awareness, where it still operates, though
usually unnoticed unless the person consciously turns to it. For example, as adults we can close our eyes and let ourselves imagine.
Also, when we go to sleep at night and when we dream, we revert
once again to the primary visual language.

To Jung, dreams are not meaningless but rather are the language
of the archetype of the Self. They are the vehicle through which this

central organizing principle orchestrates our interior life, attempting to finish the unfinished business of the day, heal wounds and traumas, meet unmet needs, and restore the sense of wholeness. We mention this language in some detail because when counseling from a Jungian framework one needs to be aware of symbolic language, how to understand it and how to use it for healing. We give several examples in the book of how to work with dreams, how to use relaxation and guided imagery to stimulate the creative writing process, and how to link writing with thinking and feeling.

Psyche as Nature. To Jung the human psyche is like Nature. It is in a process of constant evolution and periodically goes through periods of death and rebirth, of accelerated growth and diminishing growth, just like the seasons of fall, winter, spring, and summer. The psyche carries within itself regenerative and self-healing abilities which can become activated in times of crisis or stress when a person turns inward to listen to his or her dreams or meets someone he or she perceives as a helper. By turning inward, we refer to the act of taking one's inner life seriously and struggling or working to improve oneself. While this can be any number of endeavors, in this book we are specifically referring to the act of writing and recording various aspects of one's life such as one's dreams, fantasies, feelings, and desires.

This process of activation of the healing potential also occurs when a child meets and works with a caring and understanding teacher or counselor. When this adult creates a space and time—that is, joins the child for a specific time in a designated place—and encourages the student's safe expression of her inner processes (i.e., thoughts, feelings, and fantasies), the healing process begins. Once the healing potential of the psyche is "fired" or activated, the archetype of the Self takes the child to where she or he needs to go. Often this will first be to areas of wounding, pain, or confusion. In psychological jargon we would call this "unfinished business"—emotional pain or trauma that the ego (the conscious mind) first repressed and has not yet had a chance to assimilate. Getting this material out by talking, writing, or painting allows the pain to be slowly assimilated into consciousness (the ego) and finally understood. At this point, it can be "laid to rest," and new material or new growth can occur.

Teleological Point of View. To Jung the psyche is in a constant stage of evolution; it is growing, unfolding, and trying to move forward, through the various stages of life, to development, maturity, and acceptance of death. Jungian counselors try to take their sense of direction from the unfolding of the child's world through image, symbol, metaphor, play, and writing. Jung was not so much concerned with causes of the problems as he was with where the client's images and metaphors would lead. He believed the unconscious mind (the archetype of the Self) is purposeful and that, if one (client or counselor) follows its natural expression in symbolic form, then much learning and growth can occur.

In this section we have tried to describe key concepts from the Analytical Psychology of C. G. Jung. As some may seem a little esoteric or hard to ground in the outer reality of children and schools, we will next illustrate the concepts with stories or written material from students.

Examples

Metaphorical and Symbolic Language

The language of the Self, or primary process language as it is sometimes called, and how it weaves and interacts with more concrete verbal language (language of the ego) are clearly seen in the example given below.

In a classroom of twenty kindergarten children, an experienced teacher, who is learning some Jungian principles, conducts a class discussion on fear (Allan and Nairne, 1989). Many children contribute by telling what frightens them and elaborate with their stories about fearful experiences. In the middle of this, one girl, Millie, five years old, starts her story:

> One time when I was at my old house, a babysitter was with me and she was in the bathroom and someone knocked at the door and I said, "Come in," and instead of my dad it was a monster. I jumped out of the window. I felt scary. I ran around. I took my bike out the window with me, I ride it really fast, and you know what, he slipped over a car, and you know what happened again? Another monster came, and he was a giant one. And he ran fast but he couldn't catch me. So, he got runned over too, and then ANOTHER one, and he was a bigger one, and he catched up to me and he—the police came, because he had a gun, the monster,

and the police heard shooting so he came and took the monster away. He took him to jail. He took the mask off and guess who it was? My dad. And I asked him why he was trying to scare me. He said he forgot why. I felt funny inside me and then we both went back to my old house. (Allan, 1988, pp. 15–16)

Notice how the story starts off on the ego level of language (concrete and realistic) and quite quickly moves to the Self level (i.e., metaphorical and symbolic) when she says: "Instead of my dad it was a monster. I jumped out of the window. . . . I took my bike . . . with me." Later she adds: "The police heard shooting so he came and took the monster away. He took him to jail. He took the mask off and guess who it was? My dad. And I asked him why he was trying to scare me." In the painting activities that followed, Millie used a lot of red and said: "When I opened the door, it was a ghost like that with lots of blood running down."

Why would a child produce a story like that? What meaning does it have? One must bear in mind the context. This story was produced during a class discussion on fear in the presence of a very empathic and skillful teacher. Here is the special and protected setting, and the child goes to where she needs to go—to some trauma that was fixed in her psyche and not clearly understood or resolved.

At first we had no idea what it meant or what it was about, so the teacher talked with the mother. Three years earlier, when the child was two years old, she had witnessed her drunk father shoot and wound her mother. There was blood, and the police had taken the father to jail. The child had seen this, and the experience had been absorbed by her and had fixated itself in her mind. She was stuck, too, with a puzzle: how to reconcile the "good" and "bad" aspects of her father. The violence traumatized and scared her, and when she had the opportunity (the discussion and the storytelling), her psyche took her back to that scene to externalize it and to rework it. This occurred through storytelling, the painting activity, and the follow-up discussions with her teacher and mother (Allan, 1988).

Dreams

Like creative stories, dreams use the language of image and symbol to express psychological conflicts, struggles, wishes, and desires. Because they use a different language structure than waking life (ego), dreams are at first difficult to understand. However, writing them in a certain format allows their meaning, and hence message from the world of emotions, to be more clearly understood. During a class journal writing period (Buttery, 1980), a seventh-grade girl related a recent nightmare. She found the whole dream very frightening and confusing. The teacher suggested she write the dream down, draw a line underneath it, and then add an interpretation which would start something like this: "I think this dream means. . . ." The girl proceeded to do this and was amazed how an interpretation revealed itself through the writing process.

SANDRA SMITH SO DEAD!

Last night I had a dream it was about Sandra getting killed. We were driving along the road at top speed (you see we were older). Anyway we were going to Hollywood, and I was Sandra's producer and she was a dancer and singer. We were almost there and we ran out of gas. "Oh, we're going to be late for the show." Then Sandra said, "Well I'll run to the nearest gas station with the water jug and I'll be back in about half an hour." "O.K., see you later," said I. I waited for about an hour and a half. Finally I got out and went to find her. In front of the gas station, I saw gas pouring on her head and it was all burnt up. I nearly puked all over, it was really ugly. I wonder who could have done such a dumb thing. Then I woke up.

WHAT I THINK ABOUT THIS DREAM?

I think that this journal means that when Sandra punches me during Math and I get huge bruises, I really get mad and could just kill her. So I guess I was thinking about her punching me and somebody else killed her for me. I didn't cry in my dream so I guess I wasn't too sad that she got killed for punching me. This is what I think the journal means.

The writing out of this dream illustrates a number of points. The girl recorded a situation that was both frightening and confusing to her: in the dream her repressed rage surfaced and was projected onto Sandra as fire. The recalling and retelling of the dream in written form seemed both to calm her and to give her some clues as to what it might mean. Having the structure *My Interpretation* immediately after the writing of the dream seemed to help her evolve her own understanding of what the dream (her unconscious) was trying to communicate to her: namely, that she was mad at Sandra for bugging her in math class and that she felt hopeless to do anything about it. Writing itself is an assertive act (i.e., it takes an outflowing of energy to write) and one that can turn feelings of hopelessness into awareness and the possibility of action.

In the above situation, the teacher or counselor can meet privately with the student after the class and can work on the story with her. The purpose is to find out what really occurred and to help the student find a better way to handle her feelings. For example, the teacher could say:

> What stopped you telling Sandra that you were mad at her for punching you? . . . Were you afraid that if you told her you might lose her friendship? . . . The next time she bugs you, what would you like to say to her? If the student does not come up with an appropriate response, the teacher could model another statement: "Sandra, I don't like it when you hit me. It makes me mad at you. Can you stop it?"

Teleological Point of View

Writing, because it allows for a flow or stream of consciousness to occur, often demonstrates the opening or unfolding of images, ideas, and thoughts. This next example, which came out of a class discussion on crises (Allan and Nairne, 1989), clearly shows this process. In class discussions students talk about a variety of issues and then write about an experience that is central to them. A ninth grader wrote:

> A friend brought a smoke to school and offered me a drag. I said no right away. I considered it all day. It seemed so harmless so I said I would have just one drag. Once I did, I kept wanting more. We'd skip out at lunch and go back to some bushes to smoke. A grade twelve kid came with us sometimes. He always wanted to touch you in private places but I didn't want him to. Since he knew where we went at lunch, he'd come all the time. He'd even take his clothes off and want us to touch him. I didn't want to hang around these kids any more so I quit smoking and stayed with my real friends. I wrote about smoking in my diary and my mom

saw it. I was really upset. I told her that I had quit a week or so earlier and I wasn't hanging around with that girl any more. Of course, she told my dad. They treated me like an outsider and never trusted me. My dad always said cruel things to me that were totally unnecessary and made rude jokes. I got so mad at times that I didn't want to live any more. I considered running away and killing myself. I didn't though, because I knew even if they didn't act like it, my parents loved me and would be more hurt. I realize now how they must have felt and I never want to hurt them again.

This story illustrates the evolution and movement through various layers of problems and issues, from minor issues down to the most painful feelings, thoughts, and actions. She starts off with a disclosure about smoking and her struggle with it and then reveals an experience of possible sexual harassment. This leads into disclosing a parental violation (i.e., mother reading her diary) and her struggle with her dad. At this point she slips into painful affect (anger), suicidal thinking, and desperate solutions to relieve herself of the pain (i.e., running away). In containing these feelings (i.e., expressing them on paper), there is a form of transformation happening that enables her to move from her own frame of reference to an understanding of others (her parents). Another way of phrasing this is that she makes a cognitive shift from self to other that lets her see and care about another point of view: "I didn't [kill myself] though, because I knew even if they didn't act like it, my parents loved me and would be more hurt."

Transformation of Feeling and Thinking

The process of writing allows for a time of reflection about our inner world and for the opportunity to work through or transform difficult emotions and painful thoughts. Parental divorce is a common crisis for our youngsters. They seldom desire it, and it tends to shatter the archetypal image of the family—mother, father, and children together as a unit. As this next example illustrates, writing provided this teenage girl with the opportunity to record, in some depth, her feelings about her parents' divorce and then to change her own perception of its cause. The story is typical of many problem situations where normal egocentric thinking results in self-blame and an inability to hear another point of view (i.e., that of the mother). Notice how her emotional tension builds up to the point where she "had to" talk with her parents and how at that moment she can "hear" what they say and change her thinking so that she does not blame herself. This is a major step forward in her psychological development:

> When my parents decided to get a divorce I thought it was all my fault. My mother kept telling me it wasn't but still I thought I could have done something that would make them not want to be together any more. Maybe because I was born. The other night, I heard them having an argument because I didn't clear the table well. That's what I thought. My mother said she didn't want me with her, neither did my dad. I thought of running away but I knew it wouldn't help. I had to talk to them and ask why they were getting a divorce. That evening I talked to them and they said it's because they didn't love each other any more but they still loved me and wanted me to live with each of them. I finally realized it was not my fault.

This transformation of feeling and thinking is very common when students are given the opportunity to write. In the following chapters we will give many more examples of this process occurring through a variety of writing activities.

Writing as part of the counseling process fits very naturally into the school setting because so much of the academic curriculum involves written activities. Written work is a routine, daily occurrence in schools, and children find these activities normalizing; it is the "stuff" kids do at school. For those with initial reservations about working with a counselor, this familiarity can be helpful. It facilitates explanations to peers because general statements such as "Oh, we work on my journal" or "We write letters" are honest responses to queries about what they do in the counseling sessions. Written activities flow readily, especially if minimal attention is paid to spelling and grammar. The comfort thus established is carried over to other activities when the content of the written work becomes more sensitive in counseling and when curriculum requirements in the classroom are connected in writing.

Writing, at the time of need and even without the presence of the counselor, provides the child with an opportunity to externalize the pain and its images. Although the relief may not be as extensive as if a counseling session had occurred, the child does often experience an easing of the burdens by writing out problems.

Although the preferred approach for counseling is the therapeutic relationship between two people, one of the basic components of the process, the concept of a container, can be extended to written activities. Just as the therapeutic relationship provides a safe and protected environment or space in which to work on issues, the piece of paper, too, can be a secure container which allows for the transformation of painful aspects of life.

The activities included in this book have been successfully used with students in the school setting. They have received positive responses from students, who in fact often found them a highlight of their academic experience. Parents and teachers commented on changes of attitude or behavior in the children, at times small ones and at times very noticeable ones. Students even made contact with us months—and even some years—later, indicating the value of the writing to them.

Implementing Successful Writing Programs

In order for counselors to successfully implement the various writing programs we describe, careful preparation needs to occur. There are certain principles that the counselors themselves need to understand, and often preparatory work has to be done with teachers, students, and principals. Sometimes parents need to be informed and their permission given for special writing assignments that differ significantly from regular in-class school work. Since some writing topics deal with very sensitive psychological material, various precautions must be taken to protect the integrity of the work and the feelings of the writer. If violations occur (such as reading another student's "private journal"), and they will, then the counselor must know how to turn such incidents into positive learning experiences for all participants.

Counselors. Probably the most important condition for counselors implementing these programs is that they themselves have a belief in the value of writing and use writing as one means for working on their own inner development. In certain ways it is unethical to ask children to write and work on developing their inner life if the person asking does not pursue a similar course. Jung (1966) points out that, because of unconscious transference and countertransference issues, the richer the inner life of the counselor, the richer the creative development and growth of the students can be.

Key abilities of the counselor are to know what specific writing task to request of a child and how to make the writing experience profitable. Success usually occurs when the writing task has meaning and pleasure for the child and when she feels challenged by the task and wants to do it. For example, an eleven-year-old boy was referred to the counselor for throwing massive temper tantrums. The counselor saw the child individually, worked with some of the underlying feelings and issues, and then asked him to write, as homework, two imaginative stories: "The boy who threw king-sized temper tantrums" and "The boy who got himself out of a temper tantrum." If the counselor has good rapport with the child and is accurately reading the situation, a child usually shows very little resistance to the writing activity. The counselor tries to take his or her direction or suggestion from what emotions or struggles are relevant to the student at that particular moment of development. In the above case, the student enjoyed writing about all the "terrible things he did" and gained a sense of release, but he also came up with a way to get out of a tantrum when he was in one. He was then able to role play and practice this in the next session.

The issue of meaning has special relevance when the counselor is working with the whole class. Because there are always many emotional and development issues facing children, it is not that difficult to generate pertinent topics for the students. However, because of tight curriculum demands, in order to satisfy the teachers, principal, and parents, the counselor must make sure the topics he or she selects have relevance to the guidance, language arts, health, or social science curriculum. Thus, goals and objectives need to be clearly spelled out (Allan and Dyck, 1984; Allan and Dyck, 1985).

Teachers. Much of the writing work we do in the schools tends to occur in conjunction with the teachers. Usually, teachers come to us with specific problems and concerns. Some of these issues are topics like "My kids are afraid of transition to junior high school, We have a problem with scapegoating, My kids don't seem to enjoy writing stories." We then consult with the teachers to find ways to overcome these problems—checking out our ideas with them and striving for agreement on how to proceed. If it is a new way of writing (like guided imagery or problem-solving), we tend to model and demonstrate the method while the teacher sits in the class and observes. This gives the teacher and counselor a chance to debrief afterward and to identify what worked or did not work and what should be done next time to improve or enrich the program. In this way, the counselor models a particular style of working with a class as a whole. In these discussions and imagery writing formats, the counselor is trying to provide a structure or container in which a style of writing can occur which brings about a transformation of emotion and a change in perception, cognition, and behavior.

Sometimes teachers need to be reminded that the function of this approach to writing is to help students externalize and amplify inner thoughts and images. When students seek direction by asking, "What should I write about?", one can respond by saying something like: "What idea comes to you? What were you sort-of-thinking about? If you had an uncommon or strange idea, write about that." Teachers need to know that a small volume of student writing is acceptable at first if that is all the student can think about or is willing to do. In response to this, the teacher can add phrases which will help the student amplify a theme that is embedded in the brief paragraph. For example, "What happens next? What was the man thinking about? What did she do? How did the dog feel?"

Students. Just as the teachers might need some preparation for this style of writing, so will the students. They need to be told that they are going to be asked to write from the "inside to the outside," that they are going to have the chance to put down on paper their inner thoughts and feelings and use them as a source of creativity. We feel that the "creative person" inside of them is special and valuable and needs a place to be heard, seen, and expressed. This person is often first noticed in dreams, daydreams, and fantasies, and in order to help this part of them come out the teacher will use relaxation exercises and guided imagery activities (see Part Three). The students need to know that whatever comes out of their minds is acceptable, even if it seems a little unusual. They must expect that at times they might find it hard to get started or that what they want to say is frightening, but it is important to put it down and the teacher will respect the writing and keep it private. Students will also need to know what will happen to their finished products.

Principals. Principals need to be kept informed if any of the writing activities seem unusual (i.e., writing fairy tales) or deal with highly political or controversial issues (i.e., scapegoating). Counselors need to spend time with some principals talking about the value of inner world development, which also includes talking and writing about dreams and the use of guided imagery to stimulate creativity. Likewise, if small group formats are used and parent permission requested, then principals must be made aware of this. As in many school counseling activities, counselors need to work closely with the principals for maximum effectiveness of the programs.

Parents. If any of the counseling activities require the children to be seen individually or in small groups, then parent permission must be obtained. Some school districts require signed parent consent forms before a child can be seen on a regular basis. When talking with the parents, counselors need to give a brief explanation of the activity and what it is intended to do. Also, the parents need to be informed of the number of sessions, duration and times of each session, and what provisions are made for the child to catch up on missed school work. Mention also needs to be made of planned follow-up activities, telephone calls to check on progress, and issues of privacy. Parents need to know that the sessions are confidential but that, if life-threatening or dangerous issues are revealed, they would be contacted. Parents need to feel that the counselor has their interests and concerns at heart too.

Part II

JOURNALS AND LETTERS

Chapter 2

PICTURE AND WRITING JOURNALS:
A JUNGIAN APPROACH

IN THE DEVELOPMENT of our species, visual language precedes the acquisition of verbal skills: we see, look, and dream well before we talk. Indeed, some would argue that we understand and think on a visual level before we understand on a conscious, cognitive level. Later, when children enter kindergarten and the primary grades, they still express their perceptions and views of the world better graphically through drawing pictures than with the provided or written word.

Many primary teachers use "picture journals" or "picture diaries" as a means of helping their young students record aspects of their lives, giving them the opportunity to reflect on what is important and meaningful to them. In our work we distinguish between diaries, a recording of chronological events usually intended to remain private, and journals, a commentary on personal events, thoughts, and feelings frequently intended to be shared in some way. For their journals most teachers provide the children with small booklets (7¼-by-9-inch) in which the top half of the page is blank and the bottom half is lined, enabling students to draw and add words or sentences.

These journals then become very important vehicles for developing children's expressive skills, for both visual and verbal languages, and for developing and maintaining a rich interior life. As many teachers notice, these journals often provide a window into the child's soul. From a counseling perspective, these journals also offer a means of communication in which students indirectly tell the teacher about their lives and how they are surviving in the world. At times teachers become frightened and concerned by the images the children draw and by their written statements. The material could indicate sexual abuse, physical abuse, violence, depression, fear, fixation, or trauma. The teacher senses something important or fearful is being communicated but is not sure what the child means or how to respond to either the picture or the words. Many questions are raised in her mind: "Should she comment on what she sees? If so, what should she say or write? What should she do when the child keeps coloring the page in black or drawing violent pictures?" Often it is at this point that the teacher will turn to the counselor for help.

In this chapter, we will describe the theoretical basis for using journals in a school setting and briefly explain how a journal program can be established. We will also describe some of the problems teachers encounter and ways we have been able to help them. Frequently, this help consists of giving the teacher some empathic statements to say to the students, which, in turn, will help them move through blocked, trapped, or fearful material to a clearer understanding or to a direct verbal disclosure of painful incidents in their lives. We have found that counselors are in a position to help teachers understand the symbolic nature of these verbal and pictorial forms of communication. At times this understanding can allow the teacher to assist the children to move forward through certain emotional difficulties so that an actual referral to the counselor may be unnecessary.

Theoretical Basis

As Jungian counselors working in the public school system, we have a particular belief about how picture-writing journals can best be used. Because much of the structured learning time in schools focuses on the outer world, on the learning and mastery of new words, skills, and concepts supplied by teacher instruction, we feel that journal time should be the place where the child's inner world can be expressed. The task of the teacher in this situation is to provide the structure which enables the children to express or "work on" their inner worlds of feeling, images, and thoughts. The journal becomes the place where the children's experiences can be expressed, made concrete, and allowed to unfold at their own pace. In this way children can remain in contact with their inner world and continue to develop an interior life. The role of the counselor in this program is to act as a support and guide to teachers who need help in implementing this model and in working with some of the pictorial and written material that children produce from deep inside themselves.

Journal time gives students a chance to reflect on their lives and to draw, write, and think about what is important to them. Teachers should always bear this principle in mind, especially when children get stuck and ask for help because they "don't have anything to draw or say." The teachers must focus on ways of helping the children get in touch with the inner world or working with their resistances and barriers so they can express themselves on paper. For example, the teacher can say: "Yes, sometimes it is hard to know what to draw or write. Can you put your arms and head on the desk and let your mind wander? Where do you go to? What do you see?" Another approach is to ask the child to record a dream. The teacher should not then have students use their journals for writing about a science or socials project but rather should focus back into the child's inner experience.

In psychology, we have the concept of "true" and "false" self, and many problems occur later in life when the person identifies too rigidly with the false self or inflexible persona. The journal is one way to keep this inner connection with the "true self" alive. In some children, difficulties arrive with drawing or writing because they have already suppressed their true self or because they are overwhelmed with difficult, painful, or "unacceptable" thoughts, feelings, and images. Our argument, and experience, is that these difficult or painful thoughts and feelings can be transformed through the journal activity—sometimes just by the child working alone and sometimes with the right intervention, direction, or instruction by the teacher.

Time and Space Variables

Journal drawing and writing can become successful vehicles for inner and outer development when used within certain parameters and structures. Jung (1961) saw inner development as being facilitated when psychological material is given a safe and protected space within which to unfold. In our case, this occurs when a particular time is set aside on a regular basis to do the journal "work." Here the "safe and protected space" is not only the classroom and the "quiet" journal time but also the journal booklet which becomes the container or "temenos" where images, feelings, and thoughts are projected onto the white pages and blank lines. Here psychological themes can be expressed and can have the opportunity to unfold over time.

The regularity of the program is important: many teachers sense this and try to establish an identifiable time pattern and rhythm. Some conduct journal time every day of the week for ten to fifteen minutes, others just twice a week. Most teachers try to be consistent with the time: first thing in the morning, after the morning recess, or after the lunch break. In some schools and classrooms first thing in the morning is seen as the most important and least interrupted time. Some teachers believe that the children have the most to say just after recess or lunch break when they can carry thoughts and feelings from playground activities with them into their journals. For some students the end of the school day is the most productive time because they can reflect on the day's activities in class.

The drawings and writings seem to encourage inner emotional and symbolic development. Because of the sense of free choice, the journal time provides an expression and outlet for the students' unique sense of self, moving from deep within themselves to an outward or public expression. From a Jungian perspective, this is a reflective time which activates the archetype of the Self, which in turn sets in motion the inner drive of growth and development.

Setting Up the Journal Program

In order for this approach to work effectively, the teachers need to believe in its value and to arrange a structure that fits their timetables and works well with their students. The purpose of the journal needs to be stated clearly to students so they understand why they are being asked to draw or write. For example, the teacher can say:

> Boys and girls, I like to use journal time in my class three times a week. We will draw and write in our journals on Mondays, Wednesdays, and Fridays first period. I see journal time as a very special time for you to draw and write about whatever you choose. It's your time for you. What is important to you? What do you wonder or think about? What has happened to you that you like? That you don't like? What do you dream about? What do you wish for? What are you frightened of? Your journal can be used for any of these things. In our class I like the journals to be private: we don't look at each other's journals. However, if you want to show it to a friend you can, and if you want to read part of it to

the class, we can have a special journal reading time. Do you have any questions?

Role of the Teacher

A key role of the teacher is to write appropriate comments on the journals which (a) encourage the child to continue drawing and writing and also help the child elaborate or amplify various themes, (b) acknowledge the work that has been done and emphasize its importance and special nature, (c) empathize with the feelings portrayed in the story and picture, and (d) help the children move through any blocks or resistances they have to start writing or drawing.

Grading, marking, and correction pose difficult problems for the teachers. The amount of work put into journals can be voluminous, and to mark or grade them all of the time would be very time-consuming for the teacher. However, some comments do need to be made. Our suggestion is that journals not be graded and that teachers be selective in their comments, simply acknowledging some journals with a "good work" comment and making more elaborate remarks on other journals. Our experience indicates that every child's journal should be read and acknowledged at least once a week. The easiest way to manage the sheer volume seems to be by dividing the class into groups and working with one group, or about five journals, each day. Some teachers prefer to wait until part way through the journal time and then read the work in progress, commenting more extensively verbally and in some way checking or initialing the page also. Other teachers take this opportunity to have the child dictate the written part with the teacher acting as recorder. Then there is time for comments if the teacher wishes to have the child extend the content. When necessary, some teachers will read and comment on the small group's journals after school. Many teachers find that reading and commenting on an entire class set at one sitting becomes burdensome, and soon there is a lessening of interest in the program. Because the success of the program is so closely related to how much the teacher values it, we would strongly encourage as much in-class marking as possible. Sample comments in figure 2.1 may be a useful supplement to those in teachers' current repertoires and may facilitate the process of responding to each journal.

FIG. 2.1
Suggested Comments for Student Journals

ACKNOWLEDGMENT STATEMENTS:

I noticed that . . . (the little horse is back in your drawing today).
You've really worked hard on this!
You've written a lot today.
You've done a lot of work today.
There's a lot happening in your drawing!
I look forward to seeing what you put here next time.
I really like the effort you've made today.

ELABORATION / AMPLIFICATION STATEMENTS:

General
Can you tell me about . . . (this part)?
Can you tell / show me how big . . . heavy . . . old this is?
How would adding color change this?
What could happen before . . . after?
Can you tell me more?

Loss
What made him upset?
Why did he / she / it leave?
How did it feel to leave?
How does it feel to be left behind?
What do you miss most when he / she / it is gone?
What makes you feel a little better when you are hurting?

Fighting
What did . . . (the monster) . . . think / do?
How did . . . (the monster kill the dinosaur)?
How did . . . (the winner / the one who lost) . . . feel?

Help / Healing
Who can help in this situation?
What else could . . . (the bear) do?
Draw a picture of help arriving.
What does the character need?
How can the hero fix this?
What needs to happen for the child to be safe / better?
What steps does the dragon need to take now?
What would the next scene show if things were getting better?

Happy Times
What was the best thing about . . . (the picnic)?
What is the most exciting part?
What do you want to happen?
What do you think will happen?
What activities will there be?

Relationships and Friends
What else do you like to do with your best friend?
Can you tell me more about who is in your family?
How do you get to Dad's house?
When do you visit grandma?
What makes grandpa special to you?
How often do you fight / play with your cousin?

EMPATHY STATEMENTS:

Hurt
You felt really upset when . . . (your sister hit you).

It really hurts when . . . (they won't let you play).
It hurts so much that you wanted to . . . (hit them).
Sad
  When this happens you feel really sad.
  Being this sad is really awful.
  You were so upset you couldn't stop the tears.
Excited
  This was really exciting!
  It felt like you were ready to burst with so much excitement.
  Waiting was hard when you were so excited.
Scared
  You were really frightened by it!
  You wanted to . . . (run away) . . . you were so frightened.
  You were scared because . . . (you thought it was a vampire bat up there).
Angry
  You were really mad . . . angry . . . upset.
  You were so mad you wanted to . . . (shout at them)!
  Saying that out loud helped them know how mad you were.
Worried
  It's a worry when . . . (the kitty runs away).
  When that happens you worry about what could happen next.
  You really worry about this.
  You felt worried because . . . (you couldn't do anything about it).
Happy
  It was great to be so happy!
  Wow! That was wonderful.
  You felt really happy about that!

With regard to spelling corrections, the teacher has to achieve a balance between asking for some corrections and ignoring others. This will vary from child to child because some children will stop writing and drawing if the corrections are too numerous. Another way for the teacher to handle this issue is for her to simply model the correct spelling.

Child: Dear Miss Jones
          I am going to a parte. It is Trevr.

Teacher: Is it Trevor's birthday party, Pat?
          How do you feel about going to the party?

One needs to remember that a primary goal of this activity is to encourage a flow from the child's inner world onto the paper. Her second question attempts to help the child elaborate his feelings.

Teachers should try to avoid ignoring the feelings that are expressed by giving such advice as "Well, we all have bad days. Just smile and ignore them" or "Look on the bright side." A more appropriate response would be to acknowledge the feelings and make a helpful coping response: "It sounds like you are really hurting. I'm glad you

told me. Let's chat Thursday at recess" or "That must be upsetting.
Can you talk to your Mum about it?" Likewise, we discourage for-
bidding any topic or theme because the child is often showing a need
to express certain struggles and the journal is often the only place
that this can be done. It is important, then, that teachers do not
make such comments as "Don't write about your fight with your
brother any more" or "Don't use that word any more" or "Please
write about happy things." In the next section, we mention some
common specific themes that students draw and write about and
give examples of facilitative teacher statements and ideas for handling difficult issues.

Although all children know the journal is to be read by the teacher,
they should have the right to keep certain pages private. The teacher
needs to indicate that and have them devise a simple cue: usually
turning down a corner is enough. Frequently, primary-aged children
enjoy sharing verbally, and the value of their work is reinforced by
the time given to this and the quiet listening from others. The kinds
of questions the teacher may ask about the content models open-
ended questions for the class to pose also (Hipple, 1985). The teacher
may provide the option of small group sharing if the children seem
more comfortable participating in that setting. Although the primary
purpose for this work is to give the children opportunities to express themselves and to nurture a rich inner life, the academic skills
of communicating in various forms are enhanced if group sharing
is part of the program.

Writing and Drawing Activities

The focus in Jungian journal work resides in emotional and symbolic development; thus drawing and writing activities seek their
basis in the inner world of image and symbol and the outer world
of experience. By this we are referring to the way in which the children
experience their life in the world. What pleasures do they encounter,
what hurts them, what do they feel, and how do they cope? For
the primary-aged child, in order to fully capture his experience of
life, it is important to offer both directed and non-directed opportunities for writing and drawing. So throughout the week we provide a mixture of suggested topics and time for drawing, thinking,
and writing about whatever they want to record.

Directed Activities. These refer to stimulus questions or sentence stems which help the students focus on their inner world and their emotional life. These suggestions could be such topics as "a time when I felt happy . . . sad . . . fearful . . . mad," etc. Some of the topics need to be related to seasonal activities, such as Thanksgiving ("my favorite foods and what I like about them"), Halloween ("a scary time, a scary dream"), Christmas and Hanukkah ("receiving presents, giving presents"), Valentine's Day ("love"), Easter ("spring time and birthdays"), and Remembrance and Memorial Day ("sad times, losing friends, people who died"). Other directed activities include such topics as "things I like doing, things that are hard for me, when I have a problem I . . . , things I wish for, if I were invisible, my favorite dream, my worst dream." Often it is useful to alternate the "bad" (i.e., difficult or painful emotions) with the "good" (pleasant experiences): "what I like about school, what I don't like about school," "the worst day of my life, the best day of my life." We usually start with the negative experiences and end an activity with a positive suggestion or topic.

Non-Directed Drawing or Writing. At least twice a week, students should have the opportunity to "work as you wish in your journal with either a picture, a writing activity, or both." Some children will readily respond to this suggestion, while others will voice "I don't know what to do." It is important during this non-directed time not to give them a specific topic but rather to work with the students' emotional processes to help them connect to their inner world so that they can draw, write, or report on a genuine aspect of their life. In other words, so they can speak from the "true" self as opposed to the "false" or even the adaptive self.

There are two approaches teachers can take to help students make that connection to the inner self. The first is to use statements which reflect their uncertainty such as "You're not sure what to put on the page," or "You're worried about what you should put into your journal," or "You can't imagine what you want to put in there." For many children in this age group, there has been little opportunity to make decisions. In school they are often told which subject is next, how to perform a given task, even in creative subjects such as art, and generally what is expected throughout the day. At home there is frequently a similar pattern of being told what to do and when, even in the basics of what to eat and what to wear. Sometimes a completely non-directed activity is very unsettling for these children, and they may then need the teacher simply to reflect their discomfort or confusion.

A second approach needed for some children is one of encouragement: "If you did know what to do, what would you put in your journal then?" Often they do have an idea, but there may have been times when volunteered answers or suggestions were not accepted or where having the "right" answer was so important that these children are now reluctant to take the risk of being wrong. It is especially important for teacher comments to reflect genuine pleasure in the children's creativity and effort in these situations.

If there are several children who have this difficulty, the teacher may want to consider initiating non-directed activities at a different time of day—for example, at whatever time most of them have something they just "have" to tell the teacher right then. Another suggestion would be to implement this type of writing after a pre-writing activity such as a game of word association, an exciting story, a group activity or sharing time, a field trip, an unusual visitor, or special occasion. In some cases the time allotted may need to be shortened because they do not have much to draw or write about, or it may need lengthening because they never have a chance to finish. In our experience, the two things which seem to influence a deterioration in volume and quality of student work are not enough time to finish a concept and lack of teacher input. Finally, if for whatever reason the children do not have much to write or become stuck even with directed activities, we would suggest the teacher do a series of programs on relaxation and guided imagery where students are encouraged to close their eyes and go into their inner world (see Part IV of the book).

Responding to Difficult Situations and Painful Emotions

Often students use their journals to record painful events in their lives. It is important that teachers respond to these direct forms of communication by (a) acknowledging the emotions (i.e., "That must hurt") or by (b) asking for clarification or amplification (i.e., "Who hit whom first?" or "What happened next?"). When certain emotions are running high in several journals (i.e., anger, fear, hurt, shock, sadness, etc.), then the teacher can also respond by dealing with the concerns in a class discussion and art activity approach (Allan and

Nairne, 1989; Bertoia and Allan, 1988a). Furthermore, when a particular child is stuck in an emotional or symbolic theme (e.g., a dream image of a murderous dinosaur) and keeps repeating it time and time again, then without mentioning the child's name the teacher can have a problem-solving session with the class using a similar but slightly different topic or image. Obviously, when teachers become concerned over the journal contents, they should consult with the school counselor or psychologist. Next are examples of various types of "difficult" journal entries.

Hurt Feelings. A girl writes:

> My feelings are hart when My big brother calls me names in frunt of my friends and his friends. I feel embarassed and sad. Sometimes my brother hits me.

The teacher response could be:

> Yes, that must hurt. I'm glad you told me. What can you say to your brother? If he keeps on hurting you who can you ask for help?

Another child wrote:

> I get mad wen Brad trips me and I foll on my bum and my bum get wet.

The dialogue in the accompanying drawing shows one person saying, "I'm going to get you for this" with the response "Ha" and a final reply from the victim, "I hat you." The following journal page appears to carry this further with two heart shapes, the top one looking angry with "*" marks for eyes and nose and teeth showing, and the other heart looking surprised. A sample teacher comment to this could be "You're mad at Brad. You want to hurt him back. What can you say to Brad? How would you like Brad to act around you? Can you tell him that?" Or the teacher can address the symbols the child uses in the pictures. For example, near the hearts the teacher can write: "Can you tell me how the heart shapes are feeling?" If the feeling is anger, then there may be an opportunity to explore peer relations, anger, and expressions or responses to anger, depending on the reply or next entry from the child.

Angry Feelings. One child wrote:

FIG. 2.2   Hurt feelings

When I get mad
I go busrc
I get mad when
Jill right's me in her
Jrnals!!!

This example reflects the child's awareness of what caused his anger and just how severe it became. Because the figure in the drawing (fig. 2.2) is reacting to someone also saying "haha," the teacher may want to comment: "Do you feel mad if she writes about you or if she laughs when she shows you?" The teacher should also try to move the child into verbalizing his wishes: "What do you want from Jill? What do you want Jill to do?"

    Love. Many times children express affection in their entries, as this child did:

Today Jasmine gave me a LOVE kind of sine. It is purpple and pink
it is nice. and I Like it.

The teacher's reply could be:

You like Jasmine a lot and the purple and pink sign she gave you.
Do you want to make something for her?

Mixed Emotions. Sometimes the entries have several key emotions, reflecting different feelings and issues. The teacher needs to respond to all of them and then focus on the most pressing issue.

The following entry from a grade three student indicates how children are able to tap into past experiences if they are not yet fully resolved.

> Once I felt sad because somebody was calling me names so I told the teacher. When I was in grade one a boy in grade six called me names. When I was in grade two this boy in grade four told me that I was dom so I told my broter to tell his teacher so his teacher told the principal so after school he had to go outside for garbig dootei and everybody started to laugh.

Because this seems to be happening rather consistently, the teacher could comment in a way intended to gain more understanding, "Can you tell me about a time this year when you felt sad?" or "Can you tell me more about being called names this year?"

Sad Feelings. Directed topics can lead into situations which may need both verbal and written support. For example, the following example was given for a sad time: "I was sad when my anty had a hard a tack when she was sleeping and dide." Because this had just happened, the teacher spent some time with the child talking about her sad feelings related to death, rather than just writing a response. Months later, in completing a topic about frightening things, the same child wrote:

> Things that frighten me are bad dreams. My bad dreams are yousaly about monsters and Im afraid that im ded. And my mom and dad say that I talk in my sleep.

This would be an example of situations where the teacher could suggest that the student work on the material in the journal: "I'm glad you told me. Let me try to help you. Could you draw one of your bad dreams in your journal?" And later the teacher can ask: "What is the monster doing? How are you feeling? What will help the girl in the dream? What worries or frightens you most? Do you know someone who has died? Are you afraid you will die in your sleep like your aunty?" In such a talk, the teachers can disclose their own fears of death, point out the normalcy of such feelings after someone we know has died, and make helpful suggestions for coping with such feelings.

Friendships. Students often write about their peers and the variety of emotions that such interactions stir up.

> My best friend is Krystal because She is kind to me. But she dase not play whas me because Sandy dose not let me play with her.

The teacher could respond with "How do you feel when Sandy won't let you play with your best friend?", or "How do you feel about your best friend?" (if feelings needed to be accessed), or with "How does Sandy stop you and Krystal from playing?" if the situation needs more amplification.

Family Issues. Another example where both the situation and the emotions would need further work is this one: "My bad moved the othre bay in to a hows." To determine if the family had separated the teacher could ask, "Who lives in the other house with your dad?" To clarify the response from the child the teacher could ask, "What is it like for you now that Dad has moved into a house?"

Often these kinds of insights can help the teacher gain greater understanding to the child's world. The opportunity to explore the situation further in the journal can be the only outlet for the child. Another example of a child's sharing family changes comes from this child:

> My MoM dusin't like JacK so she Kicked Him out. I am not to happy so now I am gohing to Do aboat that . . . now am happy. I like to live with my mom with out JacK. I fele Much bete with out JacK. I LOVE my Mom. Just with my mom.

The teacher may want to respond with a simple paraphrasing statement such as "You are happy to live with your Mom now." Or the response could look at what else the child may be feeling: "It can be scary to think Mom might kick you out when she's mad." However, the teacher will want to consult with the counselor before going too deeply into that material.

View of Self. Children's journals often indicate a view of self. One child wrote his name and "I am dum" after it, then erased it. A few days later he wrote: "I can Look dumb" under a monster's picture that says "I Luve me" (fig. 2.3). Then he wrote "a pizza is flying . . . a flying pizza . . . AAAA I am dumd . . . No I'm no't dumd," followed a week later by "I am a potato . . . I am a dumb . . . AAAABoo, good by." When a child is so self-deprecating, even in the guise of silliness, it is very important to address the issue. The teacher can write such questions as "What would make a boy feel dumb?" "Can you tell me why the pizza thinks it's dumb?" "Has anyone ever called you dumb?" "Who?" Or even "It must hurt to think you're dumb." All these statements provide some form of opening for the child to deal with the topic. When the teacher ignores it, the child may well interpret the silence as agreement.

Report Cards. Toward report card time many children become concerned, and the journals are a way of sharing that worry. Two days after receiving the report the child wrote, "I hate my report card. I wish we nevr whated one." The child's distress can be reflected: "You're really upset with your report card. What did you not like about it? Were there any comments that you did like? Can I help you to make your next report card better? What activities do you have trouble with?" The child can be given a chance to gain imaginary relief: "Can you tell me what you would like to do with that

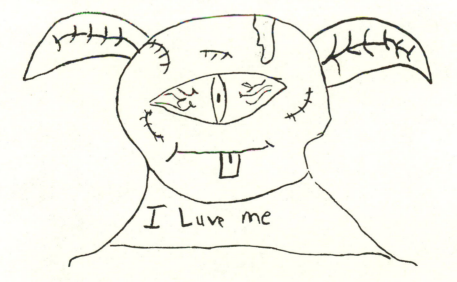

FIG. 2.3   "I can look dumb"

report card? If you wrote your own report card, what would it say?"
And later "How can I help you achieve this?"

Directed Activities. Another way of helping children gain insight
into their world is with directed activities such as "My hero" (figs.
2.4 and 2.5), in which they design an award for any hero and write
about why that person is one. An example of family being recognized
was "My Hero is MY Grandpa because he taught me." An obvious
comment in this case would be "Can you tell me in the award what
Grandpa taught you about?" It is important to help children look
to the positive in their lives also.

There will be times when a stimulus will be given, but the child's
need will be such that he or she writes about another topic. In one
example, the child responded to the day's assignment—how a bear
could handle his or her problem—but then wrote on a new topic,
a major personal loss. The teacher, recognizing the importance of
this to the child, allowed a second entry dated the day before, "April
27, 1988 if I was Bear I would take a flower out of the garden and
Put some honey on the flower. April 26, 1988 Mr. Niraweta died!"
[plus six drawn teardrops]. Instead of illustrating the day's assignment the child created a dramatic tombstone scene (fig. 2.6).

FIG. 2.4   "My hero is my Grandpa"

FIG. 2.5   Rick Hanson

FIG. 2.6   Mr. Niraweta died

Repetitious Themes. Finally, there are situations in which the child continues with a theme distressing to the teacher when it carries on over a long period. Often these themes have to do with fighting, death, brutality, sexuality, and defecation. Over several entries one boy wrote: "I see the sun crying and the Donosaurs are fieting" and "I see Dinosuars fieting echuther." While most teachers are comfortable with a few entries like this, it is difficult to know how to help the children become unstuck when they keep repeating them. Often simply reflecting the action and feeling for a few days will be enough, "The dinosaurs fight each other all the time. They are really sad and frightened they might lose the battle." If this does not change the pattern, the teacher can ask such questions as "How do you feel when the dinosaurs fight? Is there too much fighting? Who do you fight with? Do you ever feel sad because of all the fighting? Do you wish the fighting would stop? What would happen if the fighting stopped?" The teacher needs to think through the meaning of the story and ask one or two relevant questions for each entry.

When these themes continue or escalate, the teacher needs to consult with the counselor. Examples of when to consult would be with such entries as "i ess a mnstre Ding The monstre has a spiere is his bran and his uiy" and "is geting Closr to is bran" with "help" written repeatedly on the drawing. A few days later this child wrote: "The monstre is Ding he is DeDe he is not aLive when he did he was pot the monstre grave." A translation of these entries would be as follows: "I see a monster dying. The monster has a spear in his brain and his eye and is getting closer to his brain. The monster is dying. He is dead. He is not alive. When he died he was put in the monster grave." We knew that the boy who wrote this was in an acute state of psychological pain. We believed that he had experienced and witnessed violence and emotional cruelty. In the journal he tries to cope but sees death (repression) as the only solution and release of pain. Usually family interventions are needed here, but in the meantime the teacher can encourage the psychological growth by writing sentences such as "How was the dinosaur hurt? What other pains does the dinosaur feel? Has anyone ever hurt a little boy? Where did he feel the hurt? What will help the little boy? What does the little boy wish for (or need)?"

Other examples of repeated concern needing consultation would be "A monster is geting a girl. The monstr is finihct The Leg," or "The Bird Sed to the Spiter dummy, you coocoo you shont have dun

That and The Rabbit Sed Sucker Suck The Big fat Suckr to the urm-
my man," or "This is a stoped Dinosar it ets pepul wene it dint do
enething." Such themes as these of mutilation, defecation, or sexuality (figs. 2.7, 2.8, and 2.9) in either the drawings or text are
usually of utmost concern. Essentially, the teacher should be aware
of three possible options for these distressing types of entries in journals: (a) address the topic and elicit more information, (b) use the
third person in responding and reflect the content—that is, "The
dinosaur is really stupid and eats people even when they didn't do
anything." "Does it worry the dinosaur how he keeps on hurting people?", and (c) consult with the counselor. These entries could all
be indications of serious problems or circumstances in the child's
life and may need referral to others as well.

Because the journal is intended to be a safe place for children,
it is important for the teacher to write comments that do not shut

FIG. 2.7 Mutilation

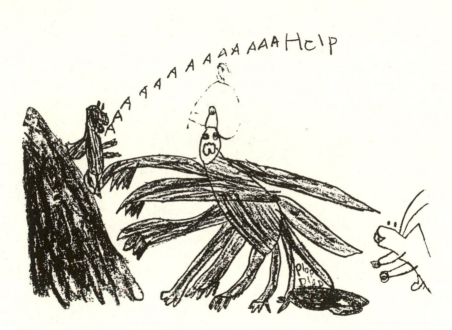

FIG. 2.8   Defecation

FIG. 2.9   Sexuality

the child down but motivate her to keep writing. Figure 2.10 offers a few suggested responses the teacher may use with difficult or troubling entries. Sometimes a child is simply preoccupied with "forbidden" words, or there has been a medical procedure in a genital area, or anatomy of the opposite sex has been seen for the first time. While we would never downplay the serious nature of some incidents in today's society, we also wish to caution teachers and counselors not to assume the worst from one or two non-specific journal entries.

FIG. 2.10

Suggested Statements for Troubling Journal Entries

BRUTALITY

The dinosaur can smash anyone, he's so tough.

The monster needs to be strong.

The soldier has been fighting every day, chopping up everything. Can you tell me what needs to change for him to stop fighting?

There is so much fighting, smashing, and killing. How do they feel about it?

DEATH

There are a lot of creatures dying. Can you tell me how they feel when they die, . . . how the shark feels when he kills them, . . . how the boat feels watching?

Something dies in each story. Can you show a way to stop the killing?

When something dies it makes us feel sad . . . angry . . . scared . . . upset.

DEFECATION

All the elephants were spitting and pooing.

They have lots of stuff to get out.

The monsters barfed and peed on everything.

How does the monster . . . boy . . . bug feel when that happens?

SEXUAL THEMES

Every puppy has a penis. You've drawn lots of them.

You know the names for the parts of the body.

You know many slang expressions for the body.

Can you tell me how you first thought about people doing this?

Conclusion

Journals provide children with a wonderful opportunity for growth. Communication skills, both written and drawn, improve with experience and opportunity if there is feedback because children gain facility with language through using it. The interest shown by the teacher gives the message that this material is important. The sharing of these inner thoughts allows greater understanding of the children, from the teacher's perspective and from the children's as well. They learn to make decisions about what will go on the paper, in the illustration, text, or in both. They make associations between personal experiences and views and the printed word. They come to value their own contributions. They realize that taking the risk of expressing themselves and their emotions is acceptable. The very act of putting some aspect of themselves on paper enhances those communication skills so basic to schooling and also nurtures a deeper understanding so essential for enhancing emotional and symbolic growth.

Chapter 3

JOURNAL WRITING AS
A DEVELOPMENTAL GUIDANCE METHOD

FOR A NUMBER of years now, we have been concerned that many school systems do not effectively deal with the developmental issues of children. As these issues tend to peak during the middle school years (Tanner, 1970; Morris, 1978), it is important that the regular curriculum should provide appropriate outlets for the normal concerns of the students (Cottingham, 1973).

The purpose of this chapter is to describe the use of journal writing as a method of developmental guidance and to show how students use their journals for "sorting out" and thinking through important issues in their lives. Examples will be used from a journal writing project developed by the teacher and used with his regular seventh-grade class during an academic year (Buttery, 1980).

Journal writing has long been used as a source of self-knowledge and self-help (Jung, 1961). In the counseling literature, journals are reported as being useful aids to both group and individual counseling sessions. Riordan and Matheny (1972) found that logs helped counselees to safely express their emotions and opinions without the effects of peer pressure. They also noted that the logs allowed the counselors to uncover real sources of conflict and unvoiced emotional concerns. Crabbes (1973) noticed that one of his clients was more at ease in writing to him than in attending sessions. He found that writing helped the client attain personal distance from her problems. Later he was able to encourage her to "be on the outside what she was feeling in the inside" (p. 390). Similarly, Carroll (1972) emphasized the integrative qualities of journal writing. She noted that journals helped the students create, experiment, and bring together inner and outer events in a meaningful way. Finally, Progoff (1975) reports that journal writing develops understanding and an inner perspective on life.

As far as we are aware, journal writing has not been specifically used as a developmental guidance tool. By developmental guidance we are referring to Dinkmeyer's (1971) definition in which the guidance program is an integral part of the curriculum, purposely organized by the teacher and geared for all students. Some of its goals are to integrate the affective and cognitive domains, to personalize the educative process, to help children understand themselves and others, and to cope with and master various developmental tasks.

A well-organized journal program can do this because it lets each student start at his or her own level of readiness and choose his or her own issues and topics to write about. Also, within this program emotional, social, and academic tasks can be integrated (see below).

Method

At the beginning of the academic year, the teacher (Mr. John Buttery) informed his students that as part of the language arts curriculum they would be writing their own journals twice a week (one in school and one at home) for the entire school year. The journals were to be called "experience journals," and in them students could select and write about any topic based on their experiences or thoughts.

They were specifically instructed that time-tabling logs (i.e., "Today, I did this and then that") were not permitted unless they referred to a common theme or thread about life and the world around them. The goal was to help children to be perceptive about their environment and their experiences and to be able to develop cohesion of reflective thought in their writing. It was hoped that such a program would provide an outlet for thoughts and feelings and hence act as a form of self-counseling.

Overview

At first, the program was difficult for the students. There was considerable resistance and complaining. The students were not accustomed to so much writing and had trouble finding topics. However, as the year progressed the content of the journals became rich in social and emotional themes. Also, the students improved academically: work skill errors dropped from 18.75 per pupil per assignment in September to 3.15 per pupil in March; writing style, grammar, and organization showed considerable gains.

The program came to play a big part in the life of the classroom. A discussion period was set aside when students could read from their journals and talk about the difficulties they were experiencing. Over time they seemed to come to value good writing and each other's opinion. They began to use the journals to solve social problems. For example, when upset they would write out their side of the story so that the class and teacher could see their point of view. Later they became effective in analyzing social situations in which they had been observers or participants.

The social influence of the journals extended beyond the classroom into family life. Children often shared their journals with their parents and asked them for help with topics, with proofreading, and in dealing with social conflicts.

Students wrote about a wide range of emotions, states, and situations which elicited feelings. The main themes were themselves, their family, their friends, and the interactions at school. They wrote about developmental issues which normally would not have been shared with parents or teachers. Some of the topics were issues of identity and career, frustrations, anger, love, fear, happiness, worries, sexual awareness, power, and stealing.

As the year progressed they showed a greater ease in expressing their feelings on paper, became more considerate of each other, and were more sensitive to the handling of emotional issues in general, especially when others were expressing their feelings in the classroom.

Examples from Specific Journal Entries

At the end of the year the writers went through the journals and found that the topics seemed to gather around seven specific themes. These were recording journals, "why" journals, family issues, national and international issues, imaginative situations, philosophical and religious themes, and emotional themes.

Recording Journals. In these journals, the students described events such as family and class outings, singing for the Christmas concert, school and sport activities. These journals were popular. The pupils seemed to enjoy recording events as they happened just as people enjoy taking family photos. A moment in time is preserved by their writing, and in doing so they are able to value their own unique past.

THE FIRST DAY

At first I hated the idea of going back to school because of all the boring work we'd have to do. Sue and I sat together while Mr. Buttery went through the basic work we would be doing and I realized it would be a little harder than I thought.

Recess came and then my friends and I discussed what we thought about being in grade seven. Sue got an earache so she ended up going home after recess. I didn't go back after lunch because I had to pick up my grandparents at the airport who were just arriving from England. My grandparents bought us a couple of presents that were really nice. I don't think that school will be that bad this year.

Typical of the beginning writer of journals, this journal tends to follow a diary format and list a series of events. It is interesting to note the change of feeling that occurs during the writing process—from hating school, to the awareness of having to work harder, to finally stating: "I don't think that school will be that bad this year."

Writing about experiences provides an appropriate outlet for feelings and a vehicle through which difficult feelings can be transformed. Likewise, in the excerpts from other journals, the reader will be aware of subtle emotional changes that occur as the pupils reveal their thoughts and feelings about developmental issues.

"Why" Journals. These journals were popular too. Students seem to have the need to understand "why"—why things happen to them, why life is the way it is—and to be able to answer some of their own questions.

WHY DO MEXICAN JUMPING BEANS JUMP?

Today my mom and I went to Richmond. When we got there, I saw some Mexican Jumping Beans and I got four of them. They are in little plastic boxes and whenever they jump they make a noise.

When I was smaller I thought that only some people could have Mexican Jumping Beans because the beans were magic. Now I read on the label that there are little caterpillars inside the beans and whenever the caterpillar takes a bite from his shell it jumps. It keeps jumping until it is out of its shell. They jump for about six months.

I guess I found the answer to my question.

The primary purpose of this student seems to be to describe and to achieve a sense of understanding of her own experience. Journals such as these often provide the opportunity for integrating knowledge. This journal reflects a developmental movement from magical thinking to rational understanding.

Family Issues. Two main journal themes emerged: siblings and parents. The following excerpt concerns siblings.

MY BROTHERS AND I

I'm sitting on my front steps doing my journal and watching the sun go down.

I'll tell you why I'm sitting out here. My two older brothers kicked me out of the house because they want to listen to their new stereo which they put in the front room and they won't let my little brother and I listen to it.

My mom has gone to Seattle until late and I didn't have a chance to talk to her about the stereo. You can hear it at least two houses down and I can't stand it. The music is terrible and I've had an earache from early this morning and now it's getting worse.

I've been thinking of running away but I haven't got the guts to because I wouldn't know where to go.

I have tried to make a big noise like bouncing the ball out in the driveway but all they have done is come down and scream at me.

It's hard living with three brothers and without a dad. Sometimes I wonder if I could ever get along with my brothers. I guess maybe in the future but right now . . . I don't really know. I guess after all my life is getting harder and harder to live and handle.

I'm sorry to have this in my journal but this was my thought for the day!

The above journal goes into considerable depth about an extremely painful situation. The girl openly communicates feelings of hurt, hopelessness, anger, and yet shows some emotional strength and maturity. The journal provides an in-depth exploration of a difficult family situation and also signals a need for help. By ending the way she does, she is asking for assurance that it is acceptable to use the journal to express herself in this manner.

The following excerpt concerns parents.

DIFFERENT TYPES OF MOTHERS

Over the past couple of years I've noticed that mothers are not the same. There are different kinds of them. I'll introduce you to some I know.

The worry-wart. The worry-wart mother is always concerned with where you are going, with whom, and when you're expected to come home. Try to reason with this kind of mother, she's not a pain in the neck, she just wants you home safe and sound!

The tired mother. The tired mother's always tired, she's too tired to do anything so if she doesn't want to do the dishes you have to. Don't fight with this mother, it's mother's day, if you do some work for her she won't be tired!

The working mother. The working mother is always working, you never see her, and when you do she doesn't talk to you as she doesn't feel good. This mother is just too involved in her work, take her out to dinner, just get her mind off her work.

The forgetful mother. The forgetful mother is always forgetting things, you have to remind her a million times until she gets it through her head. This kind of mother isn't forgetful she just has other things on her mind.

I have mentioned four different mothers but there are many other types of mothers, each one is different from the rest. My mother is all of the personalities mentioned throughout the journal and that is why I did this journal.

Mother's day is to remind you to respect your mother. You only get one true mom so if she's a worry-wart or the working mother help her along; don't make it worse.

It is significant that the student is able to analyze the roles of her mother; she abstracts some of her mother's attributes and sees them as typical personalities in other mothers. She was able to make a conceptual leap from the specific to the general. In doing so she demonstrates her own emotional maturity and her intellectual ability to analyze social-emotional issues. This insight and understanding seem to help her respond in a caring way.

National and International Issues. Here, students wrote about pressing social problems that were national or international in scope. They wrote about the current gas shortage, conservation, national unity, and war.

THAT FUNNY FEELING

Ever since the Russians have started to make nuclear weapons I
have had a feeling that any minute I could be blown up by a bomb
or nuclear weapon, because to me the Russians seem like they
would like to kill everything on Earth so that they can rule the
world. (They probably do.) I don't know why I think it but they
just seem so weird. I supposed, however, that there is a lot of in-
sane people in the rest of the world that would like to kill
everything. To be on the safe side, I will build a small radar to
make sure that there aren't any missiles heading toward me.

Most of the students wrote journals about greater social issues
only when they perceived that the issue had some direct relevance
to them. In this journal the pupil is expressing his fears about nuclear
weapons in the context of an issue which affects many other people.
The writer is able to weave his concern for himself with a realiza-
tion that this issue also affects others. In the face of such an overwhelming feeling, one solution for a thirteen-year-old is that of
humor and magical thinking.

Imaginative Situations. In these journals the students wrote about
themselves in fantasy or imaginative situations. In the fantasy they
were able to express their wishes and their dreams in a safe context, thereby deriving some emotional pleasure from the exercise.
Such fantasy projections are normal in adolescence, and, at times,
they are used to express and test career aspirations and life goals.

WHAT IT WOULD BE LIKE TO PLAY IN THE N.F.L.

I would like to play in the National Football League because you
would feel like one of the guys and that would make you feel great.
Imagine playing with the greatest players that may have lived now,
that would give you some security. I would love it so much it
wouldn't matter if we lost every game that season. I would just
say to the guys we'll get them next year, don't let it get you down.
Also, it wouldn't matter what team I was on or what position I
played. But how great it would be if we won every game, also the
play-offs and the cup. I would be almost crying for joy. Oh! how
I would like to play football in the N.F.L.

This fantasy features the writer's personality in a situation where he has to make value judgments and decisions. Through identification with heroic adult models, the boy prepares himself for the adult world and elicits a range of positive emotion—security, joy, strength, and pleasure. He is setting up an idealized goal orientation which is a common developmental theme in early adolescence (Offer, 1969).

Philosophical and Religious Themes. As the year progressed, more philosophical and religious themes were expressed. The children wrote about God, the meaning of life, synchronicity, growing old, death, and the fact that one cannot relive the past. The journals frequently suggested that they might write a sequel journal to clarify certain points.

AFTER WE DIE

What happens after we die? We don't actually know. Some people believe you go to heaven in the sky where there is a golden gate that opens up and lets you in. But some people don't believe that.

I believe that when you die you are made into a totally different person and live another life. Most people don't believe that, but I don't know because I haven't gone around asking people.

What scares me is that when you die you might never come back. I've noticed that old people never look scared but I am. I guess it's because you'll never know when you're gonna die, you could die any second.

In this journal the pupil raises questions about life after death and shares some of her own personal views and concerns. She states her own belief and is aware of the transitory nature of life and the fact that we do not know when we are going to die or what really happens after death. She allows herself to verbalize some fear over the "permanence" of death. Developmental questions of this type frequently emerge in adolescents as their distinct and separate personalities are being formed and as abstract reasoning abilities begin to develop (Piaget, 1948).

Emotional Themes. These journals were highly personal in nature and were used to provide an outlet for specific feelings. Though they were essentially statements of how the pupils were feeling in the here-and-now, they also helped the students learn appropriate ways for handling feelings.

BEING FRUSTRATED

Have you ever felt what it's like to be frustrated? Well, it's about the most horribly, frustrating feeling in the world. Right now I'm frustrated and it's down right driving me crazy! No thoughts are circulating in my head right now so it's hard to write about my thoughts. This journal is driving me CRAZY!!!

I took a break for a few hours and now my mind is circulating with new ideas and thoughts.

Today, my dad took my sisters and I to Stanley Park and we went on a six-mile walk. We had some popcorn, fudge bars, and saw the animals. I also saw Paul and his sister.

I'm not frustrated any more and my head is all clear and I'm ready for daydreaming.

This has been K.M. now signing off. Good night.

The pupil recorded her actual here-and-now experience. She wrote her frustrations out and was then able to leave the writing block behind her and return later with a new experience and some insight. The pupil had the maturity not to continue wrestling for new ideas when the time was not ripe for creativity.

Discussion

The process of writing experience journals provided an outlet for the developmental concerns of the children in a regular classroom as part of the regular curriculum. It gave them a chance to raise and discuss their own concerns and questions, to develop deeper understanding, and to find solutions to some of their own struggles.

Growth seemed to occur in three main interrelated areas: the emotional, social, and academic. The children used the journals to express such basic emotions as fear, love, anger, sadness, and caring. They became comfortable in discussing and sharing some of their deepest feelings about themselves, their aspirations, the purpose and meaning of life, death, and war.

The journals had a social value too. They increased the information flow between children, parents, and teacher. The journals were used as a method of communication and as a vehicle for solving problems, for rehearsing what could be said to peers, teacher, or parent, and for becoming aware of other people's points of view. If the child felt the teacher had misunderstood a situation, the journal was used to let him know. Likewise, many entries involved thinking through relationships with friends, parents, brothers and sisters, other adults, and classroom antagonists. They liked reading some of their journals to the class and hearing others. Many parents (twenty out of twenty-five) reported that journal writing increased communication at home, as the children read their journals to their parents and used the writing as a springboard to other discussion (Buttery, 1980).

There were also notable academic gains. Over the year, spelling errors decreased dramatically, and appearance and organization improved, along with the ability to develop clear logical thoughts and ideas. The students came to value good writing and saw it as being personally important.

Journal writing offers teachers and counselors an important developmental guidance method. It allows each child to write about and share thoughts and feelings that are current in their lives and increases the communication flow among all parties involved. This one strategy appears to benefit the emotional, social, and academic areas of a student's life. However, further research is clearly needed to evaluate this hypothesis more precisely.

Chapter 4

DREAM JOURNALS

EVERYONE DREAMS. During certain phases of sleep we dream naturally, and then upon waking we may remember fragments of those dreams. Children dream more than adults, initially remembering these dreams often. Garfield (1984) indicates that we dream less as we mature: an infant spends nine hours dreaming and adults about four hours. Yet children are encultered to dismiss dreams as unimportant nonsense, as "only" dreams, and so unworthy of exploration. This minimalization reduces the amount children remember and negates the value derived from working with their dreams. Dreams deal with emotions and symbolic life and are intrinsically related to mental health. Dreams are messages from the unconscious realm of feelings to the conscious mind. They often show us what we need to be aware of and to examine more carefully. Bad dreams do affect children; yet often because of adult downplaying, children repress these images until the power of the dream screams for attention, just as the child whose sleep is interrupted screams for a parent.

One effective way for school counselors and teachers to enrich the world of all children through understanding of their dreams and to support children who are experiencing bad dreams is to establish a program of dream journal activities. This chapter will present guidelines for working with dreams and dream journals, an outline of the method for group dream work, and case material from groups and individuals in order to demonstrate the concepts.

Guidelines

Recording. Working with dreams in a school setting is both therapeutic and fun for children. The key element is the keeping of a dream journal. For primary children who have some skill in printing, we recommend a combination of recording the dream and illustrating some aspect of it. This is best facilitated by half lined / half blank notebooks. The older the child (e.g., third grade), the more emphasis initially is placed on recording the dream. Younger children may need to write only a sentence or two and then illustrate the dream as a method of retaining the essence. Children in fourth grade and up can write the entire dream and choose to illustrate segments which "need" it. The most effective way of recording dreams is to write them out as if they are currently happening, writing in the present tense—e.g., "I am standing on a huge rock"—with no concern for grammar, spelling, or neatness on the first draft.

The simple act of recording dreams validates their significance. This validation then seems to stimulate increased incidence of remembering. The message to the psyche is that "This is important. I am paying attention. I value these dreams," and so the unconscious is better able to communicate with the more rational, conscious, ego mind. This communication in turn allows opportunities for making sense of the messages, learning from them, and perhaps even altering our outer world behaviors to respond to the directions of our deeper, intuitive inner self.

However, even the act of recording alone can change the intensity of the dream and the emotional responses to it, making the fearful, intimidating images a little less so. The child then is able to look at the emotions more objectively and so gains a little more sense of control. Some children like to record all their dreams during the week before a counseling session, whereas others only like to record one or two. Students can then choose which one will be the focus during the session.

Sharing. It is important that children have control over the sharing of their dream material. This means there should be a respect for the privacy of the journal at home and in school. A child should never be made to share any dreams, although voluntary sharing often facilitates improved communication between parent and child. There is, however, a danger of ridicule from other children and even unintentional harm from parents who may say something like "But that's only a dream," thus diminishing it, or "Monsters aren't real," thus rationalizing content as they attempt to calm and reassure the child. Whatever the intention, both responses will cause the child distress because neither the dream reality nor the emotional connections are recognized, even though they are both very powerful for the child.

Therapist Journal. Often the bizarreness of the images or the frightfulness of nightmares and significant dreams can be reduced by working with them in a variety of ways. Because different dreams lend themselves to different techniques and because children have different learning styles, counselor familiarity and comfort with several techniques is rather important. First, we would encourage the counselor or teacher to maintain a personal dream journal. Always important, experiential learning in counseling provides the increased awareness of difficulties encountered in doing something others may consider "dumb" or a "waste of time," as well as insights to the effectiveness of the technique. If counselors truly wish to help children, then they must also continue to work on themselves.

Remembering Dreams. For those who "don't have dreams" or "don't remember" dreams, some simple techniques may help. (1) While falling asleep, keep thinking, "I am going to dream and remember it." (2) Keep a tape recorder or dream journal beside the bed and write in it immediately on awakening (get up ten minutes earlier if need be). (3) There is some indication that certain foods are associated with dreaming. A glass of warm milk often leads to a relaxed state and to increases in frequency and length of dreaming (Garfield, 1984).

Additional Strategies. Supplementary techniques which the authors found useful for dream journal work in groups include various art activities, psychodrama, puppetry, and discussions. There may be times when one or two children have not written during the week, but they will always be able to remember one dream that they can "tell" during the session. There are also many occasions when typical childhood fears are shared as if they were a dream—e.g., anxiety about moving, distress about a death, and fear of the dark. If there are several written dreams or pressing outer world issues, the child is encouraged to tell the dream or story, not to read it orally. That way the affect is much easier to hear, and discrepancies or changes from the time of recording to telling may be significant.

Classroom Dream Journals

The use of dream journals with the whole class is similar to regular journal work described in chapter two. One difference is that teachers need to be aware that dream content is more symbolic, closer to primary process language, and so the flow of images and words may seem more disjointed than other journal and regular curricular writing. For example, the following story was dictated to accompany a drawing (fig. 4.1) of a girl standing under a giant eye within a triangle:

> Once there was a princess and there was a ball going on and my mother she said I had to clean up my room and then I could come out for the ball. And I was afraid that I wouldn't meet anyone there. And I cleaned my room and I went downstairs. And um, I saw this girl that looked familiar. It was my sister. And I hadn't seen her for a long time. And then I called my Mom and my Mom was so happy to see her. The end.

When commenting on dream entries, teachers need to focus either on recognition of the material or on consideration for providing alternatives. For example, if a child wrote, "A monster was chasing me and trying to shoot me with a gun and it was night time," the teacher could reply with, "What could you change if you dreamed this again

FIG. 4.1   The giant eye

to make it less scary?" When the authors used that comment with one child, the next day's dream entry showed a six-eyed monster and a ghost frightening a child in bed (fig. 4.2) and a second drawing of a vacuum cleaner sucking them away (fig. 4.3). Another child responded to the same comment with a continuation the next day on a new page. The original dream was

> I was at Stanley Park watching a whale show. Then I fell in the water and the whale was trying to eat me and it was red.

When she continued the whale story the next day she wrote:

> And then a dolphin rescued me from the whale.

If the dream was not frightening, then recognition of the content and reflection of the feeling are all that is needed. If the child wrote, "One day I was playing tag and I tripped over a dinosaur egg. In a week it hatched into a baby bronto. When it was Big I rode it," the teacher can reply with "You look very happy riding the bronto when it is big."

Often recording a dream is easier for children than other forms of writing such as poems and stories because the dream actually happened in the child's mind. Writing about dreams differs from describing outer world events because the latter are physical and readily accepted by others. The dream recording reaches much deeper inside the psyche, but only becomes concrete in the outer world if it is written or drawn. The teacher provides the space and time for children to bring their inner world out to be acknowledged.

Group Method

Rationale. Initially a dream journal group was established in one of our elementary schools for two reasons: first, the number of new referrals involving issues of fears and nightmares increased, so management of case load was a consideration. Secondly, the value of peer input was quickly recognized because there could be greater acceptance of suggestions from age mates. In hindsight there were also (a) the benefits of fewer interruptions to one classroom because

FIG. 4.2   Ghost frightening child

FIG. 4.3   Vacuum cleaner sucking child and ghost away

all the children left at one time, and (b) a greater sense of support because cross-class and cross-grade bonds quickly developed. Some children also gained a heightened sense of competency from helping others and not always being in the helpless role. One child, terribly anxious initially, directed her final entry to the counselor:

> I am a bird and you are a heart and you are flying high. You just about fall down but you get caught by me and I saved you.

Group Composition. The group was initially composed of second- and third-grade children, one gender, either self-referred or teacher referred. After signed parent permission was received, the group met for a forty-five-minute session once a week. Then two more referrals came in: a self-referral, who was having nightmares which had been somewhat resolved through medical intervention but were still upsetting, and a boy whose teacher was very concerned about his panic in any large group setting—to the point of refusing even to go into the gym for physical education. This brought us to a total of seven children in grades one to three. All were very keen to be there, and all but one were keen to share their material.

Activities. In each session every child has an opportunity to share a dream, telling it in the present tense. The counselor then summarizes the plot and reflects the feeling content, "That is really frightening when the monster bites you." The child has an opportunity to respond and correct any misunderstandings in the counselor's retelling. Often hearing it played back by an empathetic adult stimulates deeper emotions and newly remembered images for the child. This retelling and then reflecting of emotional content also model complete acceptance of all the material for other group members.

If the child is working on frightening dreams or images, the counselor then would ask what changes or new endings the child would like to have happen in the dream. Usually children can tell what different endings they would like. If the "how to" part of making the change is difficult, the counselor can suggest one or two alternatives and the child can choose one or make other suggestions. In groups, this is the time to include others in suggesting alternate strategies. Doing so allows students opportunities to practice problem-solving through creating new endings, and peer suggestions are very powerful for the children. The child whose dream is being worked on is usually quick to choose an appealing solution. The dream is then retold, rewritten, or redrawn with the new, often less frightening ending.

If the dream is being shared but has not distressed the child, then the ending can be left unchanged. The dream is told and listened to empathically, emotional content is reflected back, and the dream is summarized and then worked with in a different way. If there is a repetitive theme in the child's dreams from session to session, the counselor may ask, "How is this one like your dream about. . . ?" Once the children have learned a little about messages in dreams, they can work either individually or as a group with interpretation. It is critically important, however, that no one tells a child "This means . . ." and state or even imply that there is any one specific, correct interpretation. Dreams are a form of complex, symbolic communication from the inner self and are somewhat different for every individual. Some ideas may tentatively be suggested and may feel appropriate for the dreamer, but no one can know for certain what another's dream is about. Any interpretation by others must be cautiously undertaken.

In every session each of the children has an opportunity to share if he or she wishes, using the procedure described earlier. Before the sharing segment, however, the children are given either some dream information or a question (Kincher, 1988), such as "Why do we dream?" with a discussion following. Student responses may include "So we don't get bored while we sleep," "we need to sort out what happened during the day and this is our quiet time for that," and "what we eat before we go to bed makes different dreams." Early in the series, the children's book *The Dream Eater* (Garrison, 1986) can be read to help the children understand that everyone, even adults, has bad dreams and also that there are ways of dealing with them.

Other questions which could be used at the beginning of sessions include "Why do babies dream more than us? What helps us to remember dreams? Why do some people say that they don't dream? Why do some people dream in color and some in black and white? Can there be a message or idea in dreams? Tell us more about that" (Kincher, 1988). The purpose of these questions is to focus the group back on dreaming and leave behind whatever home and classroom issues may be at the forefront of their awareness.

In the sessions the children are given a choice of sequence for who will go first, second, etc. Often those who really need "air time" are quick to ask to go first, yet decrease requests to be first as the sessions progress. Slowly those who choose not to share will move from no sharing, to private sharing with the counselor, to a tape-recorded sharing, and eventually to group sharing in some form.

Dream Enactment. If group work is being done, there are opportunities for activities that do not lend themselves to individual work. One outstanding success is the enactment of the dream. Following the first sharing of the dream, roles are determined by the counselor (counselor familiarity with psychodrama enactment or sculpting techniques is essential), and the dreamer assigns the roles and chooses the role s/he will play. A rehearsal is "walked through" for stage direction, lines, confirmation of props, and so forth. The dream is enacted, and at the end each "character" is required to tell what it was like to be that person or thing. The dreamer is given an opportunity to rewrite any part if s/he wishes, and it is re-enacted in the new version. Occasionally the counselor will request a change in the story line as a way of assisting the child in working through an issue in a non-threatening third-party way. Obviously, having the time and props to enhance the drama is useful but not necessary.

Benefits include actually experiencing the dream or fantasy in the outer world, gaining insight from others in the group, including those chosen to be "audience," and the recognition that understanding of dream material is possible. A summary activity may be used when the counselor wants to help the child address some aspect of the dream—e.g., "go up to the monster and ask why it is there in the dream," "what message does it have," or even "overpower it in some way." One child said, "I pull out its belly button and it just fades away like a balloon shrinking." However the monster is worked with, the children can and do often gain a sense of mastery over "the fearful," thereby adding to the development of their own inner strengths. Sometimes the child's summary is as simple as "I shouldn't watch Freddy movies any more!"

Case Examples

Through dream discussions and other activities, children can resolve a concern or recognize the underlying reason for their behavior around bad dreams—e.g., "When I have a bad dream Mommy and Daddy let me come into their bed or sometimes they snuggle with me for a long time." Then the issues of parent time can be worked on privately. The group helped one child who repeated a theme about his fear of moving to a small town and not making any friends by discussing how one can make friends. His concern is illustrated in his picture (fig. 4.4) and story:

> When I went to sleep last night I had a dream about me moving. I felt scared. I dreamed I would have no freinds and I felt my puppy wiggeling my bed. I dreamed I was in a moving van, but I woke up and looked where I was. Thank God I was still at home.

Another girl heard an accident outside her window and thought "My grandma could die in an accident like that." Later that night the family received a call that indeed the grandmother, who was very close to this girl, had been killed. She felt an enormous sense of responsibility for the accident and feared that she caused it and could cause such drastic consequences again. Through writing and drawing out the images, combined with group discussion and sharing, she was able to internalize alternate, comfortable explanations for this coincidence, including the concept that Grandma may have been saying a special goodbye to her by some way we do not really understand. After three sessions on the topic, the child no longer brought it up and later left a note saying that she was not having any more nightmares about it.

FIG. 4.4   My dream

The little boy who had panic attacks on entering assemblies or gym made considerable change and was even able to participate in a small play for the whole school. Initially this child was very resistant to sharing within the group but did eventually participate in all activities. The opportunity to work through the emotional components of his fear through "dream" work seemed critically important. Several months later the child was still able to manage large group situations without going into an absolute panic.

Summary

Frightening dreams and childhood fears have a lot in common. Usually these emotional experiences mean that the child's ego is overwhelmed by the strength of feeling embedded in the experience. The counselor's (or parent's) task is to help the ego integrate the affect, understand the cause, and practice new and more empowering or assertive behaviors. Some lessening of overwhelming affect and integration of feeling occur when the child verbalizes the dream to significant others and when the feeling content is manifested by the counselor's empathic reflections. Further integration occurs in the writing and drawing and in the psychodrama activities. These activities help make the unconscious conscious. Something needing to be brought out (i.e., a buried emotion) has been externalized and explored. As a result the child feels empowered and experiences less fear. By confronting and befriending some of the frightening images, the child learns about the inner "sage" Self, nurtures the innate growth orientation, and feels more able to manage what has been most unsettling.

Articulating and encoding these inner images brings them into the realm of normalcy, of activities typical in a school setting— creative writing, word processing and computers, communication with others, and peer or social learning. Feeling comfortable with this process often leads to maintaining an ongoing dream journal beyond the time of formal group meetings. This in turn leads to more externalization of inner issues and a generalization to coping skills for life.

Although much of the material presented in this chapter is based on a remedial orientation, the ideas can be used in a developmental way also. Dream work and fearful experiences can be used in regular classroom journal writing; they can be done as a unit to stimulate creative writing or done as an opening activity to allow release of tensions brought into school from early morning awakening and home routines. Garfield (1984) and Kincher (1988) both present easy-to-follow suggestions and guidelines for a developmental approach.

Recognizing the intensity of dreams and fears and working with them in some written form decreases children's anxieties and tensions, providing a balance to the primarily cognitive focus of the educational system. This work stimulates creativity, especially for children who have difficulty generating creative writing material, because it taps directly into the inner creative self and nurtures it. Finally, dream work helps clarify that inner sense of "Who am I and what am I about?", strengthening coping strategies and problem-solving skills. All of these lead to a stronger presence within the child and a stronger relationship between the child's conscious and unconscious personalities. This deeper connection enables children to live in relationship to their "true" self, enjoying the new, the different, the challenging, becoming one who is better able to learn and to trust a personal ability to function effectively in the world.

Chapter 5

LETTER WRITING IN COUNSELING

THE MAJORITY OF children enjoy getting mail, and many will happily send it in anticipation of a response. Thus, an effective supplemental technique for busy counselors is the use of notes and letters under various circumstances. Ideally, each counselor will see the child face to face on every encounter. However, the reality of hectic schedules, frequent emergency interruptions, special classroom events, and heavy case loads necessitates alternate forms of case management at times. When, for some reason, the child or counselor has to miss a session, a brief note or letter can keep the attachment bond alive. This chapter describes several ways that writing notes and letters can facilitate counseling and emotional development.

Letters from the Counselor

Counselors can write letters or just send notes or memos. Often a personalized memo form associated with the counselor becomes very special to the recipients. Some little sketch or cartoon, especially if it is of a theme that has come up in sessions, or a postcard from the location where the counselor is on holiday maintains the attachment bond at a time when the child needs the contact. When appointments have been unavoidably missed, or when you have heard that things seem to be rocky, or when there are new developments, then a note entitled "I've been thinking of you" seems to help.

Written communication can be taken care of quickly. It provides easy access to students, even when the counselor is not in the school full time. It allows the counselor to keep in touch with youngsters whose crises are not of high priority but who at times need renewed support or just a reminder that they are still valued. Here is a brief letter to a boy who left a note saying "The shaking is back. From Jamie."

Dear Jamie,
I got the two notes you left for me. I'm pleased you can put your feelings on paper to share with me during the week. Our time together is Thursday at 1:00, unless the shaking is so bad that you need to see me before then. If so, call.

Your Counselor

Here is an example of a letter to a student who had experiences with illness and loss. This was written by the counselor when she became unexpectedly ill and had to miss six weeks of work.

Dear Andrea,
Did you have a good rest over the winter vacation? I hope so. I know you were tired a lot and got a really bad cold just as school ended.

Now that you're back in school, you may have heard that I will be away for a while. Just as the holidays started I found out that I needed a surprise operation. Now I'm home from the hospital and getting better quickly, but I still need lots of rest.

You'd laugh to see how slowly I shuffle along or sit down and get up again! I even need a nap each day! I know you've had some sad experiences with people being sick and being gone a long time. I wanted to let you know that I'll be well and back in February, just in case you heard kids talk and thought maybe I was sicker than I am.

I think of you often and look forward to our visits each week once I'm back at school. See you in February.

Hugs,
Your Counselor

Sometimes the children move to a new home and school in the middle of the counseling, when the work has not been finished. These children often benefit from a follow-up letter:

Dear Karen,
You've lived in your new home and gone to your new school for a little while now. I know you were really scared about the move before you left. How has it been?

Is your new school different from this one? Is it bigger or

smaller? Are the kids friendly? Can you describe some friends you've made there? How do you like your new classroom?

Has moving and settling in been as much of an adventure as we talked about? Which of your worries turned out not to be a problem? Wow! That's a lot of questions, isn't it!

A part of you likely misses your old school and the kids and our special times together. I miss our time, too, but I hope by now you are feeling more comfortable in your new home.

Are you still writing in your journal? That often helped when you were upset but didn't feel like sharing before. You were getting lots of ideas about what to do with those scared feelings too from working with it.

I think of you often and send a big hug with this!

Hugs,
Your Counselor

At times, when a child makes a sudden move, there is not enough time to resolve some troublesome issues. These can be appropriately addressed in a letter from the counselor:

Dear Jason,

Yesterday, I saw Mrs. M. at the club and she said you're in a new school now. How are you doing?

I know changes are hard for you and there were sure a lot of them for you this fall—two new teachers, a new counselor, a new worker, and even a new T.A.! Mrs. M. was really special to you, and it must have been hard not to work with her. I guess you were pretty angry when she started helping other kids and never worked with you at all. It's really hard to share people we're used to and like a lot, and harder still when there are so many different people all at once!

Lots of kids told me they pretend it doesn't matter when they have to go to a new school, but that inside they're really upset, angry, scared, or sad. It's okay to feel that way. But it's important to get those feelings out too.

You may find you have some of those feelings and need to get them out before you feel like you're going to burst! You may want to talk to your teacher or T.A. in the new class. There's a counselor in your school who's a really good listener and who has a playroom too. You may even want to write to Mrs. M. or to me. If you do, your teacher will make sure we get the letter.

Sometimes things seem so crummy everything just seems hopeless. Remember, Jason, you've made a lot of progress since you got to our school and people like Mrs. M., Mr. Corbett, Bill, and I have all seen that side of you that shows what a great kid you are. Please keep up that effort and let people in your new school see that side of you too.

Take care,
Your Counselor

Letters to the Whole Class

Much of the work we do in the schools is developmental and preventive in nature and involves working with a whole class (Allan and Nairne, 1989). Some of the problems we work with are complicated and difficult and involve hurt, anger, and outraged feelings. Even after an issue has been dealt with verbally, after a period of a few days we have found it useful to send a letter to the class to summarize some of the main issues and findings so that a clearer understanding and improved communications can be maintained.

This letter went out to a seventh-grade classroom where a group of boys had harassed one of the girls. Though the discussions had cleared the air, we felt it necessary to follow up and to leave openings if more hurt needed to be expressed:

Dear Grade Sevens:

Thank you for participating in the class discussions. I've read all of the sheets I asked you to hand in and would like to share the general ideas written on them.

For the most part the girls are feeling angry that this happened and scared that it could have happened to any one of them. They're thinking that it is difficult to understand how guys they've known for so long could have done it.

They seem to want the boys to know that, while they really like them, they also want them to respect their privacy rights. They do not want their personal boundaries violated.

For the most part the boys are feeling upset and sorry about what happened, and many feel badly because they believed rumors or did not intervene in any way. They are thinking that anyone being put down by a group is unfair.

They seem to want the girls to know that they need really clear communication when they are upset or mad because they may misunderstand the message otherwise.

I hope these discussions have helped you all. If I've missed anything that you want me to know or to share generally, please leave me a note or see me in my office. Again, thank you for the mature way you participated in the discussions.

Sincerely,
School Counselor

There are cautions to this form of contact. First is that whatever is included should not reflect any confidential information. It is also important to use language, both words and syntax, that the child is likely to understand without adult translation. Printing rather than writing can be very important also for the primary and the learning-disabled children. Often, judgmental terms such as "Good for you," "I'm proud of you for scoring so high," etc., can have a negative effect, which is much less readily rectified than in face-to-face sessions. It is also necessary that promises are not made in writing, especially for appointments or other situations that are difficult to guarantee.

Letters from Students

Sometimes these letters occur spontaneously when students feel a need to write to counselors and do so of their own accord. If the counselor is in another school, a note or letter helps them connect with you and to externalize some of their pain, concern, and worry and let the counselor know a session is desired. Students need to know that they can write to counselors and leave their notes or letters directly in the counselor's box in the office without having to go through the principal, teachers, or secretaries. Sometimes they write about a flare-up of an old problem, a new one following termination, a reminder that they want another session, or an update from a new school. Sometimes students use notes to self-refer. A third grader and counselor communicated as follows:

Dear Counselor,
A couple of days ago my grandpa had a heart attack.

From Curt

Her reply was:

Dear Curt:
I'm really sorry to hear about your grandpa and would like to talk
to you about it. Your teacher and I will pick a good time for you
to visit with me tomorrow.

Your Counselor

After he had been included in a new series of group sessions, he
wrote:

Dear Counselor,
Even though today is the first day at your group, I really feel better now that I have shared what I am scared of.

From Curt

If a deep rapport has been established, students will write about
some very profound hurts, as in this next letter.

Dear Counselor,
Things with my mom and dad are getting a little sad again because when my dad drops us off sometimes my dad wants to see
my mom and then they go to the basement and talk and when
they talk sometimes they get to carried away and start to yell at
each other and when they do I go to my brother's room but otherwise I'm doing fine. Sort of every thing I find that my dad gave
me, I find it in my room and I start to cry. I found this book that
my dad gave to me and he got it at Easter at 1986. I'm glad that
I found it and it is called "love helps you grow" and 1986 is when
I was about 5 years old. This book looks like brand new I haven't
seen him yet since Monday and I'm going to ask him if he still
has his wedding ring and eny of my fries read it because it is so
seisnle.

Love,
Your friend Crystal

Such a letter obviously needs a detailed reply:

Dear Crystal:
Thank you for your letter. I miss our special times together, but it helps me to know how things are when you write to me.

It sounds like you really miss your Daddy still and that you feel really sad that Mom and Dad are apart.

When they get carried away talking and then yelling, do you feel scared and sad? Sometimes kids get angry too when that happens. It's okay to feel like that, and all mixed up too.

I'm really glad you can share your sad feelings. Do you tell your Mom and Dad that you're sad too?

How do you feel when you read the book *Love Helps You Grow*?

How did your talk with Dad about the wedding ring go?

You sound like you have some things you do that really help you when you are sad. Can you tell me more about those?

Love,
Your Counselor

When students are going through or have come through a difficult period, it is helpful to ask them to write about it and to try to "put their feelings into words." Writing helps them to externalize their pain in a safe and protected space (i.e., the piece of paper or in their diary), which reduces, or relieves, some of the current emotional impact and allows them to integrate their pain and struggles into consciousness. Even when alone and struggling, they can be encouraged to think about taking out a piece of paper and writing. Here is an example from a seventh grader.

Dear Mrs. Collins:
I feel terrible. I feel lousey. Here I am sitting in the library trying to study for my socials test and I can't remember a thing I've read. I'm so scared that I'm going to fail that my worry stops me remembering. I never thought of that before but I am really nervous. Maybe I just need to relax. I'll close my eyes and go through the deep breathing you showed me. . . . I feel better now and can go back to reading and studying. Thanks for your help even though you aren't here!

Your friend Trudy

The girl starts this letter by addressing her counselor (Mrs. Collins) and simply putting her most prevalent feeling down on the paper. This seems to get the flow going, and the more she writes the more aware she becomes of other feelings and their effect on her ability to study. Soon she comes up with her own solution, can put it into practice, shows a little humor, and then gets on with her work. (She actually got a B on the test.) This school counselor had encouraged Trudy to write to her previously and to do this whenever she was hurting. She was told to start the letter with "Dear Counselor" or "Dear Mrs. Collins."

When some students have come out of a very difficult period, it is possible to ask them to write about it so that they might be able to help others. For example, one can say to them, "You know, you have just worked through a really painful experience. You have suffered a lot, but you've come through it and grown. I wonder if you would be interested in writing about it so that other students can read it. I think it would be very helpful to them. You could address it: 'To whom it may concern.'" The following was written by a girl who became pregnant and had her baby.

> To Whom It May Concern: My experience with pregnancy.
> I was asked if I would like to write a letter to other girls my age on what it was like to be pregnant and only 15 / 16. I had the option to turn it down, but I didn't want to because if I can spare one girl from going through what I had to it will be worth it. And maybe that girl is you.
>
> First of all it's obvious what happened to start the ball rolling. He was my first boyfriend and a few years older than me. We had been going together for a little over a year when I became pregnant. It was my first time, his too, and I guess it really didn't sink in what we were actually doing. All it seemed like was passion at its peak. But what it really turned out to be was 9 months of stress, painful decisions, and guilt.
>
> I tried to convince myself I really wasn't pregnant and we really did a good job. He kept telling me I wasn't and although the odds were against us we tried to make ourselves believe it. But by four months, one really can start to wonder. And I did. It was so hard! We didn't tell anyone for 5 months. We didn't go to the doctor and we kept lying to ourselves that I really wasn't pregnant although we had a pretty good idea that I was.

Finally I had to tell my mom and dad. I had always been a fairly good kid and they were shocked and disappointed. My mom seemed to never stop crying. Neither did I. I felt so ashamed. I felt like I betrayed them. The guilt level was very intense.

Then came the cruncher. All of my friends found out. I've never felt as bad as I did whenever I knew that someone else had just found out.

At 5 and a half months I started to show. I only told when I was five months along. I kept it a secret for 5 months. That was tough. That's how long it took me to get up the courage to tell anybody.

Being pregnant and fat wasn't fun. People stared wherever I went. I tried not to let it bother me but . . . well that is hard to do. Morning sickness isn't something I would like to have over either.

At about six months I realized that I had to break up with my boyfriend. Now, that was hard to do after so long of being so close—it was really hard to let go. But I knew that I had to because he wasn't right for me.

After I did that I had to face the decision of what I was going to do next. The idea of having a baby is great and it was exciting. But I really had to think about the situation and decide what was best all around. I certainly wasn't ready to be a single parent and I wouldn't want to offer my baby the immaturity of a sixteen-year-old. The decision I made was the best one for me and I know that I gave my baby the opportunity to have a proper and wonderful life. I don't want you to think that the decision was an easy one, it was the hardest one that I think I'll ever make. It was so hard to do. I know it was the best thing and I have no regrets. I really feel I did it out of love and that's the only way I think I could have shown it to my baby.

Labor wasn't the most pleasant experience. Now it doesn't seem so bad, I wouldn't go through it again for a long time, but then I thought I was going to die. You won't know what I mean until you experience it yourself.

It was a boy. After he was born it was such a relief to not be in so much discomfort (pain). But the hard part still wasn't over. For me personally, I had to see what he looked like. As I stared at him through the glass window my heart ached. It was so hard to believe that that little baby was mine. He was so tiny and adorable, thinking about it now I get tears in my eyes. I can only say that he was really here. I know that adopting was the best thing, but seeing him makes you wish that you could start all over again and not have to go through the whole experience.

I got pictures taken of him and I got to send a letter with his parents to tell him the situation and that . . . I really loved and cared about him, and I only wanted the best for him.

He will always be a special part of my life. I would rather that I had waited until I was ready to be a parent but it is too late now. I had to make the best of the situation, and for me I know I did. My life is getting back to normal as much as possible and I only hope that someday when I am ready that I will have the privilege of being a parent, because to me it really is "a privilege."

This type of letter works in a number of different ways. It helps the student integrate what has happened to her; it can also boost her self-esteem and let her feel she can be helpful to others. Also, reading a statement written by a peer can be more valuable than adult support because it provides other students with a sense of hope and can decrease feelings of loneliness.

The Unsent Letters

Everyone experiences times when emotional distress is so intense it is almost overwhelming, threatening to spill out of its own accord. In some instance, if the emotions are shared with others directly involved, even greater problems can arise. There are also occasions when it is not possible to communicate with the other person. There are times when clear, direct communication is necessary, but times when working through the emotional tangle is best done without informing the other at all. Thus, a dilemma arises: there is a need to vent the emotions in order to regain stability, yet engaging the other may well exacerbate the problem. One technique for dealing with both aspects of this dilemma is to use the "Unsent Letter."

The unsent letter is written without any censorship. The individual knows ahead of time that it is *not* going to be sent. Therefore, all feelings are more likely to be expressed. The writer is encouraged to say everything about the situation that he would like to say and to allow the emotional outpouring to flow. Sometimes students like to articulate the consequences for the person who has upset them.

Often these are severe, as when a child describes what she would like to do to the other person. Here there is safety from the consequences of one's action, as nothing will need to be enacted in the outer world. However, the deep inner images of revenge, retaliation, and re-empowerment will have gained recognition and expression. For example, one girl wrote the following unsent letter to her classmate (she gave it to her counselor for "safe keeping"):

> Peter Simpson:
> I hate you, I hate you, I HATE YOU. How could you tell Derek I loved him. It's a lie. I don't love him. I like him. Now you've embarrassed me and made a great big mess of everything. Oh, I hate you.
>   CONSEQUENCES: Because you did this to me you deserve to die. Not quickly but slowly. You can call out to your friends to help you but they will just look at you and walk away because you have NO FRIENDS NOW. You'll even call out to me and plead with me but I'll say NO.
>
> > Your enemy,
> > Lisa

Because we believe so strongly in the value of externalizing the inner conflict, we often encourage its expression in some form. Writing a letter to the other person allows two important aspects of resolution to occur. First is the clarification of what the feelings and issues are all about. By writing it out, the conscious mind is putting into words those images and feelings which are consuming energy in the unconscious. There is a structure generated for making sense of the subjective experience. Often this clarification process leads to increased understanding of related aspects of the issue. For example, if a child is really upset that grounding is the punishment for being late and so he will miss a party that everyone else is attending, the letter-writing activity may bring to the surface such issues as not being permitted to attend previous peer functions.

The second aspect of resolution is that the emotions are expressed, but without the consequences of a face-to-face confrontation. For children especially, the anticipated reactions of adults often act as a deterrent to expressing anything negative. Few children want a parent or teacher to be angry with them, yet few adults are able to be objective when a child attempts to vent his or her anger or pain. Either they become defensive, if the concern relates to them, or they become rational, helping the child understand things from the other adult's perspective. The child who is really angry with the parent for breaking a promise usually finds the parent describing how impossible it was to follow through on the promise, and if the child pushes the issue with "But you *promised!*" the parent often responds with anger rather than apologizing or owning up to a mistake. Similarly, a parent may defend a teacher who is called a liar by the child at home for a broken promise at school, thus failing to make the child feel understood even though the parent only wishes to help him or her see all the reasons why it happened. Strong emotions expressed as an accusation are usually not well received by adults, from each other or from a child, and yet a child needs an outlet for both the experience and the emotions it stirs up. A fifth grader wrote to his teacher but gave the letter to his counselor:

Mr. Jackson:
You are a liar. You said to my Mom that you didn't squeeze my arm. You said I started the fight with Sean. I didn't. He kept calling me names. You are unfair. You don't like me. I don't want to be in your class. You have favorites. You make promises and then you break them. You say we can have an outing and then you take it away. I don't like you.

Mike

It was interesting that, when Mike shared the letter with the counselor, the latter picked up on the "You don't like me—I don't like you" part:

C.:   Mike, you're mad at Mr. Jackson, you don't like him, and you feel he doesn't like you.

Mike: Yeah, I know he doesn't. He keeps picking on me. (He starts to cry.)

C.:   That really hurts. I imagine that part of you wants him to like you. Is there anyone else who you feel does not like you?

Mike: Yeah. My Dad. He likes Pat [younger brother] better than me. He always plays with him, takes him out to hockey. He yells at me, hits me. . . (starts to cry again).

C.:   You think your Dad dislikes you, loves your brother more than you, and that things will never change. (Yeah) Mike, have you actually told your dad that?

Mike: No—no way.

C.:   You don't think that would help? How about if you and I met with him together and I tried to help you two get on better. Maybe he doesn't know how you are feeling.

Mike: Okay, but I don't want Pat there.

This is not an uncommon situation, where the teacher receives the brunt of the negative projection displaced from the father. Unfortunately, in many situations, the teacher does not realize what is occurring, takes the hostility personally, and begins to dislike, or even hate, the child. When teachers experience consistently any type of strong feeling (anger, love, fear) toward a student, it is advisable to consult with the counselor to try to understand the transference and countertransference issues.

When the child is encouraged to write a letter to the adult or to other children, the benefits of "clearing the air" are often many. Sometimes there is a concern that someone will find the letter, so it is advisable to explain follow-up options also before the letter is written. There are several things that can be done. For example, the letter can be shared with the counselor and used as a vehicle for discussion within the session. It can be written by the child, sealed, and stored. For many children, having it stored in the counselor's filing cabinet, which is kept locked, adds to a sense of security and privacy. For others, having written it is enough, and so the child or the child and counselor can destroy it. We would encourage this destruction to be done with as much ritual as possible. A solemn attitude, the respect due a significant ritual, and some appropriate words such as "As I tear up this sheet of paper filled with my thoughts and feelings about the fight, I can let go of their power, bit by bit" all help reinforce the serious nature of the activity.

The Unsent Letter and Bereavement

A particularly valuable use of the unsent letter is in dealing with bereavement. One aspect of dealing with grief is the need to complete unfinished business with the deceased. Some techniques such as guided imagery and puppetry can be useful, but lack the emphasis of the unsent letter in reminding the child that "real" contact with the deceased is no longer possible. For children who need reminders of the finality of death or who need more ritual around the ending, the unsent letter is helpful.

The child writes the things that need to be said, whether matters that upset her or possible anger at the individual for dying. Often the expression of these negative aspects of the relationship then allow the child to tap into the pain of the loss. Frequently, the letter concludes with the traditional "I miss you," "I love you" types of statements.

Again, the ritual of what to do with the finished product is very important. If the deceased has been cremated, the child may wish to burn the letter. In some cases the authors have taken the students to the cemetery where the deceased was buried, and the letters were left at the grave. In another situation we left the letter in a chapel adjacent to the cemetery. Although these experiences are very emotional for the child, being in that environment with the counselor who is not part of the bereaved family can provide her or him with a profoundly cathartic experience.

The following is part of a letter written by a pre-adolescent girl, grieving the death of grandparents. They had died eight years earlier. In many ways they were parent substitutes, as her mother had been very ill for some years.

> Dear Granddad and Grandmom,
> I miss both of you very much. I wish we could go back in time and I could see you again. I remember all those lovely gifts and hugs you gave me. I also can remember your lovely smiles. But it is still a shock to me that you are all gone.
> Have many people visited your graves? I hope they have.
> I guess it's time to say good-bye.
>
> > Love, Sara
>
> P.S. Here are some cards for you to show that I love you.

Summary

Letter writing is a very important part of the counseling process and of self-healing. Letter writing allows for movement in the psyche: thoughts and emotions are expressed and emptied out into the safe and protected space (the page), thus providing relief and, at the same time, an opening for new thoughts and emotions to emerge. In writing, students take an active stance toward the healing process as they help to heal themselves by doing. There is a death–life transformational process at work here. They enter their pain by admitting it and writing about it, thus integrating it into ego consciousness. With this, repression is decreased, and more physical and psychological energy is now experienced, often as a sense of renewal. Having one's written pieces read and acknowledged by a significant adult (counselor, teacher, or parent) helps the student feel understood and more attached.

Part III

DISCUSSION AND WRITING

Chapter 6

GROUP STORYWRITING:
SOCIAL SKILLS FOR ACTING-OUT AND
WITHDRAWN PRIMARY-AGED BOYS

ONE OF THE most frequent types of referrals in an elementary school is the acting-out child; one of the most under-referred groups is the quiet, withdrawn child. Common to both is the children's difficulty with participating effectively within the classroom. Either they are busy being noisy and attention-seeking, or they are quiet and avoiding interactive involvement with the learning process. In both situations, their ability to absorb new concepts and skills is limited. The attention-seekers also interfere with the learning of all the youngsters in the room because they are distracting to everyone else and often require direct, one-to-one teacher intervention to settle or remove them.

Two aspects of these children need to be addressed. First is the strengthening of "good learner" behaviors, the confidence to ask and to answer questions, the ability to listen, the willingness to settle into a written task right away, and the ability to maintain an activity for at least a minimal time period. Second is the need to address underlying psychological difficulties which are perpetuating these inappropriate behaviors. Even primary-aged children have already learned maladaptive behaviors which help them get their needs met. These behaviors may or may not be functional for a school setting intent upon cognitive and social learning, but they are familiar and comfortable for the child. Children will not readily abandon these familiar patterns until new behaviors which feel safe and practiced are in place.

The material presented in this chapter describes a technique for working with children in a small group. While using an academic approach, storywriting, the children are learning new behaviors for working with others and are also being given an opportunity to release deeper emotional issues which are often underlying their behavior. First, the rationale for this approach is given. It is followed by a general description of a group with whom the technique was used, and then the method and products of the sessions are described in some detail. The chapter concludes with a summary of these sessions and with suggestions for other ways to use the technique.

Rationale

One way to facilitate change in learner behaviors and to address the psychological needs is to do group work with both behavioral extremes represented in one group. This allows for new behaviors to be learned over time in the small group and then practiced there first, before being tried out in the classroom. Seeing others model another way of being in the world, the children gain a clearer awareness of alternatives, even as they initially continue with their own style. In the classroom there is a continuum between these extremes, and children may not readily observe differences there.

An additional advantage to small group work is that the underlying problems need not be addressed directly: the children can learn new school behaviors as they arise in the group (e.g., not speaking out when it is another's turn). Also, the group setting provides an opportunity for the release of tensions, because sessions can be structured to meet the needs of the group. For example, if tension is building up in the students and they need to be "silly" to release it, the counselor or teacher can build in a "five-minute silly break" within the group structure. In the group described here, there was a need for "grossness" or gore to be vented but somehow keeping the atmosphere appropriate to school tasks. The venting, sometimes described in psychology as "negative practice," reduces tension so that quieter and more adaptive behaviors can be expressed.

The counselor chose to have the children discuss and write a series of group stories. Writing fits well with the language arts activities; however, the boisterousness that developed at times could not easily have been accommodated in a larger classroom. The social skills of working cooperatively, but still under counselor direction, helped the children form a sense of belonging and cohesion which their behavior prevented in the classroom. Because there were only two or three of them in any classroom, they had previously been very aware of feeling like an outsider, in spite of a great deal of teacher caring. The trust within the group eventually nurtured their self-esteem to the point they could all participate and even encourage others' participation.

Case Example

The group consisted of six boys in second and third grades. Two were very quiet and shy; the other four were management problems in their classrooms, defying authority, demanding a great deal of teacher attention, disturbing classmates, and often being very aggressive in class and on the playground. Part of the need for "gore" had to do with age and gender of the group, and part had to do with their life background. One child had not resolved his parents' divorce, remarriage, and current discussions of where he should live, including the possibility of out-of-jurisdiction custody not being recognized (if he visited the non-custodial parent, he may not be returned home again). Another had seen a severe accident and subsequent limb loss of a loved relative, while another had been removed from an abusive, alcoholic home. One child had moved repeatedly (Allan and Bardsley, 1984), living in a series of common-law families, while another very sensitive child had been distressed by divorce, calling one parent "bad and evil." The last child's father had been killed by a drunk driver.

Although each could have benefitted from a therapeutically focused group, there was a significant gap between the boys' academic performance and ability. Therefore, the decision was made to attempt a more structured learning-oriented activity whereby the counselor provided the activities (discussions and storywriting) but the students generated the content.

Method

After receiving parent permission and determining a suitable time for the teachers to have the students out of the classes, the group met for half an hour once a week over eight sessions. In the first session, the counselor met with students, got them to introduce themselves, went over the purpose of the group times, and set the ground rules.

The purpose of our group is to discuss and write stories together for eight sessions. I will be your secretary, and you will each dictate a sentence and I'll write it down. We will go around the group three or four times each session. I've provided paper, pencil, and crayons so you can draw while we talk if you wish. Once we have finished the story I'll re-read it, and you can decide on a title.

It was decided to use paper and crayons so that the students could be doing something with their hands while one student was talking and dictating his sentence. These were also used so that the images in the stories or from the child's unconscious could have a concrete outlet.

The first two stories, exceedingly violent and gory, involved such creatures as an ogre, a troll, and King Kong. At this point, one of the quiet boys suggested building a model, and we decided to use "Mad Scientist Dissect-An-Alien™" the Mattel Company, as it combined blood and gore with reconstruction and healing. From this point on, the group alternated between doing the model and writing; some of this involved the group writing of the operative report.

First Story

THE OGRE AND THE TROLL

Once upon a time there was this troll. The troll stepped on somebody. He barfed acid on the guy and the guy melted. And also when anybody crossed the bridge they had to pay him all their gold or he would kill them, unless they didn't have any gold.

One person didn't have any gold and he threw him off the bridge into the spiky waters that evil creatures lived in. And when he got into the water the creatures bit him to pieces.

Then all the creatures that lived in the water ate all of the eyeballs, head, bones, and guts.

The troll and his brother ogre picked up the house that had a man in it and ripped off his head. The head came off and the ogre stepped on it and the brain came out the ears.

The troll was still at that bridge and the ogre came over and ripped up the bridge. Then there was a big, big monster in the water and he ate up the bridge, and then he swam to another river and ate all the bridges and then he exploded!

The question has to be asked: Why did such a story appear, and what does it mean? Basically, the counselor has provided a safe and protected space (the guidance group room) and a method (discussion and writing) for the children's unconscious fantasies to be expressed and recorded. From our theoretical standpoint (see Allan, 1988), in such a therapeutic setting, children will project images and fantasies that have relevance to their personal lives and developmental struggles. This is a story about the internal struggle of "good" and "bad" feelings. Here is a safe place for the students to unload all their bad thoughts and feelings. They do not have to keep the lid on them any more, and out they tumble! Orally, they can freely express their aggressive and violent feelings—in the presence of a caring and unworried adult—which in turn provides a release of tension and in the long run will enable their egos to integrate and master their own violence and their woundedness. These types of children have often been physically abused and/or wounded by their own profoundly hurt emotions. In certain ways they need to get these feelings out, on paper, in order that change, growth, transformation, and integration can occur.

Although this story was much more violent than expected, the counselor allowed it to continue. Each boy's illustration allowed him to work on his more specific material, yet still be part of the group. There was much hooting and discussion of the content, but when one child was speaking the others were encouraged to respect his time and so the noise level dropped. They were told when it was time to give their last sentence. The session ended with a reading of the complete story and an opportunity for the boys to share their illustrations of it. The counselor thanked the boys as a group for their respect for the group's work and process, then thanked each one for a specific contribution—e.g., "The quiet way you handed out the paper at the beginning was helpful. Thank you." "Thank you for encouraging T. to share his idea." "I appreciate the way you waited for your turn even though you *really* wanted to give your idea next. Thank you."

Second Story

The following week, the boys were eager to get out of class, and two attempted to come a half hour early. One child was very quiet and "passed" on his turn twice. The following is the story from that week.

KING KONG

Once upon a time King Kong was born and he picked up this guy. And he turned him into a flat hotcake and threw it onto the Statue of Liberty, knocking it right into the water. Then it floated off like a boat and everybody can have one now 'cause there are boats in the water. Then he got really mad 'cause everybody is getting them and he picked up every boat and he crushed them in his hands. Some got smashed, and some got injured and some got crushed right into the pavement.

So he stepped on their heads and brains came out of their nose, ears, and mouths. And then he went to Scotland and picked up a whole bunch of water and sea creatures in it and turned them all into a big, humungous, humungous, humungous, HUMUNGOUS Statue of Liberty and danced with it!

He danced onto the Statue of Liberty and flattened it and threw it at the moon and sliced it into three parts and that was the end of morning, night, and day. Everyone started yelling so loud that King Kong got mad and crushed a person between his fingers and he gots flattened and thrown like a frisbee all around the world. And then he catches it and throws it in the garbage. The end.

This story continues the theme of the struggles between "good emotions" (as symbolic of the Statue of Liberty) and "bad emotions" (as symbolized by King Kong), with the "bad" clearly winning out again. Here then is the projection of their abused, damaged, and violated parts (emotions) onto others. The students are moving from a situation of powerlessness (where this pain happened to them) to a situation of mastery and power where they inflict their pain on others. Seen in a developmental sequence, this fantasy activity restores their power and coping ability. It is interesting that the Statue of Liberty gets destroyed. She, of course, is the Goddess of Justice and Protector of the Innocent. These children (our students) were not protected from early harm and violence, and so not surprisingly they are angry at the archetype of Justice.

However, they are ready now to move on to the next stage where there can be a calmer reparation of the outer violence and the heal- ing of the inner wounds and ugliness (i.e., ugly, painful feelings), as symbolized by the "Alien." After these two sessions, the group had become less rowdy and more cohesive. The children were ready to be more physically involved with a common task. Working with a model assured the participation of the child who had "passed" on some turns, yet this particular kit focused the outer as well as the inner awareness of all the children on rebuilding and healing.

First Alien Session

The mood of the sessions now became very serious, and each child was addressed as Dr. T., Dr. R., etc. The counselor explained that they had been entrusted with a very important job, and they would act as surgeons for an Alien. They determined the sequences of turns and never once challenged that decision. Before the dissection, they "scrubbed" at the sink. They maintained the cooperative roles throughout the session. When an adult inadvertently interrupted, she was eagerly told what was being done but that she could not touch because she had not "scrubbed."

In this Alien session, each boy had some body parts to insert (according to the directions in the kit) and placed his contribution inside the body cavity and added some "blood" (a thick gooey substance) around it. Surprisingly, the boy who wrote the more gory parts of previous stories was obviously very uncomfortable with touching the blood, in spite of all previous claims. The others were very supportive of his discomfort, suggesting alternatives and generally problem-solving without any adult assistance. When the sutures to close the incision would not seal the Alien, the boys made several suggestions, and finally the counselor was asked to discuss it with someone who could help.

Second Alien Session

This session consisted of a group writing of the operative report (fig. 6.1). The boys determined all the content, although the counselor provided the form.

Third Alien Session

This session was a more successful attempt at helping the Alien by correctly replacing its parts and being able to seal it up afterward. The successfully restored Alien was photographed for later use (fig. 6.2), although the children were not aware of this. The youngster who had had a problem touching the gooey stuff the first

FIG. 6.1

Operative Report

Date: 4 May 1989   Patient Name: Alien

Date of Surgery: 29 April 1989   Patient Number: 0017

Surgeons: Dr. B., Dr. K., Dr. R., Dr. T., Dr. W., Dr. P., Dr. C.

Pre-Operative Diagnosis: "Blurb outa partus"

Operation Performed: "Disectum and Transplantum"

Procedure and Findings:

1. The Alien was put on his back, and an incision was made from his chin to his tail to open the body.
2. The incision was held open, and the Branium was placed in the Branium Cavity.
3. The Stumukus was put in the body cavity.
4. The Mad Bladder was put on one side of the Stumukus.
5. The Spleenius was placed on the other side.
6. Fingers were used to put extra Alien Blood in the spaces around the organs.
7. The Liverot was nested in the middle.
8. The Heartipus fitted in the tail space, below the Liverot.
9. The Lungrass and Veinausea went on top, at the sides, of the Liverot.
10. The Intestink went into the tail on the Heartipus.
11. The Blooblob went in the very middle of the body cavity, with lots more blood.
12. The Fleshonus went in just under the chin.
13. The last organ to be put in was the Gutball, on top of the Blooblob.
14. All the spaces were filled in with Alien Blood.
15. The bandage with the sutures was pressed in place to hold the incision shut.

   All organs were placed in order. Blood was added every time. The body bulged at the end, and the sutures would not hold.
   The incision was closed with tape until a specialist could try again. The patient may get an infection if the cut is not closed soon. The patient is put in the care of Dr. B. until the next try.

Signature

---

time was very open, stating his difficulty out loud, and the other boys offered to do that part for him, but in a very matter-of-fact, not derisive way.

Fourth Alien Session

   This session included the write-up of the successful operative report, similar to the first, but with a prognosis (new vocabulary) of full recovery. The boys printed their own material this time. Comments in the "Procedures and Findings" included "Put more blood in to hold it," "Put bigger bandgeses on the top to put him together,"

FIG. 6.2   The alien

"Green slime and purple slime so we can make the body stick," and "Put the blob outa partus in beter."

These "Alien" sessions reflect a key stage in the healing process that is often possible after the violent outbursts as depicted in the first two stories. In our therapeutic experience, the expression of contained violence (i.e., in discussions, writing and drawing activities) seems to lead to the wish to repair the damage. This is called the reparatory process. The work on the Alien enables them to take an active and yet symbolic role in healing their own alien (unconscious) wounds. It is interesting that they readily take on the role of doctors and literally also help heal the group member who is most afraid of blood.

Third Story

The group went back to storywriting again in the next session, and the children described how they came upon the Alien:

When the spaceship from space came down, they were discovering Earth for their report and humans were chasing one of them, and he died because when he jumped off the bridge he thought there was grass, and he died because he fell in the water.

And when the helicopter found him, it brought him to us. And his body parts to us and they found most of his blood.

Then they bring him back to us and we put him together, but we messed him up this time and we took him apart again and then Mrs. Judi Bertoia took him to her husband and she asked him if he can put him together again and he didn't want to and she brought him back to the group. And somebody forgot to bring the purple blood to put him together again.

So we had to go out looking for it. While we were out looking for it, it came alive. It started chasing us and it couldn't catch us and it got mad and took out a bazooka. He chased us all over the place and he couldn't catch us and we set up a trap and caught him and put him in a jar and then took out his bazooka and chained it to the wall.

He tipped the jar open and burns the lid off and gets free. He tries and grabs the bazooka and gets it free. He gets into our operating room and blows it up. Then the Alien runs out and chases us. One of our shoes falls off. He shoots and then the whole building burns and we get out safely and run off. The Alien is trapped in the fire. He blows a hole in the wall and gets out and runs off. The Alien chases us to the city and gets lost and we found a place to hide. We live there for the rest of our lives.

Then later on he finds us in the city and then he chases us again and we're too fast for him so he gives up and his friends up in space are looking for him and can't find him. They come down in their space ship. Then we go home to our house and he just stays up in space and never comes down again.

That's all folks.

For the final meeting, the counselor had printed up the story and run off copies for the boys so they could follow along as the counselor read it. They laughed and enjoyed their creation as they listened and then discussed how well they worked together. They were disappointed to arrive at the end of the sessions, but we were approaching the end of the school year. Each boy was given a Polaroid picture of the Alien to remember the group by and again thanked for their unique contributions to the group. Following the sessions two of the boys sent the counselor the following thank-you note:

Tuesday June 20
Dear Mrs Bertoia
I like the Monster we pout together last week. Beefor we did storys they wer grous. Thank you for the pitcher and the reeriteid story.
From Jerry and Peter

The last story again reflects the struggle between the "good" and "bad" impulses. In the first part the emphasis is placed on putting the "damaged" self, as symbolized by the "Alien," back together again, to become whole after "accidents" and after being damaged. It is not successful. This is like the first attempts at psychotherapy: one makes progress but then regresses into more unresolved complexes. The second part deals with the surfacing of aggressive impulses again. This time the "bad" does not destroy the "good"; the "good" (i.e., the children's egos) is quick and clever and escapes to live "the rest of our lives" and to "go home to our house." In turn the "bad" is removed (repressed) to a safe place where it can no longer keep damaging the "good." The "good" here symbolizes the healthy emotions in the children or the good feelings the children have about themselves.

Conclusion

For all of the boys, these meetings provided an opportunity for tension release. At the end there was a stronger sense of self-confidence, especially since there were playground rumors about how much fun this series was and other children had asked to participate. The teachers reported various degrees of improvement. Although all the boys had improved within the sessions—in their ability to contribute appropriately, in their participation, in their self-control and self-esteem, and in their tolerance for others—there were notable generalizations for only three. The others were only somewhat better behaved. The two shy boys were now more active in class, and one of the aggressive boys was in much better control in class.

In other groups using group storywriting, similar results have been experienced. The more troubled the youngsters, the smaller the carry-over of the results. Partly that is because these children need a longer series of meeting times. They would also benefit from individual attention if that is possible. Shy children seem to show results outside the group more quickly, but it is important that at least one classmate be part of the small group.

Options for having a concrete result for each child include creating a booklet for each which contains the group stories and personal illustrations, and taking pictures of the model or a large group illustration of a story. Also helpful are sharing activities, such as reading the stories to younger classes and, if appropriate, writing a group letter to parents. In this case a letter was sent to each family from the counselor with the final report card for the year.

Group storywriting addresses both emotional and behavioral needs of the members. It provides an opportunity for students to see how others cope, especially when the counselor draws attention to behavioral issues as they arise in the sessions. A sense of belonging emerges when the children take part in fun activities with others while being accepted.

The deeper needs related to rejection, anxiety, anger, and confusion that push these children out of control can also be addressed. While a teacher may not be able to allow a child to write such material in class, especially if a specific class topic or theme is being followed, these strong emotional issues can be readily accommodated in a small group setting. The content, as it emerges, directs the counselor into the types of support activities needed to provide for fuller exploration of their issues. For example, another series demonstrated that many of the group members were very territorial (part of the classroom issues were of the "He touched my things" type of tattling), so the adjunct to the stories was a series of group illustrations. Once something was drawn, it became part of the whole, and gradually the children were able to tolerate others adding on to or embellishing their contribution. While the consistent activity is the group storywriting, it can be readily adapted to several forms and procedures and can be supplemented by many other activities.

Children can work with partners in creating chapters as a way to encourage modification of troublesome behaviors arising from participating with others. They can write out or compose on computer the stories, or they can dictate their work to the counselor for transcribing. They can each write, or one person can write and later another can do the final word processing and printing. Different members can take responsibility for different aspects of creating a finished product. However, since the process is the critical therapeutic part, there will be times when only the activity is important and no finished product is needed.

Within a school setting, the use of writing, the creative process of language arts, is supported so that there is a continuity of school activities being done in the counseling sessions. The skills and enthusiasm needed for writing are likely to generalize to the classroom if success is experienced in the sessions. Writing also provides an opportunity to externalize inner material. Group writing can enhance social skills as well. By addressing both inner and outer issues simultaneously, the counselor will be able to enlist existing skills from group members. There is power in the use of peer support when attempting to change behaviors. The peer group is where the children operate for the majority of their day, and so sharing with a subgroup and practicing with them make any larger group less intimidating. Behaviors which are disturbing in the classroom are usually more evident in this setting because there are fewer children. These behaviors can then be addressed in a therapeutic manner. The writing allows for the venting of tensions generated by behavioral change and by previous experiences and inner emotional turmoil. It also provides the counselor with insight to each child's inner and outer world issues.

Chapter 7

SENTENCE STEMS IN A "PRIMARY" DIVORCE GROUP

IN TODAY'S SOCIETY, an increasing number of children are coping with the effects of parental separation and divorce. For most of these children the changes in family structure, support, and living arrangements cause a variety of emotional responses, including anger, fear, loneliness, and shame (Tedder, Scherman, and Wantz, 1987; Thompson and Rudolph, 1983). This emotional turmoil frequently leads to behavioral and academic changes as well. The school, as a constant factor in the child's life, can provide accessible, supportive interventions to help her or him through these difficulties.

One written technique that is simple to use and especially appropriate in a school setting is the completion of sentence stems. They are short, use the written and verbal academic skills required for communication, and yet the open-ended format of stems makes them similar to projective techniques, triggering the expression of inner, personal images. Sentence stems allow for exploration of a common group issue while providing opportunity to personalize each statement. Because everyone in the classroom or group is focused on the same theme, there is cohesion in the group, even though different individuals will perceive the stem as referring to different ideas. Children will complete the statements according to their own experience and naturally reflect their own perceptions within the greater group context.

Using sentence stems with primary-aged children can be stimulating and challenging for the counselor as well as the students. The younger the children, the less skilled they are in putting their ideas on paper, and so written technique may be combined with other methods, such as bibliotherapy, puppetry, or art therapy. For children this young, opportunities to "tell" their stories are also very important; therefore sentence stems often need to be preceded by oral discussion.

The use of sentence stems parallels the typical curriculum activities such as reading and printing with which most primary children are familiar. Certainly, talking and sharing time are common activities in any primary classroom. The key difference presented in this chapter is that in a small group setting there can be a focus on the child's experience of separation and divorce, both emotionally and behaviorally. Within the counseling context, there are opportunities to explore and gain some understanding of what is happening in their world and within themselves. There is also an opportunity for the children to modify behaviors which may be creating difficulties. There is a sense of the ordinary within this setting because all of the children are coping with separation and divorce. This chapter will present an outline of the sessions in which sentence stems were used with a group and then provide more detailed discussion and case examples.

Group Sessions

There are a few general considerations which apply to all sessions. Because of the short attention span of primary-aged children and also because of their varying needs, many techniques can be combined with the use of sentence stems to effectively reach all the members of the group. In our experience, children derive great comfort from having cuddly puppets available in each session. With children this age, especially when they are dealing with loss, full body puppets similar to a cuddly toy seem to be the most preferred. Some of the children will attach to one specific puppet throughout the series, and others will change puppets in each session, reflecting their psychological state that day. The most frequently chosen puppets in the group described below were primarily animals, such as a cow, raccoon, rabbit, owl, turtle, wolf, and alligator. Flatter people puppets do not seem to appeal to primary children in groups on this topic. In some sessions the use of puppets can be a scheduled activity for all the children, but at times distressed children may choose to speak through a favorite puppet routinely. Other materials available in every session should include paper and colored pencils.

Each session begins with a puppet selection for those children who want one. Seating choices and "settling in" may take a bit of time but help the students make the transition from the classroom back into the safe and protected space of the guidance office. The adjustment time is very important when the children come from different classrooms, and they do need to have some control, even if it is only of puppet selection and a place to sit, to help them become comfortable with the sharing that will follow. For the actual printing of the ending to the sentence stem, the counselor may need to act as a secretary whenever a child asks for help in putting the words on paper. The sessions close with the counselor thanking each child for sharing and having the children briefly review what they will work on in the following week. Finally the counselor can ask, "Is this a hug day?" and provide a hug for any child who wants one. Because the adults in the child's family may be very preoccupied with their own emotions around the divorce, children are often in greater need of physical comfort at school than they would usually be.

Method

The topics for the sessions were as follows:

Session 1: Introduction. The session begins with introductions. Each child is asked to draw a favorite pet, food, or activity and then tell the group about it. This session also includes discussion of the group rules, with emphasis on confidentiality, the rule that no one shares other people's stories. The session ends with the reading and a discussion of *Mom and Dad Don't Live Together Anymore* (Stinson, 1984).

Session 2: Divorce and the Family Changes. "In my family now . . ." is the stem used. Each child completes the sentence and makes a drawing of it. Those who want to are given the opportunity to describe family changes in their homes.

Session 3: Divorce and Emotions. "In my house I sometimes feel . . ." is completed and drawn. The children tell their chosen puppet how they completed this sentence and then have the option of the puppet explaining the stem to the group or doing it themselves.

Session 4: Divorce and Emotions. *The Quarreling Book* (Zolotow, 1963) is read and discussed. "Sometimes when I'm mad I . . ." is the stem completed. Again they are given the option of the puppet showing the group what the puppet might do when it is very angry or actually describing it for themselves. They discuss a variety of other coping strategies also. Before leaving, each child is asked to describe a new plan for coping with anger.

Session 5: Divorce and Emotions. "Today I feel . . ." is completed, drawn, and discussed.

Session 6: Divorce Thoughts and Closure. Six sentence stems are used in this session (fig. 7.1), with the children having a choice of which one they would illustrate. At the end of the session each child is asked to verbally complete the sentence "I learned that I can. . . ." All the children are given the opportunity for a Polaroid photo of themselves with any puppet they choose, as a reminder of the special time together.

FIG. 7.1

Sentence Stems for a Separation and Divorce Group

One thing I like about Mom and Dad living in different places is . . .

One thing I don't like about Mom and Dad living in different places is . . .

Sometimes I . . .

Most of the time I . . .

It seems strange that . . .

If I had three wishes . . .

Case Material

The Group. Children were chosen by teacher selection. The children who participated in this group were either acting out or withdrawn, and were known to the teacher as living in a home where the mother and father or stepfather were no longer living together. The time of parental separation ranged from very recent to almost the full lifetime of the child. The children's grade levels ranged from kindergarten to grade two with one ten-year-old learning-disabled child from the Resource Room. This child had an opportunity to act as an assistant in some ways, helping with materials, offering suggestions, and describing personal coping strategies, thus giving herself, the youngest in her own family, a new role of being looked up to and being the oldest child in the group.

Content. Originally, this group was intended to focus primarily on situations and coping strategies related to separation and divorce, rather than exposing the children to too much sharing of personal emotional material. However, the children quickly indicated that, no matter what topic the stem directed the session toward, they needed to vent and explore their emotional responses. For example, one child completed the very first, introductory drawing of a "favorite thing" with a picture of a person and an animal—the family pet and only friend—beside a tree (fig. 7.2). The child explained that the pet was really sad about the divorce and, pointing to the person, emphatically stated, "That's me and I'm really mad!" The children completed their stems each time, but in telling the story to accompany the stem or the drawing, also volunteered a scenario from a troubling time. Even the children who completed the stems about feelings and used the word "happy" would then tell of a situation that upset them in some way, such as a fight, yelling, physical violence, or some form of isolation and loneliness within the home. In response to these stories, the counselor would reflect back both the content and emotion in order to empathize with the child and help her feel heard and understood.

For the acting-out children, just being in the group with other children from broken homes seemed to provide permission to express whatever emotional responses they were experiencing. For the quieter children, the use of stems was the vehicle for expression, although they were reluctant to use any word except "happy" in the

FIG. 7.2   My friend

actual printed sentence. To accommodate the amount of emotional expression, the original plan was altered so that some stems were retained until the final session, and three new stems were added specifically to elicit emotions in sessions three, four, and five. It seemed as if the children who were quiet were more often scared, worried, sad, and lonely, whereas those who were acting out in class were angry.

One rather surprising sentence completion given by these children was related to their energy: "Today I feel . . . tired." Discussion indicated that the fatigue either resulted from sleep disruptions, such as "Well, my dad always has parties and the music is real loud and I can't sleep," or referred to the general tiredness of some aspect of the divorce, such as residency changes: "I go back and forth and back and forth and my brother he gets to stay, he's happy and he gets all his own stuff." Others were visibly depressed and tired of worrying about parental behavior—"Dad, he promises, like swimming, and then says he can't come"—and family disputes—"Mom and Jason, they had a fight and Jason kicked over the plant." Several of the children were also tired of parents involving them as an intermediary or as a sympathetic listener, especially if one parent was saying negative things about the other. One of the children, who was usually tired or angry wrote, "I feel tired. Mom is always mad at Dad and me and I'm more blue than Mom or Dad or my brother." At some point in the series, all of the children indicated a feeling of fatigue or depression and a wish for a different family situation.

In the final session, all of the children could eventually complete the stem "One thing I do like about Mom and Dad living in different places is . . .," usually with some version of ". . . they don't fite eny more." However, most of them were much quicker to think of an ending for the stem "One thing I don't like about Mom and Dad living in different places. . . ." Usually the responses were about how little they now saw their fathers. Often their drawings also indicated the fractured nature of their world, such as when there were a large number of separate sections or colors used for the images (fig. 7.3), and frequently showed the hostility in the family, such as the drawing of a smiling Mom and Dad separated by the prongs of a red pitchfork (fig. 7.4). Perhaps the most poignant sentence was the completion for "If I had three wishes I": "wish my Mom and Dad loved each other. Just that one!!"

FIG. 7.3   A fractured house

FIG. 7.4   Mum, Dad, and the red pitchfork

Alternate Strategies

Although this series of group sessions provided some outlet for the children, one major change which would improve the long-term effectiveness would be to include more sessions. Given the intensity of emotions and amount of disruption in these children's lives, more opportunity for emotional expression and modification of current behavior patterns was needed. Each of the six stems used in the final session could be planned as only one day's task, or other stems to elicit emotional and behavioral responses could also be used (fig. 7.5). Sentence stems readily adapt to the group need because the counselor can simply create new stems to encourage the themes emerging, thus following the paths the children are indicating.

FIG. 7.5

Supplementary Stems for Divorce Groups

Divorce is . . .	I feel scared when . . .
Sometimes I wonder . . .	I feel guilty . . .
I can't stand it when . . .	I feel upset . . .
I think . . .	I worry that . . .
I hope . . .	I feel lonely . . .
The worst thing . . .	I knew . . .
The best thing . . .	I didn't know . . .
I hate it when . . .	Other kids . . .
I feel happy when . . .	I get excited when . . .

One thing I do with sad and angry feelings is . . .
To feel better I . . .
One of the things I'd like to ask Mom / Dad is . . .
One of the things I'd like to say to Mom / Dad is . . .

For a group of intermediate-aged children, more written work per session could be used, e.g., four to six stems per session, depending on the amount of discussion the children are comfortable with and how many other activities are planned. Children typically experience many common emotions and views about divorce (Krementz, 1984), and specific stems elicit awareness of this similarity within the group. Older children are a little less likely to experience such intense wishes for reconciliation as primary-aged children, but usually they still fantasize about the intact family.

Conclusion

Separation and divorce may lead to broken attachment bonds, which may have profound emotional and behavioral effects and result in long-term changes. While the child's age at the time of the event is an important factor, one-quarter to one-half of pre-adolescent children from homes where separation and divorce has occurred will have psychological problems one year later (Krell, 1987). Children need a safe and protected place to explore these reactions and to begin to investigate other behaviors for expressing themselves. Providing a series of group meetings in which all the members complete the same sentence stems allows individual expression of a common group theme, while remaining within the context of reading, printing, and talking, the communication skills taught in school.

Chapter 8

IMPROVING SCHOOL CLIMATE THROUGH CROSS-GRADE WRITING INTERACTIONS

SEVERAL YEARS AGO, in an article on a developmental model for consultation in the schools, Dinkmeyer (1971) wrote about the counselor's role in facilitating social interest and the capacity to co-operate. These few words seemed to herald new perspectives and new possibilities. During the past few years, there has been a definite swing in focus—away from pathology and toward the counselor's role in actively promoting conditions that facilitate growth and optimum well-being.

Recently, a flurry of books and articles has appeared on such topics as positive school climate (Breckenridge, 1976; Good and Brophy, 1978; Schmuck and Schmuck, 1979; Vacha, McDonald, Coburn, and Black, 1979), encouragement and cooperation (Dinkmeyer and Losancy, 1980; Martin, 1980; Schniedewind, 1978; Schuncke and Bloom, 1979), and self-esteem (Borba and Borba, 1982; Canfield and Wells, 1976; Felker, 1974; Purkey, 1978). In addition, counselors have been writing about their roles as consultants and as promoters of healthy learning environments (Bernstein and Splete, 1981; Kahnweiler, 1979; Podemski and Childers, 1980).

In line with these concepts, the authors turned their attention to issues of school climate and ways to facilitate cooperation and caring among students and teachers. For example, the seventh-grade teacher noticed the lack of contact that occurred among children of different grade levels. There seemed to be a high level of stratification and fear, especially in the younger children. The teacher consulted the counselor and began to devise a series of joint writing activities that would stimulate cooperation among grades. Although designed to be enjoyable, these activities were structured to have social, emotional, and cognitive learning components. The goal was a developmental counseling model that would reach and affect many children in the normal context of school activities (Gazda and Brooks, 1980).

This chapter outlines (a) how the program was established, (b) the method for generating projects, (c) four specific cooperative activities, and (d) the effects of the program on school climate. The chapter concludes with a discussion of teacher–counselor collaboration.

Establishing the Program

As with any new program, considerable planning and consultation are essential before it is introduced. Because this was a new project, it was necessary to talk with the principal, obtain approval, and then run a pilot project. The project was done with one of the new teachers, thereby broadening her involvement in the school.

The principal was enthusiastic about the program, as was the new teacher. The next step was to approach the seventh graders. First, we needed to determine whether this was a real issue. Was there a lack of contact and poor friendship patterns between this class and other grade levels? A class discussion session was held (Allan and Nairne, 1989), and the seventh graders were asked: "How many of you have friends in grade seven, six, five, four, . . . kindergarten?" The results were tallied, and, as was expected, most friends were at their own grade level, and friendship patterns and social contact greatly decreased as the grade level became lower.

Method

After this discussion, a brainstorming session was held in which the pupils were asked to list on the chalkboard activities they could do with children in the other grades. Emphasis was placed on projects that could be seen as part of the normal school curriculum.

Much interest and excitement were generated by this task, and most children contributed ideas (e.g., art, writing, dream sharing, coaching, tutor systems, science projects). From the original list of activities, twenty-five cooperative projects were devised that paired the seventh graders with every grade level from kindergarten through grade six. The activities involved all subject areas.

After each activity, the teacher met with the seventh graders and evaluated the learning experience using a supervision model that focused on sharing feelings, identifying problems, and developing solutions (Allan, 1982). The teacher also met with the counselor twice a week to go over organizational issues, problems, and any affective concerns.

Four Cooperative Activities

For this chapter four specific activities, each having a strong affective component, were selected for discussion: understanding brothers and sisters (social studies), art and dreams (art), floor hockey (physical education), and storytelling and storywriting (language arts). Each project was presented according to the following format: rationale, preparation, results, and discussion.

Brothers and Sisters

Rationale

Brothers and sisters tend to activate strong feelings in each other, and these feelings tend to persist throughout childhood and adolescence. The goals of these sessions were to help the children process their feelings and see the other siblings' points of view and to stimulate problem-solving skills. A number of activities were spread over a three-week period for grades five and seven. The projects were seen as part of social studies and emphasized oral discussion and written skills. Grades five and seven were joined for this project because many students had brothers or sisters in these two classes.

Preparation

On a blank piece of paper the students were asked to write and rank their siblings on a five-point scale ranging from *super* (5) to *terrible* (1) and to state their own position in the family (older, middle, younger, only child). After a brief discussion, students were to write an answer to the question "What are brothers and sisters like?", to comment on what they liked and did not like about their siblings, and to describe their tactics for dealing with them.

Exercise

The students from the two classes were then paired by position in the family—older with older, middle with middle, younger with younger—where possible. The classes were split up with each teacher taking one group. Each student pair was given two worksheets for writing and for describing good interactions and difficult situations with their siblings and for devising plans that would resolve the problems. Then the pupils did role playing in negative situations until they could devise satisfactory solutions. Finally, group discussion and evaluations were held.

Results

This project generated much excitement, and the students became aware of the similarity and intensity of their feelings and problems, particularly of anger, hurt, and hopelessness. There was much discussion, and some students became aware of feeling helpless and hopeless in dealing with the other sibling. Part of the discussion focused on how to extricate oneself from these overwhelming feelings and how to activate hope. After the discussion, many examples of successful conflict resolution situations were role played and modeled. Evaluation indicated that many children gained new understandings and new skills.

Dreams

Rationale

Many children report dreams and nightmares to teachers and parents, but help is seldom offered to the children in terms of understanding or working with these experiences. Dreams represent an important source of feedback to the conscious mind about how one is handling one's emotional life, unfinished business, fears, and worries (Jung, 1964).

Preparation

This project involved first and seventh graders. The seventh-grade teacher prepared students for participation by conducting a classroom discussion on dreams. The students were asked various stimulus questions (i.e., "Do any of you have falling dreams? Repetitive dreams? Have you ever died in a dream?"). The teacher suggested that they write about a dream and then interpret it. A lively discussion followed, and the students were surprised by the similarity of themes and dream-feeling states.

The first-grade teacher prepared students by reading them a children's story on dreams (Keats, 1974) and then discussing the story and some of their dreams.

Activity

The project was conducted over several days. The primary class was divided into two groups, and the seventh graders went into the primary class five at a time. Paper and paints were set up beforehand in various corners, and each child was asked to "paint a picture from one of your dreams." Later, the pupils were asked to talk about the picture and to tell a story based on it. The older students wrote the essence of the dream at the bottom or on the back of the picture. The younger children then showed and talked about their dreams to the others, and finally the pictures were put up around the room.

Results

This activity was valuable for all the children and the teachers. The young children commented on how good it was to "get the dream out" and showed signs of intense involvement and, in some cases, visible emotional relief. Considerable richness was shown in imaginative, artistic, and verbal expression, and the older children gained some understanding of the meaning and importance of dreams and how to work with their own dream material through discussion and the symbolizing process (i.e., paint, clay, drawing, and journal writing).

Physical Education

Rationale

The teachers met with their classes and found out what sports the children liked to do and what difficulties they experienced in team sports, and they discussed ways in which these problems could be overcome. New rules were devised using the philosophy and format of cooperative sports (Orlick, 1976). For example, in soccer each person could score only one goal. After that he or she had to play defensively behind the halfway mark while actively assisting those team members who had not yet scored.

Exercise

The teachers divided each class into mixed teams of nine members, and some of the most athletic children volunteered to referee and mark the scoreboards. Games were played almost every day, and each sport (soccer and floor hockey) was played for about one month.

Results

The activities stimulated intense excitement and considerable interaction in the school. For example, fourth-grade children would
come into the seventh-grade classroom seeking a team member, and
everyone cheered when children who never scored made their first
goal. The children started to make up new rules to facilitate continuous activity: no offside, use small pitches, and play behind the
goal. The objectives were met because fun, cooperation, skill development, and exercise occurred. Moreover, children who had previously
been isolated were now fully incorporated into the games, and the
more successful children experienced the new feeling of being helpers.

Storytelling and Storywriting

Rationale

Because many children did not have enough stories read to them
at home and were experiencing difficulty in writing, the first-grade
teacher wanted help in this area. The teacher felt that listening to
stories was important to stimulate interest in reading, writing, and
the acquisition of language and prereading skills.

Preparation

The first-grade teacher came into the seventh-grade class and conducted two lessons on techniques for reading to young children. The
teacher also explained how some stories dealt with psychological
themes (shyness, anger, affection) and various developmental tasks.
The students were encouraged to practice reading aloud to friends
and younger siblings and were advised about selecting appropriate
books from the school library.

Exercise

Initially, four seventh graders took a group of eight first graders
into the library and read them the story *Leo, the Late Bloomer* (Kraus,
1972). After the reading, the seventh graders used open-ended questions to facilitate discussion, stimulate recall, and activate understanding.

Results

At first only twelve seventh graders volunteered for this activity.
After three weeks, however, twenty of the twenty-four students were

reading regularly to the first graders. This proved popular with both grades, and stories were read four times a week for several months. This activity led to group discussions and other joint projects. For example, after a few weeks the seventh graders encouraged the younger children to tell or make up their own stories. The seventh graders then went back to the class, wrote out the children's stories, drew illustrations, designed covers, bound them, and gave the children back their own stories in book form. Later, these books were shown to the parents and placed in the school library.

Feedback Sessions

A critical component in the success of the program was the feedback. After every activity, the teacher met with the seventh-grade students to discuss new experiences. This was very important because it gave the pupils a chance to air thoughts and feelings, to hear others, and to learn new communication skills. Difficulties did arise ("he wouldn't talk to me," "she seemed confused by what I said"), and students complained of feeling "lousy" and frustrated after some interactions.

This led to a discussion of feelings ("How did you feel? How do you think the younger child felt?") and a search for solutions ("What could you have said? What might have worked?"). In these discussions the students asked each other questions and offered useful solutions. In this way they learned to help each other and became aware of new skills in communicating and relating to others.

It was interesting that some of the seventh graders complained about behaviors of the younger children that mirrored their own behaviors ("The child talks too much, doesn't listen to me or follow directions"). The teacher was able to use such moments to make the older children aware of this similarity of behavior and to help them change.

Teacher–Counselor Collaboration

The teacher and counselor maintained an ongoing dialogue throughout the year. This was particularly useful to the teacher because it helped to (a) assess needs, (b) evolve and refine ideas,

(c) define and focus the objectives that would provide maximum psychological gain for the students, (d) gain feedback on progress, and (e) learn counseling techniques (e.g., how to talk to the students, how to help them understand issues, and how to help them develop new action steps).

The constant feedback provided by the counselor became a source of growth and encouragement for the teacher. The counselor and teacher worked on techniques that could be used to assess and monitor the thought processes of the students before, during, and after each cooperative activity. The debriefing sessions, suggested and demonstrated by the counselor, helped give the teacher and the students a sense of purpose as well as insight into the positive and negative aspects of cross-grade interactions.

The cooperative benefits were never more apparent to the teacher than during the summary sessions with the students after each activity. Students offered positive suggestions to each other about difficulties encountered with other students during the various interactions.

One of the most important outcomes of the counselor–teacher relationship was the change in the teacher's view of the role of the counselor. The counselor stepped out of the office and into the main domain of the public school system—the classroom.

Effect on School Climate

The program has had a beneficial effect on the school atmosphere. It increased interaction (staff–staff, staff–pupil, and pupil–pupil), changed attitudes and perception (teachers and students), and generated a feeling of fun and excitement. The latter two components, although often ignored by educators, are known to greatly facilitate learning (Scarfe, 1963).

Once the program got started, it was not long before other teachers noted the excitement and enthusiasm in the staff and children and wanted to become involved too. As this happened, other teachers started to pair up for joint projects, new friendship patterns developed in the staff room, and old barriers between intermediate and primary teachers quickly disappeared.

There was also a change in atmosphere: teachers became less isolated in their classes and less possessive of "their children." As they worked and talked more with each other, they became aware that they held similar objectives and were working toward the same goals. This awareness enabled them to see the value of overall planning and pulled them together as a whole staff. The feeling of being trapped in their classrooms disappeared and was replaced by a new energy level characterized by excitement and involvement.

There was an important perception change. The children were seen not so much as "mine" but "ours," belonging to "our school." Blaming (e.g., "Your kid wrecked my gym period") was replaced by a sense of joint responsibility ("There was a problem in gym; I'm wondering what we can do to work it through").

The teachers also began to see the sixth- and seventh-grade students in a new light. They were no longer the "big rowdies" or troublemakers but were often seen as being helpful, gentle, and caring.

Effects on Pupils

The school became a friendlier place. Older and younger students would greet each other by name in the hallways, and the primary teachers reported that their children seemed to feel more secure and safe in school and on the playground. Noontime soccer, which previously was the domain of the older children, now was available to all. The importance of winning became greatly diminished; emphasis was on participation and assisting others to score. Parents commented on how nice it was to see the older children helping the younger ones.

Perhaps the most learning occurred with older children. This program apparently helped them shift some of their attention from themselves to others. They became aware of living, working, and playing within a system, namely their school, and recognized that they were but one part of this system. They became more tolerant; they noticed that the younger children varied as much in abilities, personalities, and physical development as those in their intermediate class. They observed, too, that despite the age differences, the younger children had needs and feelings that were similar to their own and were just as important.

Summary

This chapter describes a collaborative project between the counselor and the teacher in which emphasis was placed on creating a positive school environment through cross-grade interactions. Four structured interactions between the seventh graders and other grade levels are reported: class discussions on brothers and sisters, arts and dreams, cooperative sports, and storytelling and writing.

The advantages of this approach include (a) a reduction in the younger children's fear of the seventh graders, (b) an activation of cooperation and caring in the older pupils, (c) a more positive and friendly school environment, (d) greater interaction between primary and intermediate teachers, and (e) increased teacher perceptions of the counselor as a colleague actively involved in classroom life and in promoting a positive school climate.

Chapter 9

CHILDREN AND THEIR CRISES:
A DEVELOPMENTAL DISCUSSION
AND WRITING APPROACH

IN OUR WORK as a school counselor and as a counselor educator over the past twenty-five years, we have become increasingly aware of the psychological life of children and adolescents and the seeming increase in stress, strain, and crises in their lives. We wondered if there was any way in which we, as counselors, from our emphasis on developmental and preventive perspectives, could help children and adolescents cope with these inevitable stresses, strains, and crises before they happen. By helping them cope, we mean give students a cognitive map of the kinds of crisis situations that happen to children, help them understand the type of feelings and thoughts that are activated, and familiarize them with the range of adaptive responses.

As we had been doing a lot of classroom guidance work, we decided to go into grades two, five, and eight classrooms and conduct discussions on the topic of "Children and Crises." We had three goals in mind. We wanted to (a) hear from the students the types of situations they perceived as stressful, (b) understand the thoughts and feelings that they had during a crisis and six months later, and (c) activate in their minds a sense of what would be helpful to them at such times.

Method

Using a classroom format proposed by Allan and Nairne (1989), we devised a discussion on the topic "Children and Crises." The discussion consisted of six main phases spread over three forty-minute lessons. The first lesson consisted of introductory and exploratory stimulus questions. The students were asked to give their meanings of the word "crisis" and to describe the kinds of crises that children may have. The lesson ended with a drawing activity depicting a crisis experience that affected a child or children.

In the second lesson, the students were asked to write a story about a crisis situation that happened to them or to someone they knew or heard about. Following this, those who wanted to could read their story to the class.

The third lesson focused on understanding and actions. Stimulus questions were asked about how children feel in a crisis situation and what they think about both during a crisis and six months later. Students then identified what helps children in a crisis, what helped them, how they might help others, and how parents and teachers could help. Finally, the counselor summarized the main points of the discussions and asked the children what they had learned.

The project was run in two second-grade classes, two fifth-grade, and two eighth-grade classes, as part of a guidance unit on crises. All of the teachers were present throughout and at times participated in the discussions as well. (See Appendix 9.1 for a copy of the discussion format.)

Results

The discussions were well received by students and teachers alike. The topic held everyone's attention, and there was considerable self-disclosure, as well as a movement, at the end, toward resolution and closure when students were asked to identify actions that help in a time of crisis. There was much disclosure of painful experiences but little evidence of a child being overwhelmed. The genuineness of the material shared seemed to activate support and caring from most of the students. The findings from each level of discussion will now be given using written examples of the children's responses.

Meaning of the Word "Crisis." The word was written on the board and various meanings listed through the brainstorming process. From the listings, each class worked toward a composite definition. For the grade-two classes a crisis was "Trouble, bad time, a bad problem." Grade five: "When something happens that's a matter of life and death; something that really upsets you" and from grade eights: "An unexpected big problem without a quick solution, causing great embarrassment, pain, and a change of behavior."

Crisis Events That Affect Children. During the brainstorming, all the students readily filled the chalkboard with thirty to forty crisis events that happen to children. Following this they were then asked to designate the three "biggest crises that happen to children." There was considerable developmental variation here. Grade twos listed accidents, losing a friend or a pet, and illness. Teachers of these children, however, listed divorce, death, and fighting at home. Grade fives highlighted death, divorce, and fighting with friends, while grade eights listed school expectations, family problems, and peer pressures well above all other crises (fig. 9.1).

FIG. 9.1

Children's Crises by Grade Level

	Grade 2 %	Grade 5 %	Grade 8 %
Accidents	22	13	5
Moving	9	13	13
Illness	19	6	4
Death	5	15	7
Friends	17	19	22
Family Issues	8	21	18
Violence	13	7	6

Drawing and Writing Activities

These activities tended to elicit far deeper expression of feeling and more painful self-disclosure than the verbal discussions of crisis events. Also, the more introverted children seemed to find it easier to read their story or show their picture to the class than to just stand up and talk.

The question must be asked: Why and how can self-healing occur? It is our belief that when the psyche is attended to in this way (through discussion, drawing, and writing), it provides each student with the opportunity to externalize his or her own inner wounds in a way that is personal and safe. This externalization of "unfinished business" (i.e., of thoughts, impressions, memories, and images) allows for movement of repressed and dissociated affects from the unconscious and subconscious realms into consciousness. This expression both releases and transforms psychic energy that had been used for defense and protection and rechannels it into growth and healing.

Often during a crisis or trauma children feel trapped, overwhelmed, out-of-control, and powerless. Writing helps them think through and reflect on the experience at a later date, which can result in a new understanding and a feeling of control which, at times, leads to a sense of empowerment.

This pattern of externalization of painful memories and the emergence of new understanding and more positive images is seen in some of the following stories.

Accidents. This was very common with the younger children, and frequent mention was made of physical pain, cuts, bruises, broken legs, and visits to doctors and dentists. The drawings tended to indicate either the presence or absence of a helping adult; teachers noted that children who did not have caring parents tended to leave out adult figures from their drawings or stories. One lonely girl drew a sad figure of herself with a broken leg (fig. 9.2) and commented:

> This is when I fell off a trolley, broke my leg and I had to spend the rest of the summer just sitting there, not doing anything. I couldn't run around or anything. It was sunny and I just had to stay home. I was feeling pretty bad because all my other friends were out there playing. And then when I went back to school, everybody started kicking my leg to see if it hurt. But it hurt me more than it hurt them because they kicked my toes.

FIG. 9.2   Broken leg

Both the picture and story emit a feeling of isolation, pain, and loneliness. In her writing process the child does not recover near the end of the story but rather enters a more painful emotional space ("But it hurt me more than it hurt them"). The picture and story gave the teacher a deeper awareness of this girl's suffering, and a referral was made to the counselor for individual help.

Older children mentioned devastating and serious accidents, often indicating unfinished psychological work and the need to go through the experience again. An eighth grader wrote:

> On Friday after the bell rang my best friend and I ran outside, eager to get away from school. She was always so happy and always looked on the bright side of things. A real optimist and very friendly. She was staying for the night, and we planned to go to a movie, then out for a pizza. As we took our separate buses home, I thought of how much fun this evening was going to be. When I got home, I changed and then went to the phone to see if she was ready. As I dialed, I thought about her phone number and how it was as familiar to me as my own. When her mom picked up the phone, she was crying hysterically. She calmed down as much as possible and said a shaky "Hello." In a minute, after hearing her explanation, I, too, was crying. My best friend had been hit by a car on her way home from the bus stop. She was in the hospital in a very critical condition. For almost the first time in my life I felt helpless. There was nothing I could do. I lay down for hours and closed my mind. At dinner time my mom came in and gave me the news. She had died. It was the worst feeling I had ever had in my life. I couldn't stop thinking about her. I didn't sleep that night or the next. I didn't eat for almost a week. I didn't even leave the house until her funeral. I totally withdrew for almost a month. My mom finally sat down with me and helped me realize that I had to get back into life. It took a while but I finally decided to do it. It was hard, but with friends and family I did it. Although I knew I would never have such a good friend, I am going to try hard.

Moving. This situation was frequently mentioned and activated hurt feelings around leaving friends, grandparents, pets, and a favorite or special house. Often anger at parents was mentioned, as was fear of going to a new school. Once new friends were found the pain seemed to diminish. One seven-year-old girl (fig. 9.3) wrote:

> I had to move from my very best friend. I felt very bad. I cried for a whole week. I told my mom I wanted to move back. She said we couldn't. I felt better after a week because I had her phone number so I could talk to her.

One new Canadian boy wrote:

> Before I went to school I felt excited. I couldn't speak English. Then when I got there I thought I saw aliens because all of the people there had a different color of hair. I then met the teacher. She was nice and kind. All the day through I was hungry. I was looking for my lunch box just when I found it the teacher said I had to wait till lunch time. After the day was over I thought that school was fun but that I won't want to come to school again.

Illness. By illness students were referring to severe illness and emergencies that led to hospitalization. These stories and drawings (fig. 9.4) were all very personal and often had a sense of urgency about them ("My mom came rushing to the bus stop") and a sense of the dawning awareness of the reality of severe illness. A grade-five boy wrote:

> One day I heard that my oldest brother was in hospital. It was during the summer so we couldn't go on our summer vacation. The crisis was that my brother had cancer. A few days later when my parents came home from the hospital and my mom was crying because my brother could hardly breathe. And that's how he almost died. Now my brother is living and he's working with my third oldest brother. It was real shock to me. I'm glad he's not dead and that he's living.

Death. The teachers were surprised by both the number of death experiences children reported and how readily children talked about them. They were aware of how close to the surface the feelings still were even though the events may have occurred some years previously. One boy drew (fig. 9.5) and wrote:

FIG. 9.3   Moving

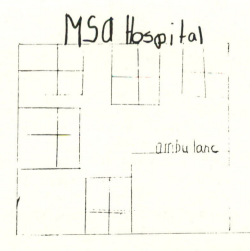

FIG. 9.4   Severe illness

A crisis is when my cat, Shalimar, was run over by a train. A crisis is when something bad happens and when my cat, Bonnie, died too. I felt bad. I still feel bad.

A grade-five student, when commenting on the death of a relative's baby, said: "My aunt told us not to talk about it. That was a crisis for us." Many of the death stories centered on pets (fig. 9.6).

One morning in the summer vacation, I woke up and went downstairs to eat my breakfast. After I got half way through my breakfast, my mom and dad told me that my dog had died, I pushed away my cereal. I thought my mom and dad were joking. My mom said, "I wish I was." I started to cry, my sister did too. I ran into the bathroom and took a kleenex. I tried to stop crying but I could not stop. My mom gave me a hug and tried to cheer me up but it would not work. They told me how she died, she got hit by a car that night. I thought and thought about her. I cried a lot too. All that week I thought about her. We had a talk with my mom and dad. We decided that we would get two more cats. Me and my sister said "yes," so about a month later we got two cats.

School. Teachers had not anticipated the number of students who found school to be a major source of crisis. This was not mentioned by the grade twos, only a few grade fives, but many grade eights. The comments centered around failure and embarrassment (fig. 9.7): "Getting a zero on a test," "Trying to learn something new," "Not doing your homework causes a crisis involving your mom and teacher." However, when the students wrote about school they tended to focus on issues with friends, especially peer pressure.

Peer Pressure. These stories reflected topics and issues that students would seldom verbalize in the class discussion. Most of the stories centered around quasi-illicit activities such as smoking, drugs, alcohol, stealing, shoplifting, sexual contact, running away, and huge fights with parents. Many of these crisis stories followed a familiar theme: a common issue was revealed, then a much deeper struggle, followed by a release of intense affect (often hurt and anger at parents), ending with a resolution whereby the adolescents were able to change their frame of reference from self to an understanding of others. Somehow the process of writing allows for a cognitive shift

FIG. 9.5   Deaths of my cats

FIG. 9.6   My cat ate my gerbil

If you got somthing wong becauso you had a crisis. You would feel stupid.

You wold feel stupid

FIG. 9.7   "You would feel stupid"

from fear into action. The following story depicts a probably imaginary situation from a teenager in a rough ghettoized school trying to separate from peer coercion:

John repeated his threat, "Well do you join us, or do you get wasted?" It was a hard decision, especially when he held a switchblade to my throat. What could I do, if I ran, I've had it. If I join them, I'm involved in a street gang fight. I decided to join them until I could think of a plan to get away. "Okay, ease up with the knife." He accepted me into the gang, told me to pick up a broken bottle, and use it as a weapon. I knew if I stayed I'm dead, they have about thirty, we have maybe thirteen. Also, this was not just a fist fight, we were fighting with knives and chains. This was stupid, I thought. The other gang said to be in the alley at seven o'clock. It was five after. Then they showed up, brandishing knives and chains. When the two leaders started fighting, I turned around and ran. I never ran so fast in my life. Somebody shouted. I ran home, sat down, and then locked all the doors. Then I was faced with the decision whether to call the police or not. I decided to call. I might get beat up at school but those gang members would get caught. I decided I made the right decision, and I was glad.

Family Issues. As can be expected, this was a major source of crises for some students. They drew and wrote about being overwhelmed by hurt and angry feelings, by being shouted at (fig. 9.8), and by being put down and physically abused (fig. 9.9). Uppermost was the pain over separation and divorce. One grade-two girl said: "Everything has been ruined and can never be mended." Another grade-two student commented: "Every single day is a crisis because no one at home likes me except my mother's help. Whenever I try to ask a question my dad just yells: 'Stay out of it.'" Teachers became aware that, in conflictual home situations, seldom did the parents take time to listen to the concerns and worries of the children, and that allowing the children to talk in class helped the children feel better and relieved. Teachers were surprised by how many children tended to use the stories to reveal much deeper issues than the topic would indicate. This story about "divorce" led into a disclosure of sexual and physical abuse. One grade-eight girl wrote:

> When I was young I went through seeing my Mom go through two divorces. I was too little to remember too much from the first one but from the second divorce I remember a lot. I was afraid to go to sleep at nights because I knew my Dad beat on my Mom. It always seemed he was so nice but then I realized he was just being nice to me and my brother. He nearly broke my Mom's arm and I could hear her crying from my bedroom. I would always want to beat him till he was dead. My Mom would go out at nights and I would cry because I was so afraid of my Dad. He would also come into my room at night when she was gone and when my brother was asleep. I was so scared to tell my mom what he did because I thought he would hurt me. Finally I couldn't stand it anymore. I told my Mom. I wish I would have told her sooner because my Mom got me and my brother out and away from that Dad as fast as she could. I was so relieved that my Mom would get no more beatings. Now I have a wonderful new Dad.

Violence. Children of all ages were concerned about the violence in the world around them. Certainly, a lot of this was derived from what they saw on television or heard about in the news. There were two main categories here: physical violence—as in beatings, murder, and child sexual abuse—and fear of nuclear holocaust. A grade-four boy wrote:

FIG. 9.8　"Go to your room"

FIG. 9.9　"My mom hit me"

Yesterday on a show [fig. 9.10] I saw a man who was telling everybody how he murdered three girls ages of eight, ten, twelve. In his apartment he had lots of girls clothing, pictures, and other things of girls. The girls' parents were on television. The mother was trying to explain how her daughter was kidnapped but she couldn't because she was crying. She kept saying she wanted to kill that man. This is a true story. The end.

A grade-eight boy drew a nuclear bomb exploding and wrote: "A crisis is what we are doing to our planet earth, cities burning, pain and war. I am scared. I want it to stop but I can't do anything" (fig. 9.11).

Understanding Phase

Once the stories and drawings had been shared, the focus of the discussion was shifted to helping the students identify the various feelings experienced during a crisis. Once again, the board was used for brainstorming and prioritizing. There was much similarity between all groups in the basic feelings of mad, bad, scared, and worried, although the older students added more sophisticated words: depressed, nervous, miserable, hysterical, shocked, stunned, desperate, suicidal, frustrated, disappointed, ashamed, embarrassed, guilty, and confused.

Young children's thoughts during a crisis tended to be of such action steps as calling for help, running away, praying, playing with toys, and trying to forget. Older children talked more deeply about their inner experience and self-blame ("Am I going to die?"), the fear of the future ("Will this ever end?", "Everything is going wrong!", "More bad experiences will come!"), and guilt ("It's all my fault," and "You blame yourself").

Six months after a crisis, younger children reported feeling "happy or glad," while older children reported feeling relieved but still thinking about it every now and then: "I was sad for over a year when my parents got divorced." "I still think about the whole thing and feel if I'd only done this or that." "Every now and again I think about him" (a friend who was killed). "I feel stupid that I didn't listen to my mum." These and other similar thoughts indicated that there was still a lot of "unfinished psychological business" present.

FIG. 9.10   Murder

FIG. 9.11   Nuclear war

Action Phase

Discussions during this phase changed the mood of the classes to that of excitement over a positive challenge. At first, in response to the question "What helps you in a time of crisis?", the students were both surprised and stunned as if nothing would help. However, once they started talking, they generated many action steps. Most of these involved talking to parents, teachers, counselors, and friends; calling help lines; and such actions as punching a pillow, crying, writing in journals, talking to pets, relaxing oneself, and praying to God. The grade eights also relied on talking to parents, counselors, and friends but also emphasized their own thinking abilities: "Think your problem over sensibly and try to find the best solution." "Finding out the real problem." "Think about what will happen afterward." "Consider options: What happens if I do this . . . or this," and "Make a decision for yourself and see how it works. Then get a second opinion."

Termination Phase

In many ways, this was the highlight of the unit, as both students and teachers responded positively to the same question: "What did you learn from these discussions?" Students reported: "Nearly all of us have had a crisis." "I'm not alone, not the only one." "It's good to talk about these things in class and learn from other kids." "I learned that a crisis is a time that will pass and you will feel better." "I learned that it is important to care about another person because, although they might look strong inside, they might be hurting."

Teachers, in a separate meeting outside of class time, mentioned how surprised they were that the students opened up so much about emergencies that were happening with friends and in their families. They also commented on the degree of accuracy with which the students understood the feelings of a person in crisis. Teachers felt that the students' feelings were very close to the surface and that the discussions seemed beneficial for class climate and peer relations. The discussions enabled them to get to know more of the children better in a short period of time. It was the first time that many children had ever really opened up and shared painful experiences.

Teachers thought that the children benefited greatly from the discussions and were able to see crises in a broader context—namely, that other children have crises and handle their feelings in a similar way to them. Finally, the discussions enabled the teachers to identify students who needed and could benefit from one-to-one counseling.

When using a guidance unit like this, the counselor needs to summarize the main points. For example:

> In this class, crises were defined as. . . . The main crises affecting children were. . . . In response to crises, students felt shock, pain, anger, despair, hopelessness . . . and thought. . . . In a time of crisis, it helped children to talk with parents, teachers, friends, and counselors, and with time and effective help, the pain of a crisis seemed to move away.

Conclusions

In this chapter we have tried to show how a guidance counselor developed a pro-active stance to meet some of the issues and struggles children face in crisis situations. Our guidance classes are very important because they provide a time when we can listen to the needs and experiences of our children and then devise ways of helping them handle their frustrations and develop adaptive coping skills. It is only by letting children and adolescents speak and by listening to them that we can truly understand their unique needs.

Every school's teachers and counselors will have to deal with children in crises. It is important that counselors help schools develop a policy on children under stress and train the teachers in the necessary theoretical understandings of crisis events and the basic communication skills required to help children. At such times children need (a) a caring relationship, (b) support and empathetic understanding, (c) structure, and (d) appropriate information. The teacher needs to (a) assess the condition of the child and the nature and severity of the crisis and (b) determine whether or not a referral is needed. Group guidance discussions and writing activities on crises help students talk about their experiences and realize they are not alone, externalize their hurt and fears, and develop an understanding of crisis events.

APPENDIX 9.1

Outline of Discussion: Children in Crises

1. Introduction
    Today we are going to talk about crisis: what the word means and what type of crises children experience. We'll have a chance to write and draw pictures about crises, and later we'll look at ways to help children who are in a state of crisis. First, what does the word "crisis" mean? Let us list the meanings on the board. [Once the brainstorming process is complete, summarize and work from the list to create a more composite definition—e.g., "For this class, a crisis is. . . ."]

2. Exploration
    (a) What kinds of crises affect children? [List on board]
    (b) Can you tell us about some of the crises you or children you have known have experienced?
    (c) On a piece of paper, write down the three most important crises that affect children.

3. Activity I
    Can you draw a picture of crisis? Imagine a crisis scene—one that happened to you or one that you heard about. Close your eyes for a moment and let your mind drift back to the crisis situation. What do you see and what do you hear? Try to get the full picture. Now open your eyes and start drawing.

4. Activity II
    Can you write a story about a crisis you have experienced? What led up to the crisis; what was the crisis and what happened later? What did you see? What did you hear? If a crisis situation has not happened to you, you can write about one you heard of or saw on television or in a movie. Remember, it must have to do with children.

5. Sharing the Story and the Picture
    I would like to hear from you now. Will some of you share your story and picture with us?

6. Understanding
    Now I want you to shift your thinking a little. Let us try to understand:
    (a) How do children feel when they are in a state of crisis? [List on board]
    (b) What do children think about when in a crisis? [List]
    (c) What do you think are the strongest thoughts or feelings?
    (d) Is it hard to help a child in a state of crisis?
    (e) How might a child think or feel six months after a crisis?

7. Let's Look Now at Helping
    (a) When you have been in a state of crisis, what helped you? [List]
    (b) If your friend is in a state of crisis, what can you do to help?
    (c) If someone in this class is in a state of crisis, how can we help him or her?
    (d) How can your teachers and counselors help you?

8. Termination
    There are two important components here:
    (a) Did you learn anything useful from this discussion?
    (b) Let me summarize the outcome of the discussions: e.g., For this class crisis means . . . . The types of crises that happen to children your age are. . . . Children feel . . . and think. . . . The following actions help children in crisis. . . . Common stages in reaction to crises are shock and denial, intense pain (hurt, sadness, and anger), bargaining, despair, and hopelessness. However, by asking for help and talking, it is possible to work through the pain into deeper understanding of life and better feelings.

Chapter 10

CLASSROOMS IN CRISIS:
SENTENCE STEMS
FOR IMPROVING GROUP DYNAMICS

IN THIS CHAPTER we describe the use of sentence stems as a written adjunct to class discussions, used when a class is in a crisis state. As nearly every teacher can attest, there are times when a group of children who are placed together in a classroom have a great deal of difficulty developing a strong sense of community. When children are dealing with so many painful aspects of their lives that they are not able to focus on school work at all, they can become management problems that trouble even the most skilled and experienced of teachers.

The goal in each case presented in this chapter was to have the grade-six students gain some insight to what was happening in the classroom and then develop new behaviors. By working through the discussion and writing process as outlined by Allan and Nairne (1989) and Barber and Allan (1989), the classes could be directed in articulating and understanding feelings and behaviors within the group. Because the children's stress levels, and hence their distractibility, were quite high, only short written activities were chosen to supplement the discussions. These provided opportunities for sharing from all class members, even those who were uncomfortable sharing orally, and also allowed for more externalization of inner material. We have often noticed that getting a noisy class to do a little writing helps calm them down.

The remainder of the material in this chapter will describe how sentence stems were used with two different classrooms. It will begin with the general method, and then specific information for the method and results from each group will be given. The chapter will conclude with a description of the activities and examples of responses from each room and then a brief summary.

EXAMPLE 1   139

Method

The outline described in depth in the previous chapter was followed generally, but with modifications to accommodate the needs of those actually experiencing a form of group crisis. The outline and activities were adapted differently in the two classrooms, but in both cases they provided an opportunity for members to be personally involved with making suggestions for helping to change the atmosphere in the respective classrooms.

In both cases there were three sessions of forty minutes each with a counselor, teacher, and grade-six class taking part. Following the Allan and Nairne (1989) outline of the five phases for a class discussion (introduction, exploration, understanding, action, and termination), the class was first introduced to the topic and given an opportunity to explore material relevant to the group. A drawing activity was also included to provide a private, and for some safer, way of sharing. In the second session, there was provision both for understanding the situation and taking appropriate action through oral and written expressive activities. Finally, in the third session, there was a review and a termination activity which varied with the need.

Example 1

The first example was a grade-six class in which nearly half the students were experiencing such a difficult time with family or peer issues that they had become management problems. As the changes of adolescence exacerbated the underlying difficulties of alcoholism, divorce, abuse, death, multiple family changes, peer pressure toward early sexual and drug experimentation, and extreme cases of cliques, the learning environment for those who were willing to concentrate became tumultuous to say the least. The teacher had indicated to the counselor that this class was a real challenge and requested assistance. Two particularly distressing aspects of the destructive behavior were the very personal "rumors" constantly being generated by many members of the class and the constant, almost theatrical, emotional outbursts manifested daily. Because some of the aspersions were based on reality in a few homes, the emotions in the room were frequently just barely contained.

Session 1

The first session began with an explanation that the counselor was aware that upsetting things were happening among the students in the classroom. Since the teacher agreed, we thought it might be useful for the counselor to come in and help out with an open talk. The students were asked to give a definition of "crisis," and the group then brainstormed components of the term. This process very quickly led to their volunteering, "Like, for example . . ." and then giving a personal account. Because there was a surprising amount of empathy for others when these accounts were shared in a structured environment, much of this session was oral. It concluded with each student creating a drawing of a crisis he or she personally knew about, either from firsthand experience or from hearing the story from a relative or friend, but not about anyone else in the class. The session concluded with the counselor thanking the class, including the teacher, for sharing and with a reminder of confidentiality. No one violated this rule during the series, a rather surprising development given the active rumor mill in effect prior to open discussion.

Session 2

The second session began with a reminder of the confidentiality rule. The main focus was a discussion of how people feel in crisis situations and how they think and act. As the students brainstormed ideas, the information was written on the board under the three headings of "Feelings," "Thoughts," "Actions." It was helpful for them to see the range of emotional responses expressed and also the commonalities of shared emotional reactions. It was also helpful for them to become aware of the thought processes and behavioral responses of others. This session concluded with an oral listing of things they did personally to respond to stress and then with the written activity of providing an ending to the stem "When I'm upset I. . . ." The brainstorming suggestions were compiled into a list for distribution in the third session (fig. 10.1).

EXAMPLE 1   141

FIG. 10.1

Coping with Crises

Suggestions from Grade Six

RELEASE THE FEELINGS

talk about it . . . with a friend
                . . . with a counselor
                . . . with a teacher
                . . . with a parent
                . . . with a pet or stuffed animal, e.g., teddy bear
                . . . with someone from the family
                . . . with someone else who's experienced it (an expert in the topic)

write about it . . . in a journal
                . . . in a letter

draw
doodle
color
scream
cry

DISTRACTIONS

upset the people who are upsetting you
run away*
try to hide it
try to forget about it
take a walk
play with a friend
do something you enjoy
go outside and enjoy the scenery
go to your room
try to be patient until it's over
ignore it
think of any good aspects
say you're sorry
be involved in decisions about the problem
see someone you like being with
go shopping
think of pleasant things

                                                        *Not recommended

---

Session 3

The final session began with a review of the term "crisis" and a request for some suggestions about what kinds of situations the students may face in the future. They were asked how they'd seen people respond right away in a crisis, and then one year, and again five years later related to that crisis. They were then given a sheet of stems to complete individually (fig. 10.2). There was a sharing time when volunteers were able to read their completions for each stem. The session concluded with their being given the sheet of compiled coping strategies from session two for future reference.

FIG. 10.2
Class Discussions

Crisis

A crisis is . . . .
To cope with a crisis . . . .
During a crisis . . . .
Six months after a crisis . . . .
Five years after a crisis . . . .
I learned . . . .
The most helpful part . . . .
The least helpful part . . . .

Results

In the first session, the definitions of "crisis" included the concepts of a negative experience, something that just happened, and something that made you feel really awful. For those who shared their stories as examples, incidents included witnessing the aftermath of an attempted suicide, seeing parents fight, seeing a serious accident, being told of a parent death, being told about parents' separation, and being molested. The honesty and seriousness of the examples evoked an empathic respect within the room. There were no reports of any violation of this respectfulness even weeks later. Those who had shared these experiences tended to draw them in the activity part. The class was reminded that, although these were powerful examples of crises, other events, too—such as moving, death of a pet, an embarrassing moment, or a fight with a close friend—could also qualify with the definitions we had given earlier. That seemed to free the creativity of some members of the class who perhaps did not have or were not prepared to share such severe experiences.

During the second session, the students expressed a wide range of feelings related to a crisis. Under "Feelings" they suggested every-

EXAMPLE 1   143

thing from being stupid, scared, dumb, embarrassed, and terrified to hurt, worried, angry, and upset. For "Thoughts" the examples they gave were of blaming someone else or finding out whose fault it was, of getting even or getting revenge, of denial, disbelief, and of fear it would be a catastrophe. Examples of "Behaviors" were usually of physical reaction, shouting, hitting, threatening, or withdrawing and running away. A few students gave examples of positive actions such as getting help, writing in their journals, and staying calm.

Each wrote out at least one thing he or she did to cope with the turmoil of a crisis. Generally, the coping activities fell into two categories, either some way of releasing the feelings or some form of distraction, either physical or mental. All suggestions from the students were listed for distribution to the class the next day, but the disclaimer "not recommended" had to be included with "run away" because that could not be encouraged. Several strategies were very effective for the students. Some were of concern to the counselor, such as "upset the people who are upsetting you," "hide it," or "say you're sorry" because these approaches are potentially dysfunctional. For example, the boy who said "say you're sorry" usually took the blame and then apologized even when he had little involvement. When the list was handed out in the final session, the techniques for emotional and physical release which were not harmful to others were strongly encouraged. There was also a brief discussion about the potential consequences of some suggestions such as "upset the people who upset you" or "running away."

By the third session, the teacher indicated there had been a calming of the emotional outbursts in class, and the rumors had decreased sharply. However, there was still a problem with some students being off task a great deal of the time.

It was interesting to note that, when given the sentence stems to complete, the class initially worked intently, but once a few students were finished and became restless, others had a difficult time completing theirs. The completion for a crisis definition was generally of the "a serious problem or something bad or terrible that happens" nature. One child wrote "a happening that a person would not like to talk about," and another wrote "something bad or a phase that you go through." "To cope with a crisis . . ." responses varied between some form of externalizing the experience and "you deal with it" types of responses. These latter were usually from students who were known for emotional outbursts. "During a crisis . . ." was completed with a variety of strong emotions, such as "you feel really sad and mad." One child suggested "you run away." "Six months after . . ." was completed with "you will probably be starting to get your life started again" or "you will still think about it and will still hurt a little bit." One child wrote "you have forgotten about it," but then for "Five years after . . ." the same child wrote "it might happen again." The majority of the students wrote "you will have forgotten about it," or "it will seem funny," or "it's no big deal" in reference to five years later.

When asked to complete "I learned . . ." most wrote some version of "how to cope with a crisis" and usually included an effective coping technique. Some students wrote that a crisis can make people feel a specific, identified emotion. One child wrote "I learned that you shouldn't tell other people's stories." One bright, dramatic student quoted a popular song, "Shout, shout, Let it all out, these are the things I can do without." The most useful part for many of the students was learning new information and coping strategies, preferably by talking. The least helpful part was either "the writing" or "the drawing" for a few of the students, but the majority of them named the technique "ignoring it" as the least helpful thing for them. Either they had used this one and found it did not work, or they understood others to say it was not effective.

It was evident that this group was highly distractable and that many of the students were coping with difficult situations. Some of them were dealing with unresolved issues from the past or with very emotional situations currently happening. Because academic work was also a challenge for several students in this class, we used limited, short written activities to provide opportunities for externalizing emotional and cognitive material in a private way. For most of the students, oral work was still preferred. The opportunity to gain an understanding of others' situations, to vent some of their own pain, and to increase their repertoire of coping strategies seemed to reduce the tensions in the room. There was a follow-up counseling support offered to some of the children as well.

The tone of the classroom improved, and the teacher indicated there was a big difference in the attitude among the students. The principal indicated there had been a major reduction in disciplinarian

EXAMPLE 2   145

matters related to these students, many of whom had been at the office daily for classroom or playground infractions.

Example 2

In another grade-six classroom where sentence stems were used in combination with discussion for a class in crisis, the underlying reason for the difficulties was not as evident. Although the teacher was very experienced and extremely skilled in nurturing group work, this particular class had still not developed much group cohesion by the spring term. Several of the students were very bright, and over half had always attended this school. There were also students who had academic difficulties, some from minority backgrounds, and a few who had behavior problems. Basically, on the surface, this was a typical classroom. Yet when the teacher had completed a sociogram to help design small groups for cooperative learning and other activities, there were almost no options for setting up groups. The decision was made to use a combination of written and discussion activities as an intervention over the following three sessions.

Session 1

In the first session the counselor simply stated there would be a series of activities where the class would work both individually and in groups. This was immediately greeted with groans and mutterings. She continued:

> One of the things we will be discussing is how we feel about ourselves and how all of us get along with others in this room. You will have a chance to do some writing and some talking. No one will have to talk if he doesn't want to, but all of you will have an opportunity to express your opinions. Everyone will listen when someone else is talking, and there will be no putdowns. All of you will complete the written activities. We'll begin with a guided imagery activity [The Rosebush] that you do alone. None of today's part will be shared with anyone in the class.

It was important to be very specific about what would happen with written material because, for whatever reason, the classroom was not perceived as a safe place to share. Also necessary for encouraging trust was the clear description of what they would and would not have to do, what the session would be about, and concrete rules about respectful treatment for everyone. From other years of working with the counselor, most of the group was familiar with and enjoyed participating in guided imagery activities. Therefore, the counselor decided to use an activity called the Rosebush (Allan, 1988), a guided imagery exercise which, when combined with its written and drawn components, provides a non-threatening perspective of the child's inner world. (See Appendix 10.1, "The Rosebush: A Guided Fantasy," and 10.2, "Post-Drawing Inquiry," at the end of this chapter.)

There were two reasons for the decision to use this as the first activity. First, because the imagery relaxed the class and worked as a projective technique in both the written and drawn portions, the counselor hoped to gain some insight into class dynamics before proceeding with oral, group work. Second, because this was not shared and did not therefore involve much risk-taking, it seemed to be a positive way to begin the sessions.

Session 2

In the second session the counselor began by giving a definition of the term IALAC (I Am Lovable and Capable, Simon, 1973). The counselor then led everyone in repeating the words for IALAC three times, increasing the volume each time. After eliciting a definition of the term "putdowns," the counselor demonstrated the destructive nature of putdowns by tearing up a sheet of paper that had IALAC printed on it. As she did this she said:

> I am lovable and capable. That's how each of us can think about ourselves. Then along comes someone with a putdown and [tears a piece off] I feel less lovable and capable. Today we're going to look at putdowns in this room.

Then the class was divided into groups of three, preselected by the teacher, to complete the following sheet of sentence stems (fig. 10.3).

EXAMPLE 2   147

FIG. 10.3
Class Discussions

Putdowns

Some "putdowns" I've heard in this room are . . . .

When I hear these I feel . . . .

A behavior that seems to go with a "putdown" is . . . .

Some reasons people may say things like this are . . . .

Some things I can do to discourage these statements are . . . .

It may be hard to stop these because . . . .

One thing I'm prepared to try is . . . .

Signatures:

The small group members were to choose someone to act as a recording secretary and someone to share the group's material with the class later. They were told that for this activity everyone had to give suggestions in the small group, but only the one person they decided on would share the material with the whole class. The session ended with the completed sentences being read out and the counselor challenging the class to think of one suggestion they could give next time to make the classroom a better place for everyone to feel like they were lovable and capable.

Session 3

The third session began with energetic renditions of IALAC. The remainder of the time was used for a class discussion on putdowns (Appendix 10.3) as outlined by Allan and Nairne (1989). The session concluded with the students regrouping in the triads from the previous session and individually writing a completed "One thing I am prepared to try to do to make this a better classroom is . . ." on the back of last session's sentence stems. They signed their statements and submitted them to the teacher.

Results

A small portion of the students in this room were very concerned about grades on a report card and resented any work being marked and counted if it involved a small group activity. Their competitive nature and performance awareness made it extremely difficult for them to help others in the group if there was a recorded mark. However, even this background did not explain why they were so quick to fling insults even in the large group.

Rosebush Activities

The results of the Rosebush activity, both the drawn and written parts, did provide some insights and suggested considerable inner turmoil in many students. In four of the drawings, the rosebush took up only a small portion of the lower half of the page (fig. 10.4). Leaving the rest of the page blank, as in these cases, is often viewed as an indication of depression (Furth, 1988). To some degree the written part accompanying each of these drawings supported this concept. For example, another child with a similar drawing wrote this description of the imagined rosebush:

> I am a small rosebush. I'm small with roses. My flowers are starting to die because of no water. My leaves are going yellow. My stems are getting weaker everyday. My thorns are sharp and I am an unfriendly rosebush. My roots are long and twisted but not as usual. I live in old, ugly yard where nothing is and I'm lonely. I don't look like a rosebush because it is dying. Nobody looks after me and that is why I am dying. The weather is good but I don't get water. My life as a rosebush is miserably. I feel wierd.

Other drawings indicate different forms of vulnerability. When words or text were included in the drawing, usually seen as the artist's concern that the reader may not get the message without word supplements, there can be verification of the intent from the story, as with this description (fig. 10.5):

> I am an only rosebush in a flower pot and I am red and not very pretty. The rose is lonely because he doesn't have any friends. My stems are branches are long and wide. They have prickles on them. No, I don't have thorns, I am friendly and protect myself by hiding in the corner. My roots are curly. I live in my own world always

FIG. 10.4   "A lonely rosebush"

FIG. 10.5   "I am not very pretty"

talking to myself there is darkness all around me and I'm lonely. Yes, I look like a rosebush. God takes care of me. It's fun. He gives me water and sunshine to help me grow. Rainy. I go to sleep. Funny, and lonely.

Yet other drawings with writing (fig. 10.6), "somebody watering the earth and letting me die," were accompanied by a text that did not match, "My gardner takes care of me and I like it very much and I love how he takes care of me because he scrubs and sprays me every morning." These contradictions suggest confusing experiences about the environment or possibly wishful thinking. When the child who did this drawing moved from the deeper, unconscious reality as represented in the drawn image and came back into the cognitive, verbal self as represented by the world in the story, there was a shift from one view of reality to another.

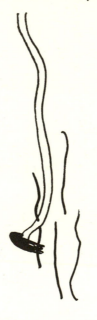

FIG. 10.6   "Somebody letting me die"

Another example of vulnerability showing on the drawing (fig. 10.7) was of a tiny rosebush, rather doubled back over itself, beside a huge trellis which dominates the page. If the rosebush could grow with that support it would be at least a third taller. In the drawing there are no thorns, yet the text indicates the rosebush does have them. Another form of denial occurs here also: "I'm not mean or friendly because flowers don't have personalities. Rosebushes don't have feelings." Although this could be simply a form of stubborn resistance from a grade-six student, given that all the rest of the drawn and written work was fully completed, it is more likely an indication of the child's functioning in the intellectual domain and repressing the emotional side.

Many students in this class demonstrated a split between their "adaptive social self" and their "true feeling self." There was often conflict between what they drew and what they wrote. The drawings indicated more hostility than the stories, suggesting that many of these students tended to bury their aggressive feelings, hence making it more likely that they would act them out against others in a more unconscious and unaware fashion. These children needed help owning their hurt and angry feelings and in accepting and handling them in a more developmentally appropriate way. Let us now give some more examples of these inner conflicts.

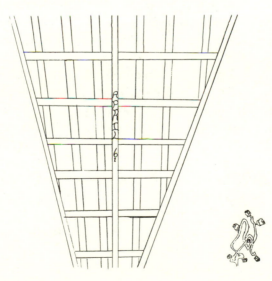

FIG. 10.7   "Rosebushes don't have feelings"

In one drawing (fig. 10.8) a small, very spiky rosebush was drawn in the lower, right corner, and a boat took up the central part with hills and a huge dark sun above. Yet the story suggests a less aggressive and more hurt picture:

> I was a red rosebush and really bushy and tall. My flowers were perfect and beautiful. My leaves are really green and long. My stems and branches are real long and tall. No, I do not have thorns. My roots are long and flat. I live by the ocean and I see lots of bats. No. No one takes care of me. Snowy. It feel a fool to be a rosebush.

By far the largest, most aggressive rosebush (fig. 10.9) drawn was accompanied by a story that again suggested a much milder person. This may reflect the wish-fulfillment process whereby the student wishes to get away from his angry destructive impulses:

> I'm a prickle rosebush. My flowers are redish pink. My leaves are a nice color green and have not holes in them. My stems and branches are nicely straight. I have thorns to protect me and they are prickled. My roots are nicely going straight down. I live in a backyard that is clean and what I see around my place is birds and more flowers. I look like the best rosebush ever produced. A man takes care of me each day he feeds me. It's a nice spring, sunny afternoon. A rosebush is nice. I get to talk to others.

There seemed to be many examples of students saying their rosebush was friendly and not having any thorns but showing aggression in another way: "I do not have any thorns. I protect myself by spitting out poison through my petals," or "I am a Venus Flytrap. I don't have any thorns, my flower protects me," or "I protect myself because I am a blood sucking bush." However, some students indicated they did have thorns but only used them when attacked (i.e., a less aggressive and more developmentally appropriate defensive posture).

Two things seemed evident from this projective activity. First, it appeared that several students did not have a clear understanding of their personal level of aggressive behavior; that is, many indicated a lot of hostility in their art, representing their inner nature at that time, but presented themselves verbally or cognitively as being "nice"

FIG. 10.8 "No one takes care of me"

FIG. 10.9 "I'm a prickly rosebush"

and "friendly." Secondly, it seemed that a few of the students were having some emotional difficulty, such as the depressed students and those who indicated their bush was dying. When these names were presented to the teacher, he confirmed the histories, and in fact, two students in these categories did attempt suicide within the following year. Obviously there were also some very vulnerable members of this class.

Discussion and Sentence Stems

Although it was important to clarify the emotions and behaviors in the room for all of the students, it was also important to be protective of the fragile students. Having the vulnerable students work in triads with at least one healthy class member seemed to accommodate both needs. Once they began, all the groups except one were able to finish the task of completing the sentence stems. In that case two group members became very frustrated because one very bright child refused to participate. The counselor worked with this triad to elicit ideas from all three, each writing his or her own material. In the end the resistant child did present to the class. In the triad setting the counselor also reflected the resistance to participating, and all members of the small group addressed the effects of the behavior.

Most of the reporting back to the class consisted of reading the small group responses, but two issues were discussed further. The "putdowns" listed by the triads ranged from swearing and rude signs to comments on academic ability and physical skills. These evoked a variety of emotions from feeling mad, left out, embarrassed, horrified, dumb, and sad to being entertained and thankful. The counselor initiated further discussion of this stem, and the class indicated that sometimes putdowns were insults made in retaliation and this awareness created relief and thankfulness. Other students also acknowledged that sometimes the comments seemed funny. After hearing concrete examples and the feelings generated by being insulted and laughed at simultaneously, many students expressed an understanding from personal experience.

When reporting the behaviors accompanying "putdowns," most groups described fighting, pushing, and laughing. Two groups showed deeper insight by saying, "they were grouchy and upset before," implying that those who were insulting others were in a bad mood when they got to school and that "they were being snobbish and foolish and then were unhappy that they put you down." The class seemed to have a good grasp of reasons why people may insult others:

> you failed a test; you were bugging their friends; because you think they are the best at everything; jealousy; trying to impress their friends; showing off; they're frustrated; they're used to it; they don't like you; you're new.

The most common response to the stem "Some things I can do to discourage these statements . . ." was some form of ignoring them. Other responses suggested running away or retaliating in some way. When asked why it may be hard to stop these "putdowns," the students responded with comments such as "They are too ignorant to get the point," "Their friends may butt in," and "They may jump out at you with a snobbish attitude." Many of the triads did not complete the stem "One thing I'm prepared to try is. . . ." Of those who did, the most common response was some form of ignoring it or avoiding the students.

From these responses it seemed there was considerable understanding among the students for why people may be so verbally abusive of others. They certainly were all aware these behaviors were occurring. They were less aware of how to deter this behavior and somewhat unwilling to commit to a new approach. However, there had been no derogatory comments during this session, including the reporting to the whole class. There was much more enthusiasm for the concluding rendition of IALAC than when the sessions began.

Because the comfort level seemed to have increased, it appeared reasonable to attempt a full class discussion in the third session. There was enough trust for sharing from many students, and, again, almost no putdowns occurred. The two times comments were made, the counselor was confrontative about the behavior and feelings of everyone in the room at that moment. One youngster was somewhat sheepish when it became evident the only reason for the comment was habit. The other student was the same one who had refused to participate in triad activity previously and who again sat sullenly and withdrawn. This session ended with everyone writing a statement of what they were prepared to do, with their signature added as an indication of commitment:

> I am prepared to try and make friends with these people. Make them feel wanted. I'll ignore them. I am prepared to stand up for myself or someone else.

The student who did not want to participate was consistent: "I am prepared to do nothing." The counselor spent a little time with this student after the class, and the teacher spent quite a bit of time over the next few weeks. Within days the child was joining in less reluctantly, and within a few months he had emerged as a positive, leading personality in the classroom.

According to the teacher, the class functioned much more cohesively after these activities. The negative comments and insults had stopped almost completely in the classroom, although they still occurred at times on the playground. Small group activity was much more productive, and the trust level had increased.

Most of the students needed only the increased awareness level and understanding of the situation and their own behavior to be willing to change and work toward more effective behavior. At a time when developmentally the peer group was becoming more important, these young people could not trust that it was safe to be themselves. Too often the peers had lashed out, and they had all been either victim or witness. Some students had also been perpetrators of the cruelty. As they gained understanding and insight, they were quite capable of some degree of change, and the subsequent problem-solving opportunity helped them determine what the change would be.

Summary

In both these classrooms, there were distressed students who were interfering with the learning process for themselves and others. They needed new behaviors, less destructive to others and more effective for themselves. The class discussions, combined with written and art activities, provided an opportunity to externalize some of their emotional distress. The sentence stems enabled the students to focus in on specific aspects of crisis situations and to think through various emotions and behaviors related to "putdowns." By relieving some of that tension, they were then able to use more cognitive processes to work through problem-solving strategies. They articulated concrete strategies and ultimately gained a sense of greater mastery over their emotions and the environment.

APPENDIX 10.1

The Rosebush: A Guided Fantasy

I would like you to close your eyes. Just be aware of your body. Forget about what's been going on around you. Just think about what's going on inside of you. Think about your breathing. Feel the air move in through your nose and mouth, down into your chest. Imagine that your breathing is like gentle waves lapping on the shore. As each wave rolls in, the more relaxed you get.

Think about your right arm. Feel it getting heavier and heavier. Feel the heaviness go all the way down the arm, down to your fingertips. Think about your left arm. Feel it getting heavier and heavier. Feel the heaviness go all the way down the arm, down to your fingertips. Think about your right leg. Feel it getting heavier and heavier. Feel the heaviness go down, down, into your foot. Think about your left leg. Feel it getting heavier and heavier. Feel the heaviness go down, down, into your foot. Feel your body relaxing and feeling heavy.

Be aware of the thoughts and images in your mind. Look at them [pause]. Now put them into a glass jar and watch them [pause]. Examine them. As more thoughts and images come into your mind, put them in your jar too. Find out what you can learn about them. Now take the jar and pour out the thoughts and images; watch as they spill out and disappear [pause]. The jar is empty.

Now I'd like you to imagine that you are a rosebush. Become a rosebush and find out what it's like to be a rosebush. What kind of rosebush are you? Are you very small? Are you large? Are you wide? Are you tall? Do you have flowers? If so, what kind? They can be any kind you want. What are your stems and branches like? Do you have thorns? What are your roots like [pause], or maybe you don't have any. If you do, are they large and straight? Are they twisted? Are they deep? Look around you [pause]. Are you in a yard? in a park? in the desert? in the city? in the country? in the middle of the ocean? Are you in a pot or growing in the ground? or through cement? or even inside somewhere? Look around you [pause]: What do you see? other flowers? Are you alone? Are there any trees? animals? people? birds? Do you look like a rosebush or something else? Is there anything around you like a fence? Does someone take care of you? What's the weather like for you right now?

What is your life like? How do you feel? What do you experience, and what happens to you as the seasons change? Be aware of yourself as a rosebush. Look carefully. Find out how you feel about your life and what happens to you.

In a few minutes, I'll ask you to open your eyes, and I want you to draw a picture of yourself as a rosebush. Then later, I'll ask you a few questions, and I'll want you to tell me about the picture as though you are the rosebush [longer pause]. When you are ready, open your eyes and draw the rosebush.

APPENDIX 10.2

Post-Drawing Inquiry for the Rosebush

Question One:	What kind of rosebush are you, and what do you look like?
Question Two:	Tell me about your flowers.
Question Three:	Tell me about your leaves.

Question Four:	Tell me about your stems and branches.
Question Five:	Do you have thorns? If so, tell me about them. If not, tell me how you protect yourself. Are you a mean or a friendly rosebush?
Question Six:	Tell me about your roots.
Question Seven:	Tell me about where you live. What kind of things do you see around you? How do you like living where you are?
Question Eight:	Do you think that you look like a rosebush, or do you think that you look like something else? If so, what?
Question Nine:	Who takes care of you? How do you feel about that? How do they look after you?
Question Ten:	What's the weather like for you right now? What happens to you when the seasons change?
Question Eleven:	How does it feel to be a rosebush? What is your life like as a rosebush?

APPENDIX 10.3

Putdowns

1. Introduction and Warm-Up
   Today we are going to discuss a topic that is of great interest to many children your age. The topic is putdowns.
   (a) How many of you have ever experienced a putdown?
   (b) How many of you have ever put someone else down?
   (c) How many of you think putdowns happen in this class?
   (d) How many don't think putdowns happen here?

2. Exploration
   (a) What are putdowns?
   (b) Are there different kinds of putdowns?
   (c) Can you tell us about a time when you were put down?
   (d) Can you tell us about a time when you used a putdown?

3. Understanding
   (a) How do you feel when you are put down? What do you feel like doing?
   (b) How do you think others feel when they are put down?
   (c) What are some of the reasons people put each other down?
   (d) Do you feel powerful when you put someone else down?
   (e) Do people who use putdowns know how the other person feels? Do they care?

4. Action Steps
   (a) What can you do if someone puts you down?
   (b) If you put someone down, what can you do after?
   (c) What kinds of things can you say instead of using a putdown?

5. Termination
   What did you learn today about putdowns?

Chapter 11

SCAPEGOATING:
RESOLVING THE PROBLEM THROUGH
DISCUSSION AND WRITING ACTIVITIES

SCHOOL COUNSELORS ARE often faced with problems such as scapegoating that affect or upset a whole class (Allan, 1981). Scapegoating of one member of a class by the other class members is a particularly disruptive and destructive problem. In addition, it seems to be a problem which is highly resistant to change through the use of conventional individual or small group counseling methods. Several factors seem to interact to reinforce the perpetuation of scapegoating.

Firstly, class members are often reluctant to give up what appears to them to be such a valuable class asset. As one child said: "You have to have a bad guy in the class. If you didn't have a bad guy, you wouldn't know that you're a good guy." The projection of the class members' problems onto the scapegoat appears to be functional for many children.

Secondly, the scapegoat, often a behavior-disordered child, comes to resent his or her role in the class and acts out. The acting-out, in turn, tends to justify the other class members' negative perceptions of the child. In this way, a continuous negative reinforcement feedback loop is set in motion.

Finally, counselors often undertake one-to-one counseling with the scapegoat in an effort to help him or her learn more appropriate ways of interacting in the classroom. However, even when more positive skills are learned in individual sessions, they do not seem to transfer readily to the classroom environment unless the class as a whole, including the teacher, also participates in discussions.

This chapter discusses a problem-solving model that can be used to deal with scapegoating in the classroom. The first part presents the model the writers developed from the approaches of Randolph and Howe (1966) and Noller, Parnes, and Biondi (1976) and from social learning theory (Egan, 1981). The latter part of the chapter describes an actual intervention in a grade-five classroom in which

a behaviorally disordered boy was being scapegoated. Writing played
a key role in helping both to calm the class and to transform some
very aggressive and hurtful emotions.

The Problem-Solving Model

The problem-solving model which follows involves several stages.
The stages are designed so that cognitive and affective (or emotional)
concerns can be expressed and transformed, and then positive actions can be stimulated. Within these broad stages are a sequence
of eight separate steps. These are (1) Introduction, (2) Fact Finding,
(3) Identification of Feelings, (4) Understandings, (5) Solutions,
(6) Blocks to the Solutions, (7) Commitment, and (8) Evaluation.
Movement through these steps enables a class to explore issues,
develop a deeper understanding, and then take responsible actions
in handling and solving problems.

Classroom management issues such as excessive pencil sharpening
or out of seat movement can usually be handled in one forty-minute
session (Barber and Allan, 1989). More deeply rooted problems,
such as scapegoating, generally require three weekly forty-minute
sessions for successful resolution. In the first session, the emphasis
is placed on steps two and three (eliciting facts and feelings)—i.e.,
on fully exploring the issue and on catharsis and verbal release of
feeling. In the second session, the emphasis is placed on a review
of the week and on deeper understanding (step four), while in the
final session the focus is on solutions, blocks to solutions, and commitment to change. These steps are now elaborated in greater detail.

The Steps

1. *Introduction.* The teacher prepares the class two or three days
ahead of time for the entrance of the counselor and for the sessions.
Later, the teacher introduces the counselor, and the purpose of the
sessions is discussed. The counselor can either elicit the problem
or present the topic of the problem to be solved. Which route the
counselor chooses is based on prior discussion with the teacher.
Specificity is very important here, as it is difficult for children to

be concrete in their problem-solving if they do not know what the problem is or how the problem relates to their lives. Spending a few minutes at the beginning of each session to describe or review the topic serves both to focus and motivate the participants.

2. *Facts.* After the problem has been isolated, the counselor starts by telling the class that, in problem-solving, the first thing that must be done is to find out the facts. The counselor writes on the chalkboard the word "facts" and then asks the pupils to call them out. With deeply rooted problems, the respondents can usually generate a long list of facts or actual things that have happened in the class. If the class is particularly rowdy, then with all of these activities it's best to ask the students to write their facts, feelings, etc., on a separate piece of paper first before calling them out as part of the class discussion.

Pacing and concreteness are particularly important when working in this phase. As a general rule, the counselor should move quite quickly with each fact, listing it on the board and moving on to another group member. If the facts are vague, the participant is asked to be more specific or the counselor tries to extract the specific fact out of the information provided. For example, when giving the facts the pupils will often relate a short anecdote. Embedded within this anecdote will be an "essence" or a fact, and it is the counselor's task to help clarify it. An attempt should be made to ensure that every class member who wants to express a fact has an opportunity to do so. Class discussion guidelines, such as "Raise your hand if you have something to say" and "Listen carefully when someone is speaking," should be rigidly enforced.

After ten to fifteen minutes, there is usually a lull in the discussion, and at this point the counselor can say: "If these are all the facts, then let's move on to the next stage."

3. *Feelings.* Here, the participants' feelings are elicited by the leader saying "If these are the facts, I'm wondering what feelings they stir up in you." It is important that the counselor remain calm, accept and write all the feelings expressed on the board, and rigidly enforce the guidelines during this critical step. The participants will tend to express a lot of negative affect, and the group must not be allowed to disintegrate into chaos. The verbal expression of anger seems to be a necessary prerequisite for the insight required to solve difficult problems. Expression is seen as part of the transformative process.

4. Understandings. This is a critical phase in the process, as the goal here is to help the class switch from blame into understanding and from self-absorption with their own feelings to helping someone else. As such, this phase needs an appropriate introduction: "We have talked about the facts and the feelings, and now I want you to shift your thinking a little for me. Why? Why would someone act this way?" The goal of this step then is to help the participants gain insight into the possible causes of the problem. This awareness can be facilitated by asking a similar question such as "Can any of you think of any reasons why some of these things [point to the facts] are happening?" If given adequate time to express both the facts and feelings, the participants are usually able to generate a number of excellent reasons to explain the disruptive behavior. Many of the teachers have been amazed by the level of perception shown by pupils regarding the dynamics of complicated problems.

5. Solutions. Once the group members have gained some insight into the possible reasons for the occurrence of a problem, they are asked to shift their thinking again to see if they can think of any potential solutions. Pointing to the problems written on the chalkboard, the counselor can then say: "Given these are the problems, can any of you think of anything we might try to help solve these problems?" Again, as before, the leader writes all suggestions for solutions on the board in the appropriate place. Later, the class is asked to rank the best solutions.

6. Blocks to the Solutions. During this step, the leader wants the group members to consider the kinds of things that might happen that could prevent them from implementing some of their solutions. The counselor at this time can ask a question like "What sorts of things do you think might keep you from trying some of these solutions?" It is interesting to note that it is usually the feelings of the participants that prevent them from both trying and persisting with the implementation of the solutions ("We'll get angry, laugh at the clowning, give up"). Another question is then asked: "Now that you know your blocks, what will help you overcome them?" ("Try to control our feelings. Don't give up.")

7. Commitment. With this step the leader tries to get a commitment from the group members to try at least one or two of the solutions. First, the counselor asks the students to take out a piece of paper and write on it the word "commitment" and list under it the things they will do to improve the classroom situation. Once the writing has finished, the counselor asks the students to sign it and send the paper up to the front of the class, asking at the same time: "Who can tell me one thing that he or she is willing to do this week to try and help solve our problem?" Later the counselor can also ask for a show of hands from those who are willing to try some of the solutions. Usually most group members are willing to try at least one solution (be specific here). If less than seventy-five percent of the class volunteers (which seldom happens), it means that more time must be spent on steps two and three. The counselor can say: "I see most of you are ready to help but some aren't. I wonder if there are any more facts or feelings that should be aired."

8. *Evaluation.* The evaluation step can also take several forms. The participants can be asked "How can we tell whether things are improving?" and "When should we check?" Or, at the end of the sessions, they can be given a piece of paper and asked to write down what they have learned about problem-solving, whether they thought the method worked, and if they had any ideas for improvement of the sessions.

In sum, through these steps the model allows the participants to air their thoughts and feelings, gain some insight into the causes of the problem, and then to find and act upon some positive solutions to it. The following actual intervention should help to illustrate both the steps and stages in this problem-solving model.

An Actual Intervention

The impetus for this intervention arose when the writers were approached by a grade-five teacher who wanted help ·with the scapegoating of a behaviorally disordered boy in his classroom. Over the months, the emotional climate of the class had seriously disintegrated, and there was considerable tension in the children. Hardly a day went by without the occurrence of ridicule, name calling, fights, and other disruptive behavior. There seemed to be an absence of positive interactions. Specifically, the teacher's request was "Could you help defuse the situation and establish a positive attitude in the class, especially toward the scapegoated boy?"

The following three-session plans comprise the basic problem-solving structure and show some of the questions asked in dealing with this specific problem. A summary of the results of the intervention—the responses of the children that were written on the board—will be found in figure 11.1. Although these responses occurred over the course of the three sessions, we have chosen to combine them in this chapter. We hope that they will provide the reader with the essence of the type of responses and transformation that can be expected with this type of work.

Session One

Introduction: (2 min.)	One of the things that teachers do is help children solve problems. Today I am going to show you one way to solve problems, and I will take, as an example, a situation from this class. I hope that you might also use this method for solving other problems that you encounter in your lives.
Facts: (15 min.)	Last week while I watched your gym class I noticed a problem. Does anyone have an idea about what problem I saw? (Many pupils cried out: "Mike wrecking all of our games.") In problem-solving the first thing we must do is find out the facts. What are the facts? What kinds of things does Mike [pseudonym] do in the classroom and in the gym? Let me list them on the board.
Feelings: (15 min.)	How do the things that he does make you feel? (List on board.)
Understandings: (4 min.)	Why do you think that Mike acts the way he does? (List on board.)
Solutions: (3 min.)	What can you do to help him? (List on board.)
Commitment: (1 min.)	Could you raise your hand if you are willing to try these solutions?

FIG. 11.1

Results of Problem-Solving Sessions

FACTS	FEELINGS	PROBLEMS	SOLUTIONS
1. Throws thing—crayons, food, worms, water bombs, books.	1. Angry—mad, really mad, frustrated.	1. He wants attention.	1. Praise good behavior; give him encouragement.
2. Acts weird—kisses you, hugs you, laughs when someone's pet dies, spits out food.	2. Sad—hurts your feelings, makes you want to cry, lousy, bad, upset.	2. He doesn't have any friends.	2. Be friendly toward him; ask him if he wants to play with you or if you can play with him.
3. Disobeys teacher—doesn't listen, rude, lies.	3. Weird—frightened, fearful.	3. He hasn't learned how to act normally.	3. Ask him to stop in a normal voice. Tell him what we do and what we don't do in class.
4. Steals—lunch kit, books, pencils, lunch, money.	4. Hopeless—feel like giving up, discouraged.	4. He wants to get you mad.	4. Ignore silly behavior; walk away. Stay calm; don't let yourself get mad; talk softly.
5. Get you in trouble—blames you, tells on you.		5. He doesn't feel important.	5. Give him an important job in the class.
6. Slams doors, yells all over the school.			
7. Kicks you, fights, screams, chases you, squishes your desk against you.			

Session Two

Introduction: (2 min.)	Last week we started working on a problem that you have in this classroom. You told me a number of facts about the problem and how you feel about it. Then we talked about why the problem was occurring, and you suggested some good reasons. I want to continue to work on this problem again today, as problems often aren't solved right away.
Facts: (5 min.)	What kinds of things has Mike done this week? Today I want to divide the facts into two parts when I write them on the board: things he did well (+) and troublesome areas (−).
Feelings: (5 min.)	How did the things that he did make you feel? Again, I want to divide the feelings into two parts: positive (+) and negative (−).
Understandings: (10 min.)	Why do you think that Mike acted the way he did?
Solutions: (15 min.)	Now I want you to shift your thinking a little bit and think about a different question. What kinds of things could you people in this class try to do this week to help to solve the problem that we have?
Commitment: (3 min.)	How many of you are willing to try some of these solutions this week? How many aren't willing to try any of them? Next week we will continue this discussion and talk about what you have tried and how it worked.

Session Three

Introduction: (3 min.)	Today is our last discussion about problem-solving and specifically solving a problem that occurred in this class. I hear from your teacher

that most of you are learning a lot from these sessions and that you are putting the ideas in practice and getting some good results. Let's look now at some of the solutions to the problem that you have tried and how each of them is working.

Solutions:
  (14 min.)

In a minute I will ask each of you what solution you tried and how it worked. I want to divide the solutions into two parts—the ones that work and the ones that don't—when I write them on the board. This will help us to know which solutions are working the best. What did you try? How did it work?

Blocks to the Solutions:
  (10 min.)

What kinds of things have you found that make trying these solutions difficult? What stops you carrying out your own solutions, and what do you have to watch for?

Commitment:
  (5 min.)

On the board you can see some of the solutions you have tried. Some of them have worked and some haven't. Which solutions do you think are the best ones? Raise your hand if you are committed to continuing to try these solutions. Raise your hand if you aren't. What needs to happen for you in order to make a commitment?

Evaluation:
  (8 min.)

What have you learned about problem-solving from these discussions? I will pass a piece of paper to each of you now, and I would like you to write down what you in particular have learned about problem-solving from our meetings and what worked best for you.

The Scapegoat

Naturally, before an intervention strategy such as this can be used, detailed preparation must be made for the scapegoated child. Following extensive consultation with the school principal and staff, a treatment approach is delineated and the parents are usually consulted. The teacher prepares the child ahead of time for what is going to happen. For example:

Teacher:	Mike, as you know, life in this classroom is rather difficult for you right now. I have some ideas as to how to help your class and you get along better. So what I'd like to do is to meet along with the class while you do some work in the library. I'll be helping them talk out their issues and come up with ways to make the classroom a friendlier place. Once I have done this I'll come down, and we'll talk about the situation from your point of view. How does that sound to you?

After the classroom discussion, the teacher sees the child alone and proceeds with a similar problem-solving format, writing down the child's responses. Usually after three or four sessions, it is possible to bring the child into the classroom and continue the dialogue directly between the child and the classmates. With skillful handling, this usually results in a positive resolution.

Discussion and Summary

These three problem-solving classroom discussion sessions helped to change the attitude of the class toward the boy, and life proceeded normally for the next three months of school (i.e., until June). What was seen as an impossible situation by most class members came to be viewed positively and as a challenge. The teacher was surprised at the transformation and pleased with the cognitive maturity shown by his pupils ("They spoke just like adults"). The pupils obviously enjoyed the discussions. There was excitement and full involvement.

Almost everyone had something to say, and "getting out" the facts and feelings cleared the air.

After the children were allowed to engage in the much needed ventilation of their complaints and feelings, they were ready to make the shift from their own frame of reference (self) to an understanding of the scapegoated boy. The class climate changed quite dramatically and quickly (in one session) from hostility to concern and caring. The problem-solving format greatly facilitated this movement, and their "new understandings" seemed to reduce their feelings of hurt and their need to blame.

The format of the problem-solving model provided an appropriate vehicle for effectively handling a difficult scapegoating situation. The format allowed the children to do the thinking, expressing, and solution finding themselves. Because of this they were more invested in working on solutions than they were before when the teacher had given them the "right" answers and told them what to do.

Behaviorally disordered children in regular classrooms present many new challenges to teachers. Despite the prevalence of scapegoating, an extensive literature review in *Psychological Abstracts* and ERIC surprisingly revealed almost no articles on the topic! In sum, the writers have found this problem-solving approach useful in a variety of difficult classroom situations, ranging from racial prejudice (Allan and Nairne, 1981; Allan and Nairne, 1989) to the mainstreaming of handicapped children (Allan and Sproule, 1985), and feel it merits further research and investigation.

Part IV

IMAGERY AND WRITING

Chapter 12

THE INNER JOURNEY: CHILDREN'S STORIES

THROUGHOUT THIS BOOK we have attempted to provide ideas and examples of different written activities or pathways for use with children, activities which will lead children inward and begin to activate their healing potential. As the case material in the previous chapters has shown, children will address painful issues and seem to know unconsciously where to go when given the safe and protected place in which to deal with their hurt. The material in this section of the book works toward accessing the symbolic and archetypal images associated with growth and healing. These activities are presented as developmental classroom exercises where discussion and reinforcement from peers are useful, but the material in each chapter can readily be adapted for individual therapeutic use also.

The theme of the journey has long been a symbol for spiritual quest and the desire for discovery, self-knowledge, and change. Indeed, life itself is sometimes viewed as a journey with different chapters and stages. In our counseling work with children, we are often struck by the way they spontaneously use this theme in their art work and sand play. For example, at the beginning of treatment, they often draw scenes of roadways, highways, and freeways where cars, people, trucks, and airplanes have crashed, are stuck, or are in need of repair (fig. 12.1). At the end of treatment the highways and airports are fixed, and cars and airplanes run smoothly (fig. 12.2). Between the beginning and end of treatment, children also create themes of leaving home (fig. 12.3), getting lost (fig. 12.4), and meeting helpers (fig. 12.5).

After pondering these images and the therapeutic process, it seemed to us that the theme of the journey was basic to the human psyche and that children who came in for treatment had often experienced damage to their personal growth process. Initially they created many broken images reflecting that experience. Something had happened to them that stopped or blocked their journey, and

FIG. 12.1   Crashes

FIG. 12.2   Running smoothly

FIG. 12.3   Running away

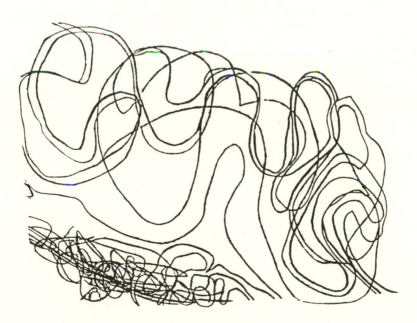

FIG. 12.4   Getting lost

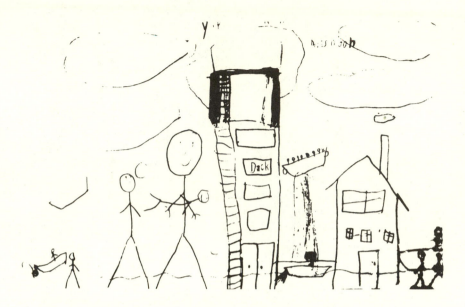

FIG. 12.5   The helpers

they could no longer function effectively—hence their referral for treatment. In the course of several decades of counseling treatment, we have noticed certain pictorial and psychological themes: The Beginning of the Journey, Leaving Home, Getting Lost, Meeting a Helper, and Returning Home.

Based on the frequency of encountering these themes in the children with whom we worked, we wondered whether such stages were archetypal and hence would have meaning for all children. As we had been working as school counselors and doing a lot of class discussions with students (Allan and Nairne, 1989), we decided to run a series of class discussions on the theme of the Journey. Not only would there be discussions of different stages of the journey but also students would have the opportunity to (a) imagine being on a journey, (b) develop a story from their imagination, and (c) paint a picture of an image or scene from their journey. This chapter describes the results of such projects and gives examples from the students' stories.

Methods and Results

This project is done over six sessions. The format for each session is the same: a stimulus word or phrase and discussion, relaxation and guided imagery, and a written activity. To activate an interest in the topic and some unconscious thinking in their minds, the class is prepared ahead of time for a series of discussions on the Journey. Best results are achieved when the teacher or instructor becomes fully involved in the theme. The classroom can be decorated with themes of travel, transportation, and journeys. Books, posters, filmstrips, and pictures can be added to the room. Stories can be read on themes that are consistent with the project and art classes used for painting their experiences. Films can be shown, such as the Canadian National Film Board's *Paddle to the Sea*. The children will need to be taught and have time to practice relaxation and guided imagery exercises.

On the first class meeting, the word "Journey" is written in bold letters on the center of the board, and free association to the word is then encouraged. The associations are then listed on the board for the class to see the diversity of reactions. Once this phase has been exhausted, the teacher or counselor moves to the second phase where the students are encouraged to:

> Close your eyes, relax for a few moments, and imagine going on a journey. Imagine leaving this classroom, setting out on your journey (by any means you wish), and having an adventure (with or without a friend). This adventure can be something that you did or a mixture of both "real" and imaginary. [Depending how involved the class seems, after about five minutes you say:] Now, imagine returning to the classroom. Take your time, don't rush back. Imagine approaching the school, coming into the building, walking down the hallways, entering the classroom, going to your desk, and sitting in your seat; imagine putting your head down, press down with your body, and feel the seat. Slowly open your eyes and join the group. What was the experience like for you?

After some brief discussion, the instructor moves the students into the third phase where they are encouraged to write a story about the experience (and if there is time or interest, later to paint a picture). In the fourth phase, those students who wish to are encouraged to read their stories to the class.

The Journey

Below are examples from the first session with a group of seventh graders:

FIRST ASSOCIATIONS

Trip I went on	Train ride	Traveling
Time machine	Center of earth	Going somewhere
Camping	Space	Hiking trip
Someone's life	Rock group	Adventure

Stories

There was much variation here: some were realistic, some philosophical, while others were very imaginative and creative. One girl wrote:

> When someone mentions the word "journey" many thoughts and words come to mind. In my case it reminds me of life.
>
> Life is to me a journey made up of many other smaller journeys, that go on until you breathe your last breath. My journey started almost thirteen years ago, and as far as I'm concerned, it will last many, many more years.
>
> Throughout my short journey, I have taken a lot of paths that I've regretted taking, but couldn't retrace. All I could do was hope to do better in the future, and not to make the same mistakes again.
>
> Life is sometimes a journey filled with disappointment and unfulfilled expectations, but in the long run, it is a journey much appreciated.

There were surprises, too. Several of the very "tough" boys wrote extremely sensitive stories, reflecting pain and various aspects of their self-concepts. A brief excerpt from one is given below:

Millenniums from now a small girl named Serena would sit crying softly as the rays from the moon danced through the window. The door to her room opened, a tall man who wore a blue suit with gold stripes down the side walked in. "What is the matter child?" said the man. The girl looked up. "I'm a Freak," she said, "I'm like no other person. Why was I bestowed with these awful powers?" she sobbed. "You are not grateful for your powers?" said the man. "No, I hate them. My parents bug me all the time, kids stare at me like . . . like . . .," the girl started crying again. "It was me who bestowed you with those powers. I thought that you with your powers could save your planet from disaster." "Disaster?" thought the girl.

"You see, many years from now your planet could possibly die from pollution and nuclear waste. You see, many people call me Starlord. I can see into the future and have other powers imaginable. To you I gave the power to alter forces and change their course and to change into any shape as a chameleon would change color; therefore, I gave thou the name Chameleon girl."

"You mean of all the people in the universe you picked me?" "Yes, I picked you because you already had a certain power that no one else on this unholy planet has!"

"And what is that?" "Love." "Love?" "Yes, I scanned your mind and noticed that you love your planet and people." "Yes, but how do you know I love my planet?" "Because years ago, as you may well remember, you could have gone to live on Mars but your love for this world helped you to stay." "But why did you pick this universe to look for someone like me?" "I was on a journey through the universes when my powers started to fade. I landed on this planet and used the last of my power to turn you into what you are." "I'm beginning to understand," said Serena. "I am grateful to you. Is there any way I can help you?"

"Yes, you can use your power to alter forces and send me back to my world." "Very well, that is what I shall do," said Serena as she lifted her finger, sending the Starlord spindaling through space back home that he left eons before.

The Beginning of My Journey

A similar process to the above is followed for each of the major themes. The title is written on the board—"Beginning of My Journey"—and associations listed. A brief discussion follows, and then the students close their eyes, put their heads down on their desks, and participate in relaxation exercises and a partially guided imagery activity. For this session, the instructor can say:

> Think about the Beginning of Your Journey. Who are you? When did your life begin? Remember this can be real or imaginary or a bit of both. It can be now, in the past, or in the future. What was life like at the Beginning of Your Journey? Who was with you? What happened? What did you see? hear? smell? touch? Just let yourself think or imagine about the Beginning of Your Journey. How do you think you *felt* about the Beginning of Your Journey? What did or might you hope for or expect to find? Just let your imagination roam.

Results

Some stories were quite literal, while others were highly symbolic and imaginative. Some stories reflected positive beginning experiences while others indicated pain ("I was born and I stepped on a tack"). At times, children used the stories to let the teacher know how they feel about themselves and to elicit a reaction from the teacher. One girl wrote:

> They called me Tamara. My nickname is Tammy. I do not really like it but I can put up with it. But now I can't stand the name Tammy. Can you? If you can, that would be good for you. But not for me. Well, I will see you later. Good-bye.

An example of a positive beginning is as follows:

MY BEGINNING OF LIFE

What's that thing looking at me? "Mrs. Johnson, you have a baby girl," said the doctor, in a loud voice. All of a sudden a thing came down, then wrapped me up in something warm. When we got in the big machine we were moving. I couldn't believe it. When we got to the place, I figured out that I was born and Mom was the big thing that wrapped me in the blanket. And the big machine was a car and I was at home. Then Mom came close and tried to make me eat baby food. "Yuc!!" It tasted bad, to me. Then Mom and Dad tried to make me say, "Mommy." So I tried. "Mo-m-m-y." I said it! Mom and Dad were so happy they were skipping around the house. They named me JulLee.

A boy who had been adopted and was having conflicts with his adoptive family, who seemed to be having a hard time accepting him for the way he was, wrote this story:

A STORY OF A SEED

One day I went to plant my seed. It was in my summer holidays. I went inside and told my mom about the seed. I told my mom I found the seed. "The seed is no good any more," said my mom. "Sure it is," I said. "I think I saw it before," said my mom. "I think I know what one you mean." "Oh," I said. "I'll go get it." I picked it up. I ran to show it to my mom. "Let me see," said my mom. "I think it must be mine. Yes, it is no good any more." Just then my dad came home from work. "Hi Dad!" I called. "Hi!" he called back. "Look what I found." "What is it?" my dad asked. "Yes," I said. I told my dad about the seed. So that's the story of the seed. At supper my dad said: "I don't think it is good seed, you should throw it out." "I agree," said my mom. "You should." "All right," I said grumbling. "Good!" said my mom. Soon it was bedtime for me.

"Good night mom and . . . dad!" "Good night!" said mom and dad. When I went to bed I still thought about the seed. I would never forget it. The next morning my alarm watch would ring at seven. I got up as fast as I could so I would not miss the school bus. "Nicholas!" my mom called. "Yes mom!" I called back. "I have a surprise for you." "What?" I called. "I am going to buy you a seed at the seed store." "Oh good!" I cried. "That's what I've always needed." "Never mind now!" said my mom. "I don't know how much it costs. Anyway, hurry up and eat your breakfast." After breakfast I kissed my mom good-bye and I hurried to the bus and told the kids the good news!

Other stories centered around such themes as getting off the mother's lap and crawling away from her into other rooms and also the learning and mastery of specific skills:

MY JOURNEY

I remember the first time when I could ride my bike. I was only two years old. I could beat some of my friends and I was on a two wheeler bike. And most of them were three and four years old. I like my bike that I used to have. I was so proud of myself that my Dad timed me. And I went around the block five times and it took me ten minutes.

Another child wrote:

BEGINNING OF MY JOURNEY

I started gymnastics when I was around five or six. It wasn't very exciting because it was only a recreation class. All the classes had a different name and color of badges. (That is for kids that passed.) When I did my first "Cartwheel" I fell on my head because my arms gave out.

The first coach I had was "Anne." She was nice and had long blonde hair. My second coach was a short lady with short brown hair but I've forgotten her name. My third coach was "Charleen." She wasn't short but she wasn't tall I think. Charleen was really nice.

After my recreation gymnastics I signed up for the "Gym Club." After a while my two coaches picked a few people to come to a harder class and I am in it now. And in 1996 I hope to be in the 1996 Olympics.

Leaving Home

The guided imagery for this topic was as follows:

Think about leaving home. Have you ever thought about leaving home? Remember this can be real or imaginary or a combination of both. What was the first time you thought about leaving home? What was going on in your life at that moment in time? What had happened? And what were you thinking and feeling? Did you, would you, just get up and go? Or would you plan it? Would you go in the day time or the night time? Would you go alone or with friends? Where would you go? What age do you think is the best age to leave home? Just let your imagination roam.

Results

Most of these stories centered around angry confrontations at home, guilt, shame, or unpleasant home life. However, they also showed intensity of feeling, humor, anger, the desire and wish that their parents would be kind and understanding of them as people, and an awareness of what a special safe place home can be. Some of the stories were as follows:

LEAVING HOME

Good-bye, Jardy I thought in anger. I'm leaving home for good. I got my bags and packed: clothes, food, money, drink of orange juice, and blankets. I'm going to go to Angela's house for four nights—then to my Aunt Susan's for a few nights. Then I'll go anywhere (but home). I got on my bike and rode to Angela's. On the way I stopped at the store and bought bubble gum. I met Laura there and told her I was leaving home. She said I was doing the right thing. When I got to Angela's house she said "you can stay as long as you want." So I stayed for five days. Then I went home and my family was nice to me.

LEAVING HOME

I want to tell you when I was around eight I went to a forest because my mom and dad were fighting. I tried to stop them, then whoosh, I went. Then I said to my mom and dad: "If you fight again I will run away." So they had another fight about the electricity bill so I ran away. I ran day and night. I ran and ran and ran. Then one day I made a tent. A couple of days after that I felt lonely so I went home. I took down my tent and ran and ran. About a day or so after I was home and I said "I'll never run away."

LEAVING HOME

I was nine years old when I ran away. You see I broke my mom's best butter dish and I was really mad at myself. So I got on my bike and rode off to Port Guichon school and back. I felt better after that.

Getting Lost

The guided imagery for this topic was as follows:

> Think about getting lost. Have you ever been lost? How old were
> you? Where were you? What happened? How did you feel? What
> was the worst moment? How long did it seem like that you were
> lost? Did you learn anything new from the experience? Now I want
> you to imagine being lost again. It can either be real, imaginary,
> or a bit of both. Just let your mind wander to a situation where
> you find yourself lost. Where are you? And what happens?

Results

Most of these stories centered around an actual experience of being lost when young. Usually this was in a store while shopping or
at a beach or park. Frequently, scared feelings were identified as was
the sense of relief when found. Often, the children mentioned meeting
helpful adults who took care of them and helped them find their
parents. Occasionally, children mentioned that their parents did not
even realize they were missing, while other children experienced loss
as being killed by wild animals. Many children commented on what
they learned from the experience: "If I got lost again, I know I'll
be found"; "My parents were really worried about me: I felt they
really loved me"; "Some adults are friendly and will help you"; "I
learned that big department stores have PA systems!"

LOST

Oh no! I'm lost in Woodwards. The shock had just settled into
me. I started to cry. "Mom!" I screamed. The sound was deafen-
ing. I felt sick to my stomach. My legs were weak. Suddenly I saw
my mother's coat! I ran, fell, was I hurt? No! I hugged my mom
so hard I'm sure I stopped her blood.

LOST

One day when I was around six I got lost. I felt scared. I started
to cry then a lady saw me and she said to me, "How come you
are crying?" I said, "Because I'm lost." So I went to another lady.
She said, "What is your name?" I said, "My name is Arlene." She

asked how old I am and I said, "Six." The lady then said into a strange thing, "There is a girl named Arlene, six years old, please report in the reporting room." And a couple of minutes later my mom and dad came. I felt much better.

LOST

One day I got lost and nobody knew that I was lost. I didn't even know that I was lost myself. I wandered deep into the dark scary woods. Then I heard a noise like a scream from a girl in the distance. It got darker and darker and the screams got louder and louder as I went deeper into the dark scary woods. I heard a noise above me and all I could see was two bright eyes. Then a cougar jumped out and that was the end of me. Good-bye Cruel World.

This story is interesting because it comes from a boy who was experiencing some severe emotional difficulties. In a certain way he is "lost" in his own overwhelming emotions, does not know it consciously but does realize unconsciously that he is lost ("I didn't even know that I was lost myself"), and is also aware that "nobody knew I was lost." This could mean that unconsciously he is aware that parents and teachers are unaware of his internal pain. The emotional theme in the story does not reflect any recovery (or helpful) process but rather leads to his death. His hurt and aggressive impulses are turned inward in a masochistic pattern. His story was viewed as a signal for help, and the boy was referred to the school counselor.

Meeting a Helper

This guided imagery also focused on helping the students think about the helpers they had met in their lives.

Think about the word "Helper." What does it mean? Who has helped you in your life? As you look back over your life, who have the different helpers been? For example, who helps you when you are doing something? Who helps you when you are in trouble? Who helps you when you are physically hurt? Who has been the most important helper in your life? Now can you think about or imagine an experience where someone or something helped you? What was happening before the helper came along? Who was the helper? What did the helper do? And how did you feel immediately afterward? And what are you left feeling now about the helper? Just let your mind mull over, dwell on the scene.

Results

Though children depicted friends, parents, and teachers in the role of helpers, most commonly seen were animals, especially their pets. It was as if in times of need the students could talk to their pets and receive comfort from them. Pets in stories, as in dreams, tend to symbolize a deep emotional and "knowing" instinctive side of ourselves.

MY HELPER

I had a fight with my Mum and Dad. It was so unfair. They don't listen to me. I got mad and ran to my room and SLAMMED the door. The whole house must have shook. I dived on my water bed. It was warm and my cat Tiger was there. He's such a fine cat. I stroked him on his long belly and he purred. He always purrs when you touch him. Nothing upsets him and I told him my whole story. After a while I felt better and I went out and talked to my Mum and Dad. We made up and now we are a happy family.

THE HELPER

My friend and I were walking home from school and we came to a cross walk. A car was speeding down the road. My dog was in the house window. She was barking and waving her paw at me. My friend said, "Who cares about your dumb dog." He ran out in the middle of the road and got killed. This is a true story. My dog was the helper because she tried to warn us.

THE HELPER

I can't speak well. I stutter and pronounce my letters wrong. I can't speak well because I have a high roof in my mouth. Me and my speech teacher look at flash cards and I have to say them. One time I got to bring a friend. Jason came with me. I mostly have trouble with my S's and R's. I've been going since kindergarten.

Returning Home

The guided imagery for this activity was as follows:

> Imagine it's many years in the future. Where are you? What are you doing? You begin to feel a little restless and slowly become aware you wish to return home for a visit. Imagine preparing for the homeward journey. How old are you? What do you look like? You are returning to your parents' house, the one you remember and like the best. Are you alone or is someone with you? How do you feel as you approach your parents? How do they greet you? What do you do together? What do you tell them? Is there anything special you want to tell them? Do you sleep over at the house? How do you leave and say goodbye?

Results

Many of these stories showed great excitement at the thought of having been out in the world and returning home. Most carried the themes of independence and mastery, success in work and relationship, and a wish to let the parents know what they had accomplished and that they could cope effectively with life. There was a great deal of humor and also feelings of appreciation and generosity, as the children now lavish presents back on the parents.

RETURNING HOME

Ding-dong! The doorbell rang. "Hi Mom," I said, "it's me, Ian."
"Why Ian, you've grown a beard," said my mother. "Take your coat off."

"I was planning to spend the night," I told my father as he hung up my coat.

"Oh that's fine," he said. "By the way Ian, have you found a job yet?"

"Why yes I have," I said. "I'm working for the C-FOX radio station." The next morning I had to leave early. When my Dad turned on his radio this is what he heard: "Fairly cloudy with a few sunny breaks. It's 50°C right now. I'm Ian Morrison, and this is AC/DC on C-FOX."

COMING HOME

"Hi Mom, I'm home from my long business trip. Now guess what, Mom, I'm married to Angela King. I've made lots of money. Now, I'm living in Dallas, I've made $20,000, and I've also got 1,000 acres. Can we stay for a bit because our plane leaves tomorrow morning? Can we have dinner too? Will you make us your baked apple turnover? I miss it."

"Well, son, you're back. Sure I will. I saw your Rolls Royce out front so I came down. How'd you get rich? Fill me in."

"Well, I sold and bought land and oil wells. We have to go to bed. See you tomorrow. Good-bye Mom and Dad. See you in ten years."

HOME

"Hey Dad, I just earned another five hundred dollars for our new house and I'd like you to meet my wife, Amber. I see you're living in the same old house. You would never guess where I'm living now."

"Where son?"

"Quebec and I joined the Quebec Nordiques hockey team."

"What position do you play?"

"Goalie."

"That's terrific son."

"Dad, that grey hair suits you and Mom, that cane suits you too. Bye Mom and Dad. Hope you see me play in the next game against the Vancouver Canucks."

RETURNING HOME

"Hi Mom and Dad! I miss you. Guess how old I am. I'm twenty and I've got no job but I got married. Can I see my room?"

My Dad said, "Arlene, where have you been? We have looked all over for you even in Hollywood."

And I said, "Do you miss me? Dad and Mom, do you mind if I go to bed now and sleep in my old bed because I'm sleepy."

Summary

This project often stirs up considerable interest on the part of both students and teachers. Because of their archetypal basis, every student can relate to each of the themes, and because time is set aside for relaxation and imagination, the students can and do bring to each theme their own unique experiences. There is then meaning embedded in the activities and to some extent the opportunity for some personal psychological development and growth. The students in the class get to know each other better, and the social and emotional climate of the class improves. Students write a lot about themselves in the stories, about their family, friends, and teachers, and start to open up and disclose more with the teachers at other times. Not only are serious concerns shared, but also the project seems to stimulate creativity, humor, and play. There is often a lot of laughter when students read and share their stories, especially when they bring their friends and classmates into the stories and give them key parts.

In reading the stories over the weeks, teachers and counselors can become aware of consistent themes and patterns in terms of how children respond to their inner drives and the world around them. Some of the themes to look for are as follows: dependence/independence; inclusion/isolation; hopelessness/mastery; blame/self-responsibility; apathy/excitement; failure/success; inner directedness/outer directedness; and "stuckness"/growth. Teachers have found that, while many children grow through this project, it is also possible to identify, through the writing themes, some children who are trapped by their problems and need a referral for counseling.

Chapter 13

WRITTEN PATHS TO HEALING

THIS CHAPTER CONTINUES the archetypal theme of the Journey described in chapter twelve but provides a specific guided imagery experience that allows for the opportunity for healing. Well-designed imagery activities enable the students to tap directly into the self-healing abilities of the psyche that are located in the deeper structures or archetypal layers. Jung (1964) is insistent that, if a person is given an appropriate setting and relationship (to teacher, counselor, or therapist), the psyche both has the ability and knows how to heal itself. This capacity, he believes, developed over thousands of years and is embedded in the archetype of the Self, the key organizing principle of the psyche. The self-healing ability emerges at night when the control of the ego and ego defenses weaken during sleep and the dream process becomes activated. The healing process can also become engaged when individuals close their eyes and turn inward during guided imagery activities. Here again, the ego moves aside a little and becomes receptive to spontaneous fantasy images from within, organized by the archetype of the Self. The dreamer or imaginer is often led to images that reflect wounding, healing, or core psychological struggles. Students report that experiencing these images and feelings during classroom guided imagery activities often leaves them feeling inwardly calm and with many more ideas for writing activities. Such inner journeys seem to replenish and strengthen the students' egos, better enabling them to continue the heroic journey of learning, working, and self-development.

The intent of the material presented in this chapter is twofold: (a) to provide the children with specific guided imagery and written exercises which they can use toward repairing some aspect of their lives needing healing and (b) to give students greater understanding of their personal decision-making process. The series begins with a typical classroom activity, the reading and discussion of a poem, Frost's "The Road Less Taken." This introduction leads into a group discussion of the decision-making process. Through the relaxation and pathway visualization activities which follow (see Appendix

13.1), students are then taken into their own inner world. Finally, the series concludes with opportunities for externalizing this individual experience through drawing, writing, and responding to a series of questions about it.

The majority of these activities require two two-hour sessions, with the revisions to the written story and its final copy being completed within the language arts period over an additional three half-hour sessions. The first session includes the introduction, discussion, relaxation, imagery, and drawing. The second session includes a brief review of the previous week's activities, an explanation and discussion of the story guide questions (see Appendix 13.2), writing the story, and completing the evaluation questionnaire (see Appendix 13.3). The questionnaire functions both as a summary activity for the class and as a guide for evaluation of the student preferences and the growth value of various activities. The following material in this chapter includes a description of the introductory activities, the response to the relaxation and guided imagery, presentation of the drawings, and then an overview of the students' stories. The chapter concludes with a review of the discussion questions and an evaluation of the project.

Introductory Activities

Poetry. The class was told that they would be doing a series of exercises, some of which would involve the whole class in discussion. They were told that some of the activities might be a little uncomfortable for them because they would be asked to share opinions with others and try new and maybe different ways of stimulating their creativity. They would be asked to take some risks in trusting others and their own inner images. They were also told that all of them would be involved by participating, but they would not be forced to participate orally in the class discussion. Finally, they were also told that none of the material they created would have to be shared in class, but they would have an option if there was enough time to display pictures and stories. Following this, they were told a little about the poet Robert Frost: that he wrote in the early 1900s, lived in the New England states, and wrote mainly about life in relationship to nature. The teacher then read his poem "The Road Less Taken."

Discussion. The meaning of the word "diverged" from the first line of the poem was discussed, and two questions were also posed: "What did the poet see?" and "What did the poet do?" This part of the activity served two purposes: it provided an introduction to the image about to be explored, and, more importantly, it helped to develop the awareness that making choices or choosing pathways is a common human experience. It was important to keep the discussion concrete and to keep the focus on choice or decision-making thoughts. Therefore, there was no further in-depth discussion of the poem but rather a switch to generating ideas for later activities.

The students were asked to imagine what might be included if one path indicated "hurts" or "upsetting feelings" a young person may have experienced by his or her age. Their responses included everything from major traumas—such as family breakups, a death in the family, moves, separations from best friends, and physical injury in some form—to lesser pains, such as fights with friends, getting into trouble at school, or temporary embarrassments. They were then asked: "What kinds of things do students your age have to make choices about?" The class responded enthusiastically with everything from the clothes they would wear that day, cheating, and what to do after school each day to careers and marriage partners. When asked what went through their minds when they made choices, they again shared many ideas. Consequences from teachers and parents, results in school, and popularity were a few examples. Simply to generate ideas, all of these thoughts were shared orally in this part of the activity. No material was pursued in any serious discussion in order to avoid leading the whole class into a single train of thought, but many ideas were generated, hopefully stimulating a personal issue and so allowing students to benefit more fully from the imagery.

Relaxation and Imagery

The students were told to get comfortable and then taken through a relaxation and guided imagery activity (see Appendix 13.1). The majority of students appeared quite relaxed in their seats and seemed to enjoy this "journey." During the imagery, some students felt as if they were watching themselves in a movie and not as if they were really there. Others could not see themselves because the imaginary journey seemed to actually be happening. Usually, these possible reactions are explained to the children before the imagery and again in the text of the journey. One student described the experience slightly differently:

> It wasn't like I was in the picture. It was more like I was there but I couldn't see myself. Like unless you look in a mirror you don't really see yourself, but you know that you're there. I could see myself but not my face, because really you can't see your face without a mirror.

It is important to reassure students taking part in an imaginary journey that whatever they experience is acceptable. This encouragement seems to stimulate the imagination. Such affirmation from the leader provides comfort for what is often an unusual image to the child and also informs the deeper levels of the unconscious that creative expression is valued.

Another important component of guided imagery is to tell students that they are totally in command of what they place on their inner screen. If any of the images or locations suggested in the text bother them in any way, they are to change it to something they like, something that feels right to them:

> If I were to say, "You are walking along a sandy beach at the ocean," and you hate the ocean, change it to walking along a lakeshore or walking through the woods, somewhere you really like.

It is important to empower students to take control of their own visualizations, to image things that are positive. It is especially important to have them in control in this imagery when they must make a decision and where there is not an opportunity for individual debriefing of really frightening experiences.

This "healing path" journey includes the usual sensory stimulus to evoke as much involvement as possible, plus several other images. The trip begins with a relaxation of the body and the nurturing of a sense of safety and confidence. The images start in a sunlit field and proceed along a path to a wooded area within a clearing. The path separates in the clearing, and the children examine the directional signs, one of which is left unclear in the instructions so they can fill in details appropriate for themselves. The verbal directions

have them choose one pathway and follow it, and then return to
the clearing, the meadow, and finally to the school. This provides
for some common experience and also for individual expression in
the details.

Drawing

Immediately following the relaxation and imagery, the students
were asked to draw something from their journey while the image
was still fresh. For many of the students, the uppermost image was
the point in the journey where they faced the divergence in the
pathway, so they chose to illustrate this. A few students chose the
initial, or final, meadow or woods to draw, and some selected a visual
impression of the experience they had after making a decision about
the pathway. The following illustrations (figs. 13.1 and 13.2) suggest the variety of images stimulated by the same text.

Because of time constraints, this group was encouraged to make
line drawings with an option of using colored pencils or felt pens
if the students wanted to add color. These restrictions worked well
but did stifle creativity somewhat. Giving options of collage work,
oil pastels, paints, and even three-dimensional creations would be
useful if time permits. Some of these children had asked if they could
make the sign they imagined, such as with wood or papier-mâché.
Another change which may be useful, depending on the group
dynamics, would be an opportunity for students to work in small
groups. Several students asked if they could join desks for the activity and later worked very well when given a choice in this. Some
students wanted only to talk as they worked and to share materials,
especially for coloring the drawing. The authors' concern for the
contamination of one student's image by another's was unfounded,
both because many of them moved about in the room anyway and
also because they were very enthusiastic about creating a representation of their own journey.

Written Activities

The second session began with a review of what had been done
together the week before. The students quickly named the poem and

FIG. 13.1   Sunrise

FIG. 13.2   The wood

described what it was about. All of them had completed their pictures by this time and had handed them in to the classroom teacher. It was interesting to note that none of the students asked for the drawing back when it came time to begin the written activity. The two activities seemed to be related, but separate, expressions of the same experience.

Story. Following the review the students were told that they would be doing written activities about the pathway imagery from the last session: writing a draft of a story about it and then answering a questionnaire. They were reminded that this draft stage of writing was for getting the ideas on paper and that there would be opportunities for doing revisions later. The story guide (Appendix 13.2) was used to elicit suggestions for describing their imaginary journey. This was first discussed in a group, both to help generate ideas for those who had more difficulty with written activities and also to stimulate creativity for all of them. For example, the first suggestion is "Describe the signpost," and in the discussion the students suggested that could include listing materials the signpost was made of, describing its color, age, or height, and telling about the wording on the sign. They were told that they could use these suggestions or could simply write whatever was important to them personally from the guided imagery journey taken the week before.

Their stories tended to deal with one of three general categories or themes. These were the decision-making process, wish-fulfillment fantasies, and the reparation process. These first two examples focus in part on the decision-making process:

PATHWAY

The signpost I saw was a rugged log in a square shape in a small clearing surrounded by a dense forest. Going through the forest was a narrow path which divided into two paths at the signpost. At the top of the signpost is another piece of wood attached lengthways to the post. The two ends were pointing each in a different direction. The right side of the sign says "Path to Healing." The other sign I can't read and is fuzzy. The entire imagery was really fuzzy. In the picture, I'm walking along the path and stop at the signpost, not sure which way to go. I felt confused and not sure which way to go because I couldn't see what the sign on the left said, and I wasn't sure what there was at the end of either path. I stood there for a while, not looking at both paths, not sure which way to go. All around me are trees close together. The air is really clean. There's not much around at all. The forest is kind of dark, but in the clearing the sun's shining down. I was thinking which way should I go? What would be at the end of the paths? Would I get lost or would I find my way back? If I chose one path would I miss something because I went that way? What would happen along the path I chose? Finally I decided to go down the path to "Healing" because I wasn't sure what the other one led to and what was at the end of it. I didn't meet or see anyone and there wasn't any talking in there either. Walking along the path to "Healing" was very fuzzy and not clear at all. I don't think I got to the end of it before I turned back because the path was very long. The path was like a normal path through the forest, but it was really quiet and peaceful. I kept walking and walking through the forest, and finally I turned back because I had been walking for a very long time and wasn't really getting anywhere. Along the narrow path there were some tree roots sticking up, and there were little patches of sunlight shining down on the ground. On my way back I felt very content, relaxed, safe, and secure. I felt like that for the rest of the day. I felt more sure of myself. This helped me learn a little about myself.

THE PATHWAY OF BEAUTY AND WONDER

As I was walking along one nice sunny day I saw a signpost. I had walked a long way through the overgrown forest. Everything was green and blooming. The grass was tall and all the plant life was growing with life. The fresh air smelled of sweet flowers. But as I went deeper into the clear green forest, I saw a big signpost. It was dug into the ground, and there was a long big board nailed across the long piece of wood. It looked pretty old but I wasn't sure. One side of the sign said "Path to Healing," while the other was squiggled and I didn't understand what it said. I stood there wondering what to do. I didn't want to go back, but I didn't know which path to take either. Puzzled I looked about at the two paths. The path to "Healing" looked peaceful and green, but I had a feeling that on my way on this path it would turn out all wrong. Then I looked at the other path. It was also very peaceful looking, but I had a stronger reaction toward it. Trees, plants, and flowers bloomed happily all around me. I felt much safer toward the unknown path. I kept on thinking if I should listen to myself or against my feelings. I looked about questioningly, if I should go one way or the other. At last I decided to trust my feelings inside for the first time. So I started to walk on the path, and it got more and more pretty and peaceful. The trees stood nice and tall. There was a fresh clean smell of pine in the air. The grass shined brightly. The flowers brought color to the happy woods. The sun shone down brightly with golden yellow rays of light. As I came to the end of the path I felt as if little eyes were watching me and I was being watched. I saw a clean bright blue lake, and in the lake were pretty little silver fish swimming around. Everything was bright and very relaxing. Just as I was about to sit down by a big oak tree, I heard some rumbling and shuffling in the bushes nearby. I froze right there. I stood up with shock. All of a sudden, all kinds of different animals popped out of their hiding places. They told me that they were upset and afraid because other human beings had treated them badly because they could talk, dance, sing, and do everything I could do. We talked about school, feelings, and more. After the talking we had a wonderful party. The animals taught me native dances, new dances and also old dances. Then everybody sang at least one song. Afterward they had a big cake, cookies, punch, and other sweets. After the big celebration all the animals and I had a quiet peaceful nap. Pretty soon it was time to go home, and I didn't want to go because it was so peaceful and quiet. I wanted to live in this new land forever. I felt very sad as I walked back home. But maybe I'll come back another day for a real vacation. Oh well, until then I had to say goodbye.

A second theme which arose was that of fantasy, and here the stories tended to be either upbeat and humorous or rather frightening. The frightening stories typically came from students who needed referral to counseling. Here are examples of each:

THE SIGNPOSTS

When I got to the signposts I saw a three foot high post that had another three foot long board nailed onto the post. One side read "Healing Street," and the other side read "Fantasy Street." In my picture I wasn't on the page. I was just coming to the place that I drew. This place looked like a cartoon. The trees had eyes, noses, and mouths and they all smiled. I even saw a deer and it talked too. Everything seemed so alive. It was almost like the movie *Roger*

Rabbit. While standing there I was feeling curious. I was wondering how this land came to be. I wanted to find out more about this place. It was so unreal it was almost scary. I was trying to figure out if I should say something or if I should run back to school. I was trying to figure out if I liked this place or not. I chose the mystery path because I met some trees and some animals. I was really amazed with this and it was neat. These trees said a lot of things. They explained where I was and answered all of my questions. I told them that I was glad to meet them and to find this place. Along this path I discovered a lot of new things. As I was walking back to school I felt really cheerful that I went down that path. I had a fun time and was happy with the choice I made.

HEAVY METAL

One day I was walking down a gravel path just off Seaciveam. I started to look really far down the path when I saw a small post-like figure. I finally came to the post. On it were two signs. One of them said "Healing street" and it had an arrow pointing down a gravel path. On the gravel path were thousands and millions of footprints. Then I looked at the second sign and it said "The Healing Power of Heavy metal" with an arrow pointing down a gravel path. On this gravel road there were large patches of grass all over the path. So I decided to take the grassy path.

I started to walk and then I saw a sign run past me yelling, "Watch for the . . ."; then he was gone. I thought to myself, "Watch out for what?"; Then all of a sudden there it was. Yes you guessed it, Heavy metal music. It hit me. The band that was playing was METALLICA. Then they stopped and the singer and head guitarist, James Helfield, came down and said, "Can you play?"

I said, "I'll try, but don't expect anything fancy." So I got up there and put on the guitar. Then I felt some sort of urge to play the song "The Four Horsemen." So I did. When I was done he said, "Pretty good. Want to go to the pizza parlor for a large one?"

I said, "Of course, let's go. I can't wait." When we were finished with our pizza I started to walk back. Then James stopped me and said, "Here, keep this guitar and some day start up your own band."

I took his best guitar and walked home. My sister stopped me at the stairs and said, "Where did you get this?"

I said, "James Helfield gave it to me," and then I ran into my room. Then she said, "Fine, he wouldn't believe me either if I said I got my drums from Jon Bon Jovi."

The pathway to healing was bright and the sun was shining and there was a rainbow. But on the other path I never knew what the sign said, but it was dark and there was a forest. I went down the unknown path, and every step I took it got darker and darker. I started to hear things and see glowing eyes. I felt determined to make it to the end of the path. As I was walking along the path I heard footsteps and they got louder and louder. I saw a fence up ahead and went to it, but before I got there a dog on a leash came out with a man holding it. He was an executioner. To the left of me was a fence and to the right was the man. So since I had made it to the end I decided to run back, and when the dog jumped at me I took off. I fell back into a whole bunch of color-ful circles, and the next thing I knew I was in the classroom.

With regard to healing or healing images, themes of guilt and reparation emerged. It was obvious that some students had trou-bling feelings and thoughts on their mind and wanted to do some-thing about it. These two examples illustrate that point.

THE PATHWAY

One day when I was camping with my parents I asked if I could go on a walk in the forest because I was feeling very guilty. I was walking for about a half an hour when I reached this peaceful meadow. The meadow had tall grass swaying back and forth, beautiful trees, birds chirping from the tree branches, and a clear stream leading way off into the meadow. The sun was glaring in my eyes. I decided to follow the stream. After about an hour of walking I came to a clearing with a signpost and two paths. One read "Healing," and the other one said something but I couldn't quite see what it was. When I got right up to it I still couldn't read it, but the first two letters I could read were a "G" and a "U." I stood there wondering what word that sign could have said. In a few minutes I decided to give up and choose the path to take: "Healing" or the other one. Since I was so curious about the path that I couldn't read, I decided to take that path. As soon as I entered the path it got pitch dark. I couldn't see a thing! After a few

minutes of wandering through the darkness I saw a light ahead.
I ran as fast as I could toward the light, and when I reached the
light I saw myself sitting on a bench in the middle of a basketball
game. It was my old basketball game that I had last week. I went
back in time, and this is the game where there were twenty-seven
seconds left, a tie game, and the other team was on a breakaway.
I jumped while trying to get the ball away, but I hit the guy on
the breakaway and he smashed against the wall and broke his arm.
Now it was in the fourth quarter with three minutes left to go.
My shift was on next. The coach said to me angrily, "Get on the
court, NOW!" We were losing by five, and then there were two
minutes left in the game. I went for a dive to the basket, made
a shot, scored, and was fouled all at the same time. I was standing at the foul line, took the shot, and now Glen Canyon was winning by only two points. Glen Canyon took a shot, stuffed
Webster's ball, Webster shot and scored! Tie game with twenty-
seven seconds left in the game, Glen Canyon is on breakaway. I
stopped all of a sudden because I remembered how I broke his
arm. He and I got the ball, three seconds left. I shot and I scored.
We won. On my way back I was not feeling guilty any more and
I was feeling good now.

THE UNKNOWN PATH

It was a beautiful day so I decided to take a walk. I went to a grassy
meadow where the sun shone brightly. As I walked through the
meadow, the grass tickled my legs and feet and the sun shone on
my eyes. I went further and saw a path that followed a sparkling
brook. I decided to follow the path and went a long way until I
came to a dense forest. The path went through the forest to a big
clearing. On the other side of the clearing were two roads that
diverged in the middle. The sign on one of the paths said, "To
Healing," and the other sign was blurry because the sun shone on
the letters. The signposts were nailed on a tree with the branches
pointing the way. You could see holes on the signs because someone was using the signs as a target practice while they were hunt-
ing. I was curious about the one that I couldn't read, so I decided
to follow the path. As I walked, I could hear people talking in
the distance. I ran toward the talking but I couldn't find where
it was coming from. I walked on further, and then I finally recognized the voices, my two best friends, Kyle and Kevin. I looked

all around me, but all I saw were trees, birds, and some chipmunks collecting nuts for the long cold winter. I was wondering why I heard those voices because we all had a big huge fight. It was because we always had to do what Kyle wanted to do. I couldn't go on without my two best friends. I went back to the signposts and saw that the other sign said, "To Apologizing." I went home and apologized and forgave my two best friends.

Issues typical of this age emerged in many stories, such as those involving relationships, environment, and view of self. The fantasy material frequently included wishes for the future, animation, and dealing with fearful things. Many of the students spent a lot of time describing the signposts and struggling with the decision of choosing a path. Also, considerable description was given to the peaceful, relaxing aspects of the imaginary journeys. Several stories included humor, and several more serious students who did not usually enjoy creative writing seemed able to enjoy the freedom of these writing activities. For one student, who was experiencing a difficult time personally, there was an expression of futility and hopelessness in the story's conclusion, that nothing could help. On the whole, the written content seemed to consistently reflect in some way the issue uppermost in the students' minds as they worked on the activity.

Discussion Questions. Before this session ended, the students were given the list of discussion questions to complete (Appendix 13.3). It was explained to them that the questions were meant to help them think back through the choice they had made in this activity and to help them in future decision-making situations. They were also told that the form was for the authors to keep, as a guide for making changes in this activity in the future.

The first five questions related to the choice of path the students made in the guided imagery. The first question, asking why they chose the path they did, was frequently answered with a version of "I was curious about what was down there." Three other types of responses were also common: following a feeling about which path to take, picking the exciting or unknown one, and choosing the safer one. A few students also made their decisions on the basis of being drawn to or wanting to avoid certain images they could see on the pathways. About half the class responded that they did not learn anything, with reasons ranging from "There was nothing there to learn," "I was too relaxed to learn anything," to "All I did was have fun." For those who did believe they learned something, it was often a significant new insight:

> When I have a decision to make I used to make it quickly without thinking and often regretted it. But now I know I should think before I make decisions.

> I learned that I can trust myself and my feelings.

> I learned that people can help if they want to and that you do have a choice.

Over seventy percent of the class was surprised about something. Most of the unexpected material was related to the dream-like vividness of the images and the emotions they elicited. One especially rewarding comment was "I was surprised by the fact that I actually went back in time and made myself not feel guilty." Another insightful comment was "When you try to help someone and they are depressed they may get very angry at you." Only two students were not happy with their choice of path, both thinking they may have had more excitement on the other path. The others were pleased because they felt better physically or emotionally in some way (i.e., often more pleasurably relaxed). The only ones who regretted not taking the other path were simply curious about what it may have contained.

When asked how they make decisions, the students were divided between making an immediate response or a delayed one. Those who indicated they decided right away either "just did it" almost impulsively or "went with what was in my heart," an intuitive response. Of those who consider the decision for a while, many weighed the consequences and possible outcomes. A few consulted with parents, especially on serious matters, thus influenced by others they value. Decision-making issues covered a wide range of examples from the mundane, "whether or not to wear a coat," to the serious, "deciding if you should stay home or run away" and "taking part in different things, like some kind of club that vandalizes, but is very popular." A great many students were well aware that they may have to face decisions about using drugs, smoking, or becoming sexually active, as well as making classroom decisions such as when and how well to do homework and how to behave toward the teachers. The list of things to think about before making these decisions was primarily related to consequences. These included how they would feel about themselves, how it would affect their reputation, how others (parents, teachers, and peers) would feel about them and act toward them, whether or not it would be physically harmful to themselves or in any way to others. For many students, decision-making involved the weighing of the advantages and disadvantages and at least some time for deliberation.

The final two questions were related to the instructional activities. Generally the students were really enthusiastic about all of the exercises, but tended to prefer either the drawing or storywriting. However, clearly the most popular was the relaxation and guided imagery sequence. As one child said, "In grade seven you work hard and need to relax." For many students this activity was a very different approach to creative writing and provided a less pressured time for them. Another said it would be better still if "You did it every Friday."

Conclusion

Heightening student awareness of different aspects of the decision-making process was furthered by most of these activities in themselves. By doing them in combination, using so many modalities of expression, we were better able to access each inner child and strengthen the understanding of the process in meaningful ways. The series also provided some students with insights about opportunities for going inward and beginning to heal some of their own hurts and wounds.

APPENDIX 13.1
Which Path? Guided Imagery Activity

This activity has two parts to it. The first part is a relaxation exercise and the second part, imagery and imagination. Get settled into a comfortable position. Many kids find that resting their heads on the desk is relaxing. Most kids prefer to close their eyes so the imagination is really clear, but some may want to keep theirs open. You choose the way best for you. Now slowly breathe in . . . and out . . . in again . . . and out . . . once more in . . . and out.

Now make your hand into a fist . . . and hold it . . . hold it tight . . . and now relax it. Make the other hand into a fist . . . and hold it . . . and hold it . . . and relax. This time tighten up your whole body, your arms, legs, your stomach, and back, even your face. . . . That's right . . . hold it . . . and relax now. Feel those wonderfully relaxed muscles through your whole body as you breathe slowly in and out.

Let your muscles stay relaxed as you imagine a cloud of warm air floating around your feet. Imagine that warm, comforting air slowly drifting up around your legs, making them even more relaxed. Let the air drift higher and higher so it's around your knees . . . and now all the way up to your waist. Feel all the leg muscles relax even more. As the warm air floats up around your bottom and your stomach, you start to relax even further. . . . Imagine the air drifting around your chest and your back, and gently all the way down your arms to your fingertips. Then it slowly drifts around your neck, your face, and even the back of your head . . . as you feel more and more comfortable, lazy, and relaxed. You may find your body feels lighter as if it could float, or it may feel heavy as if it were sinking into your chair. Just enjoy the wonderful, safe, lazy feeling. . . .

In your imagination, you will see a field or meadow. You may see yourself there, or it may seem as if you really are standing in it. As you look around the meadow in your imagination, what do you see? flowers? trees? birds or animals? Feel the warm sunshine on your skin and perhaps a light breeze. . . . Take a deep breath and see what smells are in the meadow. It may be grass, or flowers, or perhaps the ocean is nearby. Whatever sounds you hear in this meadow, they help you feel even more relaxed; it may be an airplane, people talking in the distance, music, or just the sounds of nature. Then you notice a stream near you and decide to follow it. Feel the grass against your legs as you go over to the path. You see the sunlight sparkling on the water as you follow the path beside the stream. . . . You don't need to concentrate on what I'm saying now; you can just let your mind wander into whatever is happening. The part of you that needs to hear my voice will listen. . . . That's right: keep on following the path by the stream.

As you look up from the stream, you notice you are coming to a wooded area. The path changes a little, and there are a few roots crossing it. As you enter the woods, notice how the scenery changes. Is it cooler? Can you see the sunlight filtered through the trees, or is the path still quite wide? As you pause for a moment to listen to the woods, what sounds do you hear? Keep following this path. . . .

Just up ahead you see a clearing. Walk into that clearing until you see a signpost, indicating two directions. What does it look like? Is it tall or short? Is it new or really old? What is it made of? What color is it? Now look at the words on it.

One sign says "Path to Healing." But you can't quite see what the other sign says. Pause for a moment and think about which path you want to take now. . . . That's right. . . . There may be something in your life right now that needs healing, a fight with someone you care about, a time when someone hurt your feelings, a worry inside you, something that really is bothering you and that could use some help to heal. Think about it for a moment. . . . Do you want to take this opportunity to work on it now and see what happens on this pathway? What good will come from healing? What changes will happen if you go this way?

Now consider the other pathway. . . . Look at the other sign. You can't quite read it yet. You have to get closer. What does it say? Can you make it out now? Let words form in your head or on the sign. . . . Does it give you any clue to what's along this pathway? If you choose to go this way, what might you come across? Take a moment to think about which path you'll follow now. . . .

Now begin your journey down the path you've chosen. As you go along notice how the scenery changes. Are there people, or animals, or buildings, or fantasy shapes you've never seen before? That's it; keep on going. . . . What's happening now. . . . Whatever happens as you go along, you will know what to do. . . . You may have a job or task given to you: go ahead and tackle it if that happens. . . . You may meet some special person or special animal; you may find some gift or some special reminder of this place. . . . There may be a fearsome character to talk to or a helpless creature to take care of. Take your time and enjoy all of this. . . . Now that you arrive at the place of healing, or at the end of the other path, do whatever you must on this path; find out what this opportunity is all about. . . . That's right. . . . What is it like here? Look around you. Who do you see? What do they say to you? Spend some time here. . . .

Soon it will be time to turn back. Take a look around you to really remember the things that are here. Think about how you feel right now in this place. . . . What did you learn, or do, or think about here? After one last look around, begin to follow the path back to the signpost and the clearing. . . .

Stop here in the clearing by the signpost for a minute and think about your experience. . . . Are you pleased that you chose the path you did? Next time what would you choose? What valuable thing did you learn from this choice? . . . Would you change the signs in any way? . . . Think back for a moment about what was down the path you followed. What image comes to your mind? . . . Remember, you can come back to this place anytime you want to.

Now it's time to take the very first path through the woods and along the stream to the school. You may notice the changes along the way, or you may be thinking about your experience. Follow the path back to the first meadow. . . . Look around the meadow filled with sunshine and warm air and breathe in slowly . . . and out. . . . You have just had a very important experience, and you are really aware of the feelings and ideas inside you. . . . As you breathe in . . . and out . . . you get ready to return to the everyday world. Take three deep breaths. That's right.

Now you begin to be aware of your body and the return to school. Slowly you think about stretching. Then you breathe in and out once more. Your mind can still see the picture from your experience that you will create in class. Now wiggle your fingers, stretch your back and shoulder muscles, and push down on your seat. When you are ready, open your eyes, stretch, and rejoin your class.

APPENDIX 13.2

Suggested Guide for Written Pathway Story

1. Describe the signpost(s).
2. Where are you in this picture?
3. Describe what you see around you.
4. What are you feeling as you stand here?
5. What are you thinking as you stand here?
6. Which path did you choose?
7. Who / what did you meet?
8. What did it / he / she say? What did you say?
9. What happened along this path?
10. What were your feelings as you left?

APPENDIX 13.3

Which Path? Discussion Questions

1. What made you choose this path? _____

_____

_____

2. Did you learn anything? [ ] Yes [ ] No. Explain _____

_____

_____

3. Were you surprised by anything? [ ] Yes [ ] No. Explain _____

_____

_____

4. Do you think you made a wise choice to take this path? [ ] Yes [ ] No. Explain

_____

_____

_____

5. Do you have any regrets about not taking the other path? [ ] Yes [ ] No. Explain

_____

_____

6. How do you make important decisions in your life? _____
_____
_____

7. In this class some of the decisions I have to make are about _____
_____
_____

8. Before I make these decisions, some of the things I will think about first are ____
_____
_____
_____

9. This would be a better activity if _____
_____
_____

10. The part of this activity that I enjoyed the most was [ ] the poem, [ ] the relaxation, [ ] the imagination, [ ] the drawing, [ ] the writing, [ ] the questions because _____
_____
_____

Chapter 14

Writing Fairy Tales as Training for Problem-Solving

TODAY'S CHILDREN ARE faced with a myriad of difficult situations in which they must either simply react to circumstances or attempt to define the problem and arrive at some strategies for resolving it. The fast pace of society tends to push young people into an almost instinctive response, which can lead to less than desirable consequences for them. Given ample opportunities to practice problem-solving, these students can replace the pattern of reacting with one which involves anticipating potential outcomes for different responses and selecting the one which best meets their needs.

Within a school setting, counselors can assist children with the problem-solving process by providing practice opportunities. One rather unique, and safe, way is to have them write fairy tales. The material presented in this chapter explains the rationale for using fairy tales, describes the method used with several grade-seven classrooms, and provides examples of material from these classes. The chapter concludes with a discussion of the method.

Rationale

Writing fairy tales as problem-solving will usually be included within curriculum guidelines in two areas, language arts and life skills. For example, in most school districts the language arts or creative writing curriculum will define the desired outcomes of its programs to include divergent thinking (generating ideas), determining purpose, narrowing topic, and communication of thoughts and feelings (Hipple, 1985). Schools hope that students will develop their ability to listen, speak, read, write, compute, and think productively.

Secondly, some form of life skills or health and guidance material will focus in part on problem-solving. For instance, in British Columbia, the Ministry of Education has included a problem-solving model in the new Family Life curriculum. The intent is to provide practice in clarifying problem and goal definition, and to set up opportunities to brainstorm various options for problem-solving and anticipating possible consequences of each strategy. Although the writing of fairy tales provides a slight variation on this model because of the creative writing component, the basic structure of a fairy tale (Furth, 1987, August) is the same in that it provides for clarifying, brainstorming, and anticipating consequences. The "introduction" includes problem and goal definition as well as descriptions of the characters and setting. Emphasis is placed on helping the children clearly define what the problem is and what task must be accomplished for the goal to be reached. For example, in "The Seven Ravens" (Grimm, 1944), the problem is that the brothers have been cursed and turned into ravens, and the goal is for the sister to find her brothers and so end the curse.

The "ups and downs" (or "peripeteia") are the initial attempts to solve the problem. Fairy tales are a good vehicle for children to brainstorm various ways of problem-solving because there are usually some attempts which do not work, and the students can enjoy causing complications in the lives of the characters as they work toward a solution. This part of the process helps with the real life problem-solving also because often the first one or two attempts do not work.

The "climax" is the attempt that is successful. By completing a certain task, or series of individual tasks, the characters reach some form of solution to the original problem.

The "resolution" (or "lysis") is the "happily ever after," or not, that ends the tale. Some stories end with everything being wonderful, and some end with a tinge of sadness, as with the mermaid who becomes a girl with legs but is always in pain as she walks, and who does not, in fact, marry her prince charming. Some fairy tales even just sort of run out of steam.

From a counseling perspective, there is an established tradition of using storytelling (Allan, 1988; Brandell, 1988; Lawson, 1987). On one level the material presented by the child is just a story. On a symbolic level, however, it is significant because it is a concrete representation of the images from the child's unconscious. Whether the child is working through a difficult crisis or is processing a normal developmental issue, the theme of the fairy tale reflects current, often unconscious, concerns. Working with a fairy tale is like working with a dream. Both come from the archetypal layer of the psyche and deal with the major emotional struggles in our lives, especially the theme of "good" versus "bad" and the integration of our impoverished and undeveloped self. In writing the fairy tale, the students often go through a similar emotional struggle as the hero or heroine in their story and in doing so frequently strengthen their own ego.

Furth (1987, August) indicates that individuals use "myths" to help develop a symbol of self. Those fairy tales which have significance for an individual touch part of the inner self. By realizing that one fairy tale is more meaningful than another, the individual can access some part of the self which is important at that time in life. For example, the polarities of good and evil represented by fairy tale characters help the child to understand the difference between the two and to make choices about who one wants to be (Bettelheim, 1975).

Archetypal images within fairy tales date back historically twenty-five thousand years, and until recently these stories were shared with adults as well as children. Because fairy tales contain less conscious cultural overlay than legends, they tend to touch more basic patterns of the unconscious, making them significant to a greater range of groups, in a sense making them a form of international language (Von Franz, 1982). Therefore, fairy tale writing accommodates at one time children from a wide range of ethnic backgrounds.

Bettelheim (1975) describes the value of fairy tales as follows:

> In order to master the psychological problems of growing up . . . a child needs to understand what is going on within his conscious self so that he can also cope with that which goes on in his unconscious. He can achieve this understanding, and with it the ability to cope not through rational comprehension of the nature and content of his unconscious, but by becoming familiar with it through spinning out daydreams—ruminating, rearranging, and fantasizing about suitable story elements in response to unconscious pressures. By doing this, the child fits unconscious content into conscious fantasies, which then enable him to deal with that content. It is here that fairy tales have unequaled value because they offer new dimensions to the child's imagination which would be impossible for him to discover as truly on his own. Even more important, the form and structure of fairy tales suggest images to the child by which he can structure his daydreams and with them give better directions to his life. (P. 6)

Simply providing an opportunity for writing, which brings out the inner world issues, is useful for the child. However, the counselor, in reading both the written content (Furth, 1987, August) and the illustrations (Bertoia and Allan, 1988b; Furth, 1988), gains greater insights to current issues, either crisis or developmental, by what is symbolically represented within the story. Another indicator of where the emotional attachment lies frequently occurs when the author reads the fairy tale out loud (Furth, 1987, August). Significant variations in vocal inflections are clues for the counselor; for instance, as stronger emotion is shown in the oral reading, the counselor can hypothesize that the author has some difficulty with this part of the symbolic meaning from the unconscious. By incorporating fairy tale writing within the curriculum, the counselor gives children an opportunity for self-expression on two levels, the story itself and the metaphor of symbolic value.

Method

Day 1. On the first day, the counselor introduces the topic to the class, explaining that they will be working on a new unit combining problem-solving and creative writing. The counselor reads a fairy tale, such as "The Seven Ravens" (Grimm, 1944), to the entire class and, using an overhead or blackboard, explains and elicits the parts (introduction, ups and downs, climax, and resolution) of that particular fairy tale from the class as a group (fig. 14.1, Fairy Tales: Parts of the Tale, Class Activity).

Day 2. The counselor again reads a fairy tale, such as "The Shoes That Were Danced to Pieces" (Grimm, 1944). This time, the class is divided into triads to work cooperatively in identifying the parts of this fairy tale using the above form. The group members should be preselected by the counselor or teacher so that each triad has a creative student working with those who have more difficulty. After fifteen to twenty minutes, the class members reassemble and share their results.

Day 3. In the initial activity, the entire class brainstorms possible ideas for the four components of the introduction in a fairy tale. All responses are accepted and may be clustered at times; for instance, in the introduction, "characters" could be grouped under "royalty," "villagers," "animals," and "mythical creatures" (trolls, ogres, etc.). For the written assignment, the children work individually to choose some suggestions from the class list or to generate new ones, which appeal to them for their own fairy tales. They write these on their own "Parts of the Tale" form (fig. 14.1).

FIG. 14.1

Fairy Tales: Parts of the Tale
Class Activity

---

1. INTRODUCTION
   a) Characters:
   b) Setting:
   c) Problem:
   d) Goal:

2. UPS AND DOWNS: (attempts to solve the problem, events)
   a)
   b)
   c)

3. CLIMAX: (final task)

4. RESOLUTION: (what happens)

Day 4. Again, using an overhead or board, the counselor has the class generate problem-solving strategies by brainstorming ideas for the "ups and downs," the "climax," and the "resolution." Their assignment is to begin to record some of these ideas or to generate some of their own for their personal fairy tales on their Personal Fairy Tale form.

Day 5. Individuals select those choices which appeal to them and, in point form only, write them in sequence on the "Storymap" page (fig. 14.2).

Day 6. This is the time of actually writing the draft version of the fairy tales. The points from the storymap are written into proper sentence form, but there is no emphasis on the mechanics of writing at this stage.

Day 7. The class is again broken into triads for sharing of drafts. The groups have two tasks after hearing each member's story: first, each listener states one thing he or she really liked about the fairy tale, and secondly, each listener suggests another possible idea for the "ups and downs" or climax if the author requests group assistance.

FIG. 14.2
Personal Fairy Tale: Storymap

	INTRODUCTION	UPS AND DOWNS	CLIMAX	RESOLUTION
Characters				
Setting				
Problem				
Goal				

Day 8. Illustrations. Because these can take such a long time, they can be done over two lessons. At this time the children create three illustrations for the fairy tale: one from their introduction, another for any of the ups and downs, and a final one from either the climax or the resolution.

Whether or not there is any further work on the fairy tales depends on three factors: time, facilities, and interest. Both the time required for other curriculum needs and time constraints on the counselor (although classroom teachers can easily complete the creative writing part) must be considered. Facilities for producing more polished copies or whatever form a revised version would take must also be taken into account. It is the writers' experience that most children want to share their stories. Therefore, the revisions that allow for easier reading are necessary. In many cases, the children have taken the tales to the "publish" stage, either to leave in the school library or to share with younger grades.

From the perspective of the creative writing process, completion is useful because the technical skills of revision are part of the curriculum. From the problem-solving viewpoint, just writing a draft stage provides the experience of generating options and looking at subsequent consequences of those decisions. This approach can also be used as an introduction to learning other models for decision-making. Because the fairy tale format presented here includes directed, small group activities, there was benefit to the students in increased brainstorming of ideas and in supporting a sense of accomplishment and pride in the product. Finally, the value to the counselor of gaining insight to the psychological state of the children is also met by this point—the story giving much information which is enhanced by the illustrations.

Results

The following examples clarify how a counselor can learn more about students through their fairy tales.

Example 1

Betty is a shy, gentle, seventh-grade girl whose fairy tale is titled "The Magic Horse."

Once upon a time in a beautiful kingdom called Fantastica there lived a King and a Queen. One day the Queen became very sick and died. A few days after this, the King died of sadness over the loss of his wife.

The prince and princess were very upset about the death of their parents and were also very worried that they might not rule their land well enough. Now the princess owned a horse whose name was Kywa. He was very gentle and was very responsible with the princess.

One day, while she was brushing him (because she always liked to do things by herself) he said to her, "Do not get too excited that I am talking, but I must tell you what I have heard!" The princess was very surprised to hear her horse talking but managed to control herself. She asked Kywa what he wanted and then sat down to listen to him.

"I have very sharp hearing," Kywa began, "and when I was watching you play in the courtyard, I heard your uncle and aunt talking. They are planning to kill the prince to stop him from becoming King."

The princess gasped. "I must warn him," she cried.

"Wait!" said Kywa. "Your aunt is going to put poison in the prince's breakfast. Tell him to say he is not hungry."

The princess did this and instead of eating his breakfast the prince made something for himself, and so the prince lived.

A few days later Kywa said to the princess, "Your aunt and uncle have sent guards to get you late this night when you are asleep. We must leave until we figure out what to do." The princess agreed and ran to tell her brother.

"But how do you know all this?" asked the prince.

"Kywa told me," she answered. The prince was very surprised to hear of a talking horse, but listened quietly as Kywa told them of his plan.

Later that night the prince and princess snuck away from the castle into the stable, where they took Kywa and the prince's horse from their stalls.

But just as they were about to leave, five guards appeared at the stable door. The prince and princess leaped onto the horses' backs and galloped through the side door and into the woods. The guards ran after them but finally gave up.

At last Kywa slowed to a confused canter. "Do you know where we are?" he asked. But neither the prince nor the princess had been this far into the woods before.

Finally, they settled down for the night in an old cave. Some time later Kywa said in a worried voice, "I smell wolves!" Just as they stumbled out of the cave, a whole pack of wolves bounded through the bushes. Kywa and Satin, the prince's horse, even carrying the prince and princess, could easily outrun the wolves and since the pack had a bit of food anyway, the wolves gave up the chase.

The next day, while trying to find their way back, all four fell through a hole. They landed on a soft bed of leaves. They were in a beautiful underground world where two deer gazed at them. Kywa, Satin, the prince, and princess had a long drink from a stream and then began to walk.

A while later they heard beautiful music coming from a flute, and in a clearing before them they found a dwarf. "Do you know how to get back to Fantastica?" the princess asked.

"Of course," said the dwarf. "Go up!"

"But how do you get there?" asked the prince.

"Oh," replied the dwarf, "go on for about a mile until you see a waterfall. Go under this waterfall and you will find a staircase leading to Fantastica."

They thanked the dwarf and began to walk again. Just as the dwarf had said, they came to a waterfall. They went under this, but instead of finding a staircase, they found a huge, green dragon with ruby red eyes.

"To get to Fantastica," said the dragon, "you must solve this riddle. What is small in the morning, big in the afternoon, and gone at night?"

"A king eating pie?" the prince asked.

"No, I believe he means your shadow," Kywa said calmly.

"Correct," the dragon said. "You may pass."

Up the stairs they went until they came to a wall which they thought they could never get by. The prince felt along it until he touched a stone that opened a door on the side. They went inside and saw a gaping pit under a narrow ledge. On the other end of the ledge was the doorway out.

The prince and princess began to cross the pit when they realized that the horses could never get across the narrow ledge. They looked back just in time to see Kywa close his eyes tight. Wings grew out of his and Satin's backs. They took off and flew alongside the prince and princess. "Get on," Kywa said.

"You can fly and talk!" said the princess in excitement.

"We must get back to the palace," Kywa said.

Soon they reached the village and then the palace gates where two guards stopped them. "We are the prince and princess."

"You are supposed to be dead," said one confused guard.

"My evil aunt and uncle were trying to get rid of us to prevent us from becoming King and Queen," the princess explained. They were quickly let by and told their loyal servants to get their aunt and uncle imprisoned and to call the villagers to a meeting.

The princess took Kywa back to his stall, gave him a flake of hay, and later went to join the prince. He had just finished telling the villagers the story, and as soon as the princess appeared they began to cheer.

The prince and princess became King and Queen, and Kywa the magic horse lived happily for the rest of his long life.

This fairy tale can be interpreted as a written version of "rites of passage." There is a forced separation from parents and a challenge to survive. Certain problems must be successfully overcome for survival and maturity. Forests often represent the unconscious; caves, a place of transformation; waterfalls, a place of crossing, as in a baptism or crossing into a new life. The flute is often associated with emotional anguish, which is certainly part of leaving childhood behind. Both the dwarf and the dragon can represent some ambivalence around inner knowledge and struggles. The horse, often a symbol for energy and frequently drawn by latency age girls (Allan, 1988), helps them throughout, reflecting in a sense the author's own inner strength. Finally, in order to regain the kingdom, the magic horse answers the dragon's riddle by identifying the importance of one's shadow, or inner unrecognized self. The children then face one final gaping danger which the horses' power and strength overcome so that they can return, no longer as dependent children, but now as individuals who can struggle against great odds and survive. Even their titles change to adult terms, "King and Queen." The illustrations (figs. 14.3, 14.4) further clarify the psychological image in that only the princess and animals are shown. The other inner aspect of self for a female writer, the male (animus) or prince, is written about, but never appears visually. The reader is given insights to

FIG. 14.3   Kywa

FIG. 14.4   Riding out

this young lady's present psychological development, the intensely difficult task of leaving behind childhood and entering adult life, even if it is done in symbolic form only.

Example 2

Ron is a typical, outgoing, and somewhat disorganized seventh-grade boy.

CITY OF THIEVES

Once upon a time, long long ago when the world was dark and evil lurked, living only on mortal flesh, a young boy was born and he would soon be known as the Giver of Light. As the boy grew he was taught how to use swords and bows and arrows. The young boy was ready for his first quest with his father, Dirk, who was a barbarian. Young Dak, at age ten, set out with his father to save their small village from the ORK soldiers, who continued to harass the village day after day by setting fires on the huts and taking the women. As they trudged through the marshy forest floor, Dak could hear branches and twigs breaking. Dak, his father, and companion, Romulus, walked for hours. At the last few minutes when they looked back and were ending their walk, Dirk saw that Dak was gone. Romulus and Dirk hollered for Dak but they got no reply. Dirk continued to look for his son. Meanwhile, "Dad! Are you there!? Oh, great. I'm lost. But I must complete my quest." So Dak moved on.

Two hours later . . .

"Ahh, I can't walk another step. I think I'll just—yawn—rest here for a while." Unsuspectingly, Dak fell dead asleep and was carried away by three goblins, Pinch, Boo, and Click. The boy grew to thirteen years old living with the three goblins. The goblins taught Dak many tricks and special powers which Dak would find very helpful, such as how to fly. "OH, NO, the ORKS!! HELP!!"

Dak was taken that night out of the big hollow tree where the goblins lived. But the goblins soon got wise to the ORKS' plans and decided to get the boy back. That night the three goblins caught up with the ORKS, but how could three small goblins defeat such huge, green, heavily armored lizards? The goblins didn't even have weapons! but they were very smart. So the Goblins released the ORKS' gwak horses. These horses were twelve feet long and

ate ORK flesh. So that was the end of the ORKS. The goblins freed
the boy and set off to finish their quest, but now with the aid of
the ORK-eating gwaks. After days of riding they finally reached
the caverns of the dead. These caverns were dark and filled with
creatures of the night. They slowly crept into the caverns, but they
were fully aware of the dangers. Dak slowly walked down the hall
with the goblins following closely behind. Finally, they came to
a large corridor, marked with Satan's symbol. They pushed the
door open with great trouble. It was well worth it; what luck, Dak
and the three goblins found the golden sword. Dak claimed the
sword off the wall and with the beauty of the sword forgot about
the princess. The end.

As for Dak, he became a great warrior and saved many people
with his companions, the goblins. But that's another story.

When interpreting this complex fairy tale, we see the dominant
theme of the good/evil polarities: darkness and light, mortal/im-
mortal, barbarians/teachers. The story begins with a pervading
gloom, brightened by the promise of one who will become a giver
of light, or knowledge. The first illustration (fig. 14.5) supports this
with a shaded land and huge mountain, suggestive of a struggle,
dominated by a sword with two roses, one on either side, and thought
to be wielded by the Hero to overcome demonic powers. Specifically,
the two-edged sword symbolizes the duality of life and death (Cooper,
1978). The rose is associated with the ambivalence of heaven/earth
and life/death, and the thorns signify pain (Cooper, 1978). Certainly,
the struggles and choices of growing up are painful, as are the situations faced by the fairy tale hero. The separate pathways in the illustration suggest alternate routes. Abduction by "teachers" is common
as part of the rites of passage in many aboriginal cultures. In this
fairy tale the teachers are goblins, often seen as evil, yet here clearly
aligned with the hero and representative of learning. They capture,
teach, rescue, then accompany the hero on his journey. Ultimately,
the hero and his companions face Evil directly on its home territory
(figs. 14.6, 14.7) and seize the Golden Sword. The foursome goes
on to many adventures, typical of the action-oriented individuation
process of young males. It is interesting that the beauty of the sword
and what it represents temporarily cause the hero to forget about
the princess or feminine aspect of self at this time, for this is also

FIG. 14.5   The hero's sword

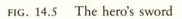

FIG. 14.6   Doorway to Hades

FIG. 14.7   The door

common in the necessary self-involvement embedded in the transition of leaving childhood. Finally, the promise of a further story indicates that this one is not yet truly complete (Furth, 1987, August), and one could then anticipate further work within this polarized struggle, again suggestive of the life-long individuation process.

Example 3

Linda, a physically handicapped seventh grader from a rural community, wrote a fairy tale about a princess who mysteriously lost her little finger each night.

> Once upon a time there was a princess. She woke up every morning and her little finger was cut off, yet every night before she went to bed it was there. The King wanted to know why it was not there in the morning yet was back every night. But one night when it was still not there, the King sent a soldier to hide in her room overnight. In the middle of the night an Elf came and said, "Now let

me take your finger until tomorrow night. After dinner when you go into the bathroom, I will meet you there." So the next morning he told the King all about it. The King said that he needed more proof. So the soldier went to the bathroom and put the tape recorder in there just before dinner. He turned it on, and when she went into the bathroom the soldier listened. When she came out, he went in.

Then he tried the tape recorder and it did not work. So he hid in the room again, and when he heard the Elf wake her up he turned on the tape recorder. He taped the thing they had talked about, and in the morning he let the King hear the tape. After he heard the tape he asked the princess if it was true and she said, "No." For a few days the soldier thought about it, and then he asked her if it was true. She said she was not allowed to tell or my [sic] finger would stay cut off. The next night after dinner the soldier went into the bathroom and after her finger was there, the soldier killed the Elf and then she told the King the whole story. The soldier got to marry the princess and they lived happily ever after. The end.

That it is the baby finger could certainly symbolically represent helplessness in the situation, and the loss of childhood could be symbolized by its being "cut off." Here the perpetrator, the Elf often represents the amoral forces of nature (Cooper, 1978). The bathroom is usually a place of privacy, yet here is "the scene of the crime." Often associated with killing, a soldier here does kill the elf or evildoer, thus becoming a rescuer and enforcer of justice. The first picture (fig. 14.8) the girl drew showed a house with many, many windows, which can be associated with vulnerability (Furth, 1987, January). The second picture shows a female figure lying in bed, with the elf above and almost straddling the figure's head, and the soldier saying "Now you are my bride." Although certainly not a concrete disclosure, both the story and the illustrations could be seen to support our prior but unsubstantiated concern that the girl was being abused.

These three cases demonstrate that only one activity—the writing and illustration of fairy tales—can help a counselor understand some aspects of the inner worlds of an entire classroom of children. There may be developmental issues which are most significant at the moment, especially in relatively functional situations, or indicators of

FIG. 14.8   House with many windows

serious distress in non-functional environments. In either case, the information provides the counselor with some direction for future interventions.

Evaluation

Evaluations from the students indicated both strengths and weaknesses in this activity. Many said it would be improved by hearing more fairy tales, both prior to writing their own and as a sharing activity afterward. All enjoyed doing their own fairy tale, although some had a strong preference for the writing activities and others had an equally strong preference for the illustrations only. Several liked the opportunity to use their imaginations with no constraints. Many indicated they would like more group sharing time, while others wanted less. Many, especially boys, wanted more violence. While many students indicated that they learned more about writing a fairy tale from the detailed pre-writing activities, some also indicated that the process was boring and they did not like it. A few indicated that they learned more about problem-solving. One said that she learned "that fairy tales are more than just a story for little kids. Now I know they are more than that and now I enjoy reading them again! I didn't before."

The teachers thought it was a good activity to use. They noticed the group sharing went very well, especially given that these particular groups usually had difficulty with sharing without using put-downs. Yet with this activity they responded within the guidelines of "I liked . . ." following the readings. The teacher also indicated that the task generated considerable involvement from all the students, many of whom were frequently non-compliant behavior problems. Several of those students, as well as many better students, wrote a greater volume of material than they usually produced.

One suggestion for improvement was that future attempts include showing videos of traditional fairy tales for those children who learn better from visual stimuli. In fact, between counselor sessions, one teacher had done this and was pleased by a very positive student response. Also, longer time to complete the activities was suggested. One teacher thought it might be more effective with sixth graders because students at that age would be more comfortable with the concept of fairy tales.

It is difficult to evaluate the actual transfer of learning to greater skills in daily problem-solving. Student awareness of the process of problem definition and working with possible options was certainly clear. Many children verbally indicated increased skills by statements such as "I think it out more now and try and think about what might happen if I do this or that." In addition, staff and student enthusiasm for the project and the insights gained certainly make this a worthwhile activity.

Chapter 15

VISION QUEST:
A GUIDANCE CURRICULUM FOR TRANSITION
FROM CHILDHOOD TO ADOLESCENCE

MANY PARENTS AND teachers are worried about the lack of adequate educational and psychological preparation our children have for their transition into adolescence and young adulthood. Frequently one sees on television and in the newspapers concern over the "troubled" youth of today—their drug problems, unwanted pregnancies, cult involvements, suicides, and delinquent acts. One hears too about violence, fear, and destruction in the schools. Obviously, there are many causes to such behaviors, but the question that arose in our minds was: What, if anything, can the public school system do to help in the transition from childhood to young adulthood so that some of these problems might be reduced?

Transition from one developmental phase to another usually involves changes in personal awareness and necessitates the learning of new behaviors. Any major change in our life pattern seems to require shifts in our identity and in the way we function. Jung (1969) said this quite poetically in 1931 when he wrote that what is true in the morning of our life is often a lie by the afternoon. On a psychological level, change often involves pain and ambivalence, confusion and dismemberment as the old identity dies and the new one emerges. At times there needs to be a hiatus, an empty period, a period of incubation between the death of the old and the birth of the new.

Recently, counseling psychologists have written quite extensively on transitions (Adams and Hopson, 1977) and on the need for intervention strategies to cope with them (Brammer and Abrego, 1981). While most of this material has focused on midlife crises, divorce, and career change, the transition from childhood to young adolescence largely has been neglected.

School counselors have written about transition from elementary to junior high school and have developed some useful coping strategies (Allan and McKean, 1984; Bent, 1976; Childress, 1982;

Friedman, 1976; Nisbet and Entwistle, 1969). However, these researchers did not address the deeper developmental issue of change of identity from child to young adolescent.

While working in the public school system as counselors and teachers, we realized that children need to understand and be prepared for this change. To meet this need we set about designing a developmental guidance curriculum on transition for grades six, seven, and eight. This chapter provides the background to our thinking, the methodology, and some of the children's responses to the material. Specific objectives, materials, and twelve lesson plans are contained in the manual (Allan and Dyck, 1985).

Background

In many ways, our present day Western civilization is an anomaly: most cultures have had rites of passage for young adolescents. Though some formal rites still do exist (confirmation, bar mitzvah, graduation, and the driver's license), most of the young are left to make or discover their own challenges or rites of initiation. Historically, this is unusual, for in other cultures the rites of passage involved all levels of the community—from the elders who steered the process to the very young who joined in the celebrations. Because of this lack, we turned to other cultures for an understanding of some of the psychological principles embedded in the rites of passage. In particular, we examined the work of such anthropologists as Van Gennep (1960), Turner (1967), Freed and Freed (1980), and Lincoln (1981), and we read writers of stories about initiation and transition (Niehardt, 1972; Salerno and Vanderburgh, 1980; Waldo, 1980). From these works we tried to identify some of the key components in transition so that we could use these in designing a curriculum of transition for today's youth. For example, certain patterns stood out:

—Just before puberty, children are aware of bodily changes and the impending change of status from child to young adult.

—The times or moments of transition were occasions for specific and vital learning.

—There were three clearly defined stages: separation and preparation, test or ordeal, and celebration with a change of status and re-incorporation.

—All of the phases involved the use of "significant others" from the family and community.

—The preparation phase often involved separation into single-sexed groups, the learning of new knowledge and skills, and actual preparation for a test or challenge.

—The activities were different for each sex. The boys needed the formal break from mothers, while girls needed the involvement of the whole community, especially adults.

—A celebration, or recognition ceremony, was held. This often provided an experience of renewal for the whole community.

—The psychological effects of the rite included the internalization of a positive self-concept for each initiate as a competent and capable young adult, ready for new responsibilities.

—The rites helped the young adolescent become a responsible carrier of the future.

Though we could not incorporate all of these principles into our guidance curriculum, we attempted to adapt some of them for contemporary life. We did involve parents in the project, and the grade-seven classroom became the "Community."

One children's story, *Nkwala* (Sharp, 1978), seemed to contain many essential components of a rite of passage. We decided to use readings from this novel in conjunction with the manual. Nkwala is a young Native American Salish Indian boy who, at the time of puberty, must make a solo journey to the mountains to attain his manhood and to find his guardian spirit (vision quest). The journey involves physical tests, self-discipline (i.e., fasting), overcoming childhood fears, and finding his own personal symbol or totem through the dream process. Once this has been achieved, the youth returns to the tribe and is welcomed with a ceremony marking the young adulthood status. The failure to pass the tests simply means the youth must try again. This process may occur several times over a two- or three-year period, and no social stigma is attached to not passing the tests the first few times around.

Broadly speaking, some of the psychological functions of rites of passage seemed to include the act of separation from the family of origin, coming to terms with childhood fears, learning new coping skills, the process of psychological death of the old childhood identity, and the emergence of a new outer and inner identity. The outer identity as a competent young man or young woman is established by passing tests and challenges, while the new inner identity occurs through receptivity to the dream or vision process. The dream or vision often provides both the sacred totem or personal guardian spirit and a new name to reflect one's new status.

In designing the curriculum, we thought it was important first to show the students how other cultures handled transition and then to include units which dealt symbolically with some of the major themes: i.e., the journey, childhood fears, and devising modern rites of passage. We saw as new coping skills for the students (a) awareness and understanding of the process of transition, (b) learning about fear and how to overcome it, (c) devising and passing their own tests, and (d) communicating their thoughts and feelings to their parents. We hoped these processes might help strengthen the new emerging self-concept.

Method

The curriculum consisted of three major units: Awareness, Understanding, and Challenge. Each unit was composed of three or four lessons which involved the presentation of stimulus material, class discussions, written activities, and the sharing of individual projects.

Unit 1—Awareness

The purpose of this unit was to help the students become aware of the concepts of transition: rites of passage, death–rebirth, and psychological transformation. The goal was to give them a cultural perspective and a frame of reference to help them understand that the changes they were going through (or were about to make) are universal and are a normal part of life.

In this unit, the students were introduced to the words "anthropologist" and "*Rites de Passage*," shown slides of Australian aboriginal puberty rites (Scollay, 1980), and read excerpts from *Nkwala*. The unit closed with a discussion of the theme of life as a journey.

Unit 2—Understanding

The goal of this section was to facilitate a deeper understanding of the process of change for each of the students. The unit focused on memories from childhood; signs that indicated they were growing up; and past, present, and future fears. Part of this understanding of change concentrated on their life line by helping them see where they have come from, where they are now, and what they hope to achieve in the future.

Unit 3—Challenge

A critical component in becoming a successful young adolescent is the ability to face difficulties and to overcome them. In this unit we set about designing simple challenges and providing students with a structure for handling and mastering certain developmental tasks. The unit starts with the students developing their own modern rites of passage and ends with a "Declaration of Dependence." Many of the challenges in this unit relate to communicating and sharing certain thoughts and feelings with parents. One of our goals was to increase the communication flow between young adolescent and parent, realizing that this can be a very difficult task for some adolescents and for some parents.

After each written activity, time was set aside for students to read and discuss their work with the class. Though this activity was optional, many students volunteered to participate.

The project was introduced as part of guidance to a regular grade-seven class, and the students were informed that for the next twelve weeks (April, May, and June) they would have the opportunity to learn about themselves and the stage they were in. They were also told that this work would help prepare them for adolescence and young adulthood.

Results

Though space does not permit a detailed analysis of each session, a brief overview utilizing the students' written reactions will be provided.

1. Australian Aboriginal Rites of Passage. The focus here was on the concepts of "death-of-childhood" and "re-birth-into-adulthood," and photographs and slides were shown of young aboriginals with their faces painted white, lying as if dead, in shallow graves (Scollay,

1980). There was a stunned response: "Are you for real!" "This is a joke, right?" and "You're making this up!" However, when asked to list the similarities between the initiation ceremony and a North American funeral, they drew several comparisons: "They lie still in a shallow grave, like a coffin; their faces are white or grey like a dead person's and have no expressions; and the relatives come to see them—the last look." Slowly, the students came to understand the symbolic act of "dying one's childhood" in order to release new energy for growth.

The last slide showed bodily tattooing that occurred as preparation for acceptance as an adult. The concept of having the adults in a society look physically different from children was initially hard to understand. However, some children commented that in our culture we can tell the difference between the two groups based on looks (i.e., looking older), clothes, and the driving of cars.

2. *Vision Quest.* The second, third, and fourth sessions focused on the vision quest experience of North American Indians. The story *Nkwala* was read to the class, and questions were asked regarding key concepts involved in the vision quest.

The unit led to many interesting discussions in the class. The idea of "proving oneself" and passing tests to be an adult intrigued some of the students. When tradition was mentioned, several students shared their experiences with confirmation and bar mitzvah. Other students were surprised by the length of time the preparation took (a year) for these experiences. Fear of failing was discussed, and this led into a discussion of other fears. Although the concept of rites of passage was new to the students, they quickly grasped the idea and could draw parallels between Nkwala's culture and their own.

3. *Journeys.* The last session in this section dealt with the theme of Journey. The word "Journey" was written on the chalkboard, and students were asked to share their first thoughts. Their free associations were listed on the board. Later, they were asked to study the list and to note the underlying theme. They noticed that a journey involved going somewhere, and one child commented that life was like a journey.

Students were then asked to focus on themselves and write a story about "My Journey." The story could be real or imaginary but would need a beginning, middle, and end. A girl who had been very withdrawn wrote the following story and later read it to the class:

I'm going away from home with a friend on my summer vacation; we go to a quiet place where no one can bug us. We get there by bus and walk into a quiet place; all we can hear is birds whistling and singing, and we can see squirrels running down and up the tree. We lay out our things on the ground and take out our tents. When we've done that we make our food and later clean up.

We have a lot of fun by seeing a lot of things in the woods and going swimming. A couple of days later we have to go home, but we don't want to leave our animal friends or the woods where there's a lot of things to enjoy. We tell our little friends that we'll be back.

My Mom's calling me and I find myself on my bed. I was only daydreaming. I'd like my dream to be true some day.

An important component of the journey discussion occurred when part of the class time was set aside for the students to read their own stories to the class. Attention was riveted to the story, and a strong, supportive group bond was formed. It was as if they were listening to one of the great mysteries and wonders of life.

4. Past Experiences. The lesson was introduced by writing the word "Metamorphosis" on the board, and leading questions were asked about the life cycle of various insects, animals, plants, and trees. Students were then asked to identify changes in the way they were treated which provided evidence of their own metamorphoses. Some examples of this were:

> You are punished physically less often. You have more responsibilities. Bedtimes become later. You have more say in the clothes you wear. Parents don't hug and kiss you as often. Parents stop fighting your battles.

When asked about situations when they felt most like a young adult, the common responses were:

> When Dad lets me help him at work. When Mom leaves me alone without reminding me to . . . When my parents let me sit in on adult conversations. When adults ask for my opinion.

Students stated they wished there were more times when parents treated them like adults. Two boys admitted they lost their parents' trust by abusing some privileges.

5. *Anticipated Experiences.* Students then responded to the question "What events might you experience in the next ten years that will cause you to feel more like an adult?" Some suggestions were:

> You may drive a car. You may move out of the house. You may look for a job. You may go out on your first date. You may travel alone. You may graduate from high school.

When the list was completed (twenty-eight ideas), the class was asked how they felt while focusing on future experiences. Two-thirds reported feeling anxious and nervous, especially regarding high school, job seeking, graduation, and traveling alone, while less than one-third felt excited about adulthood. This led into the next discussion unit on fears.

6. *Fears.* The acceptance, understanding, and mastery of fear are important to growing up. In order to help the students deal with this developmental task, they were asked to brainstorm (a) childhood fears and (b) present fears. Examples of these are given below:

CHILDHOOD	PRESENT
Getting lost	Older teenagers
Doctors/dentists	Getting beaten up
Ghosts	Failing school
Lightning	The future
Dogs	Arguing parents

They were also asked to write a short story about what life would be like without fear. The purpose of this activity was to help them see that fear has embedded in it some very useful components. Two examples of this are as follows:

> Life would be sad without fear because it would be like missing an arm or part of your body because you need fears in life; it's part of what you do. Also without fear you would figure you'd be macho or tougher than others.

> If I had no fears in the world it would be fun because I could walk

anywhere I wanted to go and do anything I wanted to do. I would
be like a king walking around, and when I did something it would
be fun getting chased by the cops or the guy you bugged.

When I did do something wrong it wouldn't be fun because you
would just walk around as if it was your own world. No one would
like you because they would think you a Mr. Macho.

The second story presents an obvious shift in thinking processes going
from the first shallow reaction to a deeper intuitive level, demon-
strating some empathy and understanding of human interactions.

The initial discussions on fear revealed that typically most students
do everything they can to avoid or run from fear and painful situations. Such comments were made as "Hide it, run away, avoid it,
fight it, cry, and pretend it doesn't exist." We tried to help them see
that some fearful experiences are best overcome by talking with
others, by assertive behavior, and by problem-solving techniques.

A class discussion was held on problem-solving techniques for
dealing with fear (Allan, 1983), and the students were shown how
to (a) list facts, (b) identify feelings, (c) define the problems,
(d) develop solutions, (e) note possible blocks to solutions, and
(f) evaluate the outcome.

This unit ended with a writing project where they had to describe
a fearful situation that turned out to be positive. One girl wrote:

ARGUING PARENTS

One night I was at home doing my homework, and all of a sudden I heard someone arguing. I went out into the kitchen and saw
my parents. I don't know why they were arguing.

I was kind of scared but I didn't say anything to them. I thought
to myself I better just go in my room and finish my homework
while they work it out. A thought came that I am going to leave
this place and never come back if they don't stop it. They were
constantly fighting, it seemed they would never stop.

I wished we were a family again but I really felt like getting up
and leaving, going anywhere just to get away from here. I yelled
at them to stop fighting for once and then left for my sister's for
the weekend. It would show them how ridiculous they looked when
they were fighting.

The fighting decreased a lot after that because my parents knew that I knew. I was happy with my Mom and Dad because they quit fighting. And now we are like a family again.

7. *Challenges.* This section sought to stretch the students by having them write letters of advice: one to themselves and one to their parents. These tasks took the form of written activities in class. An optional challenge was offered whereby they could give these written assignments to their parents or to their teacher.

a. *Advice to Myself.* The purpose of this session was to help the student develop and use some introspective analysis. The lesson was introduced with the sharing of times when advice is given and when advice is needed. This was followed by an activity inspired by the instruction "Knowing yourself better than anyone else does, write an honest letter of advice to yourself." Some of the many times when advice is both given and needed were:

ADVICE IS OFTEN GIVEN	ADVICE IS NEEDED
Report card time	When I'm depressed or sad
Before parents go out	Funerals
Before day or overnight trips with friends	When I'm confused
When I do something bad	When I'm really angry
Before a game or concert	When I'm screwing up
Birthdays	Before a game or concert
	Which courses to take in school

When the students were asked to write advice to themselves, the results demonstrated honesty, accuracy, and sincerity. One boy in the class, noted for his denial of any blame or fault, wrote:

ADVICE TO MYSELF

Get involved in more activities
Improve my behavior at school
Work better with others
Be more patient at times
Do the things I don't want to do
Be more active in events.

This boy's behavior had been characterized by impatience, disinterest in many activities during school, and difficulty working with peers. If a teacher was questioning him verbally, it probably would have been difficult for him to have accepted any responsibility for his actions.

The results of this activity were refreshing and awakening for the teacher because most of the students were far more aware of their weaknesses and shortcomings than others realized.

b. Advice to My Parents. The students were keen to contribute their own ideas on this topic but had to be reminded of the three criteria of advice (honesty, accuracy, and meaning to help, not harm). Some students took the opportunity to get even, thus reflecting unexpressed hostility and perhaps a need for some brief family counseling. However, many of the statements were well-meaning, and one example is given below.

ADVICE TO MY PARENTS

Sometimes   You brought me up
You worry too much   To be a good person
About me   And I'll do my best
And the things I do   Not to let you down
But relax
Don't worry
I'm grown up
And I know
What's right and wrong

Many of the letters and poems reflected the themes of worry and trust. In essence, the students told the parents to worry less and trust them more. This was done in the context of love: "Look, you've brought me up well."

c. The Challenge. Once both these activities were finished, the students were "challenged" to share both sets of advice with their parents. This challenge was initially soundly rejected. The fear of vocal objectors, who stated they would not do this, exerted a definite pressure on many of the other students. This led into a discussion of fear, the acceptance of how frightening it is to share certain feelings, and the value of not being afraid to be what you are. In the end, fourteen out of twenty-four students accepted the challenge, and seven gave the letters to the teacher.

In the follow-up discussion a week later, all but one were glad that they had done it. Most students reported that their parents really appreciated the insight the letters gave them. Two parents actually telephoned to mention how informative the letters were and how they were unaware that their children had such "deep" thoughts.

8. Modern Rites of Passage. Using the classroom discussion procedures again (Allan and Nairne, 1989), and with the knowledge gained about rites of passage, students are asked to discuss what tests they might like to design for themselves. In order to activate ideas for tests or challenges, a brainstorming session was held, and the following themes developed:

> Plan and prepare a meal for the family or grandparents. Learn a new skill, i.e., baking bread or changing the car oil. Do the weekly shopping for the family. Dig up the garden and prepare it for planting. Do your own washing and meals for a week. Sleep without a night light. Teach a class for a period. Wash and clean the family car without being asked. Plan a family outing and make all of the arrangements. An overnight bike hike.

Although all of the children took on a challenge, the greatest degree of success occurred with parent involvement. We also noticed the students needed help in focusing on fears or worries that they wished to overcome. An example of two tests are given below. The first test reflects a girl's experience with overcoming her fear of sleeping in the dark. This fear was an old fear from childhood. She felt that, as a young adolescent, she should be able to sleep in the dark. This test, then, represented for her a symbolic step into adolescence.

NAME OF TEST:	TAMING MY FEAR OF THE DARK
Preparation:	I will need my Dad to help me with this test. I plan on being able to sleep without the hallway light on. Dad will have to put a dimmer switch on the hallway light. This test should take ten days to finish.
Action:	With the dimmer switch in place, each night I plan on turning the dial slightly so that the light becomes gradually dimmer. I think by gradually turning down the light until it is off, I won't notice the change and I'll be able to

sleep in the dark. Success happens when I've made it without a light for a week.

Reward: My Mom and Dad will appreciate this because they think I'm too old for a light and besides it wastes electricity.

Parent
Comment: We've tried to turn the light off for years and nothing has worked. It has been weeks now and she hasn't had the light on or even mentioned it. My husband and I said we're taking her to her favorite restaurant to celebrate. Thank you.

The girl's test possessed all the essential ingredients for a meaningful rite of passage. She designed and prepared herself mentally for the test. She arranged and set up the necessary environment. The parents were involved in supporting the activity and recognized the feat as a meaningful growing-up experience.

Two boys worked on a challenge together. Their experience was as follows:

NAME OF TEST: BIKING AND CAMPING
Test: We will bike to our property (six hours), camp for the night, and bike back home the next day.

Preparation: We will fix our bikes up, get in shape by riding one hour a day for two weeks, map out our route on country roads before we go, take along camping gear and food for meals. We will do it on a weekend in June.

Completion: The test will be passed if we do it all without any help from any adults. That means no phoning home like E.T.

Reward: Our parents will give us a barbecue party at the beach.

This test turned out to be quite a feat. The boys got stuck in a heavy rainstorm and found they had to walk their bikes up some long hills. It took them eight hours to get there instead of six. They could hardly sleep at night because of strange sounds (trains, animals). However, they arrived home by four P.M. on Sunday, feeling very proud of themselves. Later, one of the mothers telephoned to say the two families (nine people) got together for the beach barbecue at which there had been "speeches" to honor the two "adventurers."

When students devise their own tests, there is increased motivation and commitment to pass them. The test of these boys contained many of the essential components of a meaningful rite of passage: preparation, separation, challenges, and celebration with family members.

For the last test, the class was challenged to plan, organize, and run a year-end class graduation party. The teacher provided the structure: "What factors must you take into consideration while organizing a party?" while the students planned the agenda and organized the decorations, food, speeches, and awards (every class member gets one award), music, and dance. Needless to say, it was a great farewell celebration.

9. *Declaration of Dependence*. Another closing activity in the curriculum focused on drawing an analogy between the life cycles of countries and humans. Using a well-known document, the teacher shifts the students' thinking from gaining independence to recognizing and appreciating dependence. During this stage the students are asked to "brainstorm a list of things adolescents depend on or need from their parents."

After a slow start and many groans, the list grew quickly to thirty-three items, which surprised most of the students. Among these items were the following:

> To encourage you when you are down. To give you advice when you need it. To love you no matter what you do or look like. To wake you up. To help you remember things. To feed and clothe you. To look after you when you are sick. To drive you places on the spur of the moment (even when they are busy)!

Once the list was completed, the students were challenged to let the parents know how they felt about them and what they will probably still need from them during their adolescence. The document was called "The Declaration of Dependence" and was to be sent as a letter.

A follow-up discussion allowed the students to share both their reactions and their parents' to this task. Responses varied widely. Most felt nervous and awkward just before giving the letter and greatly relieved afterward. Common comments were "My Mom felt privileged when I told her what I needed her for" and "I learned how much my Mum needs me and how much I love her." The parents, too, responded positively, thanking their son or daughter for sharing their feelings. One mother, who had been in a difficult phase with her daughter, was deeply touched and cried when she read the letter. One father, who had been over-protective, after reading the letter approached his son and told him he deserved more responsibility and freedom now that he was growing older.

In sum, this activity seemed to help both students and parents be aware of the changing nature of their roles and their interdependence.

Discussion

In many ways, the curriculum passed our expectations of what it could achieve. There were more worthwhile benefits than we planned, especially in the extent of both student and parent involvement. By the end of the school year, most students felt challenged by their developmental task and believed that they would have some support for this from their parents. We felt that they did have an understanding of the changes they were going through and what might be expected of them as young adults.

The identification of their needs and the communication of these to their parents seemed to be a big step through fear into responsibility and honesty. Students wrote in their journals of changes in themselves and of improved relationships at home and with friends:

> I felt good about the sharing time with my Mom. I learned how much she cared about me when I was young. I knew my Mom felt privileged when I told her what I needed her for.

> I really liked the activities. They showed me how much my parents love me. I really like the Declaration of Dependence.

Several parents telephoned the teacher and thanked him for the sharing activities (i.e., the Advice and Declaration of Dependence Challenges). One particular parent sent the following note to the school:

> I thought the activities were very worthwhile and beneficial. They put us more in touch with our children's feelings, made us think and remember.

Another parent commented on how pleased he and his wife were that the school system was apparently finally changing with the times to meet the needs of the children.

There was also an increased awareness by parents of the students' needs to participate in some of the decision-making processes in the family. One girl in the class was very upset by her parents' decision to send her to a private school the following year. After participating in the sharing activities, the girl proudly announced that her Mom and Dad would allow her to make the decision as to which school she would attend next year. It was interesting to note that the girl eventually chose the private school.

Many of the activities contributed to an improved understanding of the adolescent by the parent. A frequent comment, during the last parent–teacher conference of the year, made mention of how the parents never knew their children had such "profound" thoughts. One mother was "astounded" that her daughter could be so sensitive. She went on to thank the teacher for creating such a meaningful experience.

We felt good about the program in that it attempted to integrate the developmental needs of the students, especially their social and emotional concerns, into the regular school curriculum. The students had an opportunity to share their thoughts and feelings about current issues in their lives and to understand these in the broader context of growth, development, and society. As the program involved considerable writing and sharing, the skills involved in oral presentation, listening, spelling, sentence structure, and grammar were constantly being strengthened and reinforced.

We noticed the class became more manageable and the atmosphere more cooperative. A deep sense of trust developed between students and teacher, and the trust between students improved. Clearly, though, these were just our evaluations, and more formal, independent evaluation and follow-up need to occur to ascertain more precisely the nature of change. Plans are underway to do this and to add a unit for parents and students on the physiological and psychological aspects of puberty.

Implications

Rites of passage, whether formal or informal, are an essential aspect of education. Although our culture seems to have dropped many of the formal aspects, the process of initiation continues to occur in the psyche and lives of our adolescents. Some of this process is seen in their peer group activities, their escapades, sporting activities, music, and in their creative writing projects (Allan, 1978).

Our argument is that so much more can be done by parents, teachers, and church groups. Our experience is that these adults want to do more. They feel something is missing but are not sure where or how to start. The key issue is consciousness—being aware of the need and its importance. The second component is awareness of the right time, and the third component is willingness to provide an appropriate structure or container for the experience.

Based on some of the principles mentioned in this project, we have found that other parents, teachers, and adolescents have been able to devise some of their own rites and celebrations. For example, on reading this material, one father set about designing a small family celebration for his daughter's tenth birthday. First, the girl designed her own party for her girlfriends. This included the food she wanted, the special activities (roller skating and sleep over), the type and order of games, how the presents would be opened, a timetable of events, and the sleeping arrangements. Second, the father planned another party just for the extended family (fourteen members). During coffee and cake, the father said:

> I'd like to spend a few minutes talking about Larissa and the changes she has made over the past year because she was nine and now she is going to be ten. During the year I've been aware of her changing and growing up. I remember she failed one swimming test, but worked hard at it and later in the summer she passed it. She was very brave when she had two teeth pulled. She became a seconder in her Brownie pack, went away to camp, and loved it. She started gym and ice skating lessons. . . .

Following this, the other family members spontaneously added their images and memories of Larissa in the past year. There was no flattery but, rather, statements of what occurred and humorous anecdotes. The following morning, the daughter came to the breakfast table and announced this dream:

> I lose my bag at Zellers. I couldn't find it so I came home and told Daddy and Daddy said, "Come with me in the camperbus and I'll help you find it." But we couldn't find it. So Daddy bought me a new, bright red one, then went home. Mummy said, "What a lovely new bag you have. Since you've been so good I'll buy you a pair of new roller skates." Then we went out for an ice cream and in the ice cream parlor we met Nanny and Nanny said, "Larissa, I have a surprise for you. Here it is." "Oh, goody," I said. "It's $500.00. Let's go to Hawaii." Then we all went to Hawaii and I woke up with a happy feeling inside.

This dream reflects loss, newness, excitement, and affirmation of self.

There are many activities that teachers and parents can do to facilitate an understanding of change and transition. Various activities and concrete representations can be built on the rituals that already exist within the family or school environment. In another family, a book was created to acknowledge the son's coming of legal age. Family members and friends were each given a page and asked to help celebrate the birthday with some remembrance from "The First Nineteen Years." The poems, stories, anecdotes, photos, and other creative endeavors were then bound and presented to the young man at the traditional birthday dinner. A similar activity occurred for another family when a new baby was born, and pages of advice to her were contributed by those who knew her parents. Class yearbooks are yet another example of activities which can reflect the sense of what was and what is developing. One school took a shoe from each seventh-grade student, covered it with papier-mâché, and mounted the class set as a collage heading toward the door, a creative reminder of their final year in the elementary system and forward movement to secondary school. Successful rites usually result in a release of energy and a sense of renewal for all.

Chapter 16

My Guardian Spirit:
A Guided Imagery and Writing Activity
for Intermediate Students

JOHN ALLAN WRITES:

My first experience with the concept of the Vision Quest was a visionary experience in its own right. Of all places, I was sitting in the large, beautiful lecture room at the C. G. Jung Institute on Lake Zürich, Küsnacht, Switzerland. I was spellbound listening to Louise Mahdi describe the Vision Quest experience of Wabose, a young Ojibway girl in 1826 (Schoolcraft, 1851). Being a teacher of children and adolescents, as well as a counselor educator, I began to see how important these ancient *rites de passage* were and how, in a traditional sense, they are for the most part missing in our contemporary society. An effective young adolescent *rite de passage* not only helps the child with inner and outer identity issues but also provides a sense of change and renewal for significant others in the culture surrounding the child. Hearing Louise talk and imagining Wabose leaving her village, finding a safe and protected space, fasting for six days, experiencing her visions, and receiving her new name and "work" identity made me think of attempting to develop and write a guidance curriculum for transition. On returning to Canada I set about devising and implementing these programs in the regular public schools with the help of my graduate students Pat Dyck and Bill Brechin.

This chapter focuses on one aspect of the Vision Quest material called "My Guardian Spirit" and shows how intermediate students experienced their own inner guide.

Preparation Phase

The "Guardian Spirit" activity is often used as part of a unit in the transition curriculum or when studying Native American Indian cultures. The students read about the first North Americans and about the Northwest Coast and Plains Indians (Zieman, 1973). The topics of various spiritual beliefs, including vision quests and guardian spirits, are introduced. Then the story of Nkwala (Sharp, 1978) is read with the students, and various questions are raised. Nkwala is a young Salish Indian boy who, at the time of puberty, must make a solo journey to the mountains to strengthen his individual personality and to find his guardian spirit through the Vision Quest. The journey involves physical tests, self-discipline, fasting, visions, dreams, and unique self-expression through dance.

In order to give the students a feeling of an authentic Vision Quest, we read parts of Wabose's 1826 experience, as recorded by Henry Schoolcraft (1851). Wabose describes how, at the age of thirteen years, with the onset of menstruation, early in a winter's morning she ran off as far as she could from her village. Later her mother found her and helped her make a small lodge with the branches of the spruce tree. Her mother told her to keep away from everyone, to fast, and to "not even taste snow." Two days later her mother returned bringing no food but saying: "Now my daughter listen to me and try to obey. Blacken your face and fast really, that the Master of Life may have pity on you . . . and favor you with visions from the true Great Spirit. . . . If your visions are not good, reject them" (p. 392). Wabose continued to fast until the sixth day when she fancied a voice called to her and said: "Poor child, I pity your condition, come you are invited this way." In her vision, Wabose saw a thin shiny path, which she followed until she saw a flame rising from the top of a new moon and the Everlasting Standing Woman, who gave her a new name. She continued on until she met her guardian spirit, Bright Blue Sky, who gave her songs and gifts of life to help her endure life's difficulties. When her mother returned, Wabose related her visions to her. Her mother said it was good, took her home, made a feast in honor of her success, and invited a great many guests. (As this story is quite long and rich in imagery, teachers and counselors wishing to use it should read Schoolcraft's original version, condense it, and select appropriate parts for their students.)

Broadly speaking these *rites de passage* activities involve such psychological functions as separating from the family of origin, purification of the body, overcoming childhood fears, death of the "old" childhood identity, learning new coping skills, and the birth of new inner and outer identities. The outer identity is that of a competent young man or woman who can pass tests, challenges, and survive in a society. The inner identity occurs through receptivity to the dream or vision process where initiates receive a sacred totem or personal guardian spirit that comes to them from the depth of their psyches. Often new names are given that symbolize and represent both their inner direction and their newly acquired adult status.

Imagery Activity

The students are prepared for the guided imagery activity by practice in relaxation techniques and instruction in the imagery process itself. They are encouraged to place their heads down on their desks and close their eyes and to let their minds wander wherever they want to go. In this relaxed state, they are then prepared by the teacher for what to expect from guided imagery:

> This activity is like seeing pictures in your head. It's a bit like both dreaming and imagining at the same time. During this activity, on finding your Guardian Spirit, I will talk to you in short sentences, and you can follow along in your mind. This experience may be part real and part fantasy [imaginative]. It's okay for you to use places and pictures you've seen, but also many children imagine pictures and places that they have never seen. At times you might be busy and active and at other times quite quiet, sitting and waiting while things happen in front of you, like watching a movie that you are in. If something too scary comes up—which seldom happens—you can look away, become involved in some other imagery activity, or simply open your eyes. Okay now, I'll give you five minutes to let your mind go wherever it wants to. . . [allow for five minutes of silence]. Okay, become aware of the sound of my voice, bring your attention to your body sensations, press down first gently and then firmly with your head, hands, and bum on your desk and seat, and slowly open your eyes. Now after that little practice run tell me where you went to, what you saw, how you found it, and any questions you may have.

Once questions have been asked and discussed, the teacher can move into the actual imagery activity or delay it for another class period. The ellipses (. . .) indicate a pause of about thirty seconds to five minutes to allow the students to use their imaginations. The imagery is as follows:

Close your eyes and let your mind wander for a while. . . . Now imagine that you are living many, many years ago . . . long before white people came to this land . . . and it is approaching time for you to leave on your Vision Quest in search of your Guardian Spirit. Let's get you a home base first: Where are you living? on the Plains? by a lake? in the woods? near a desert? . . . Who is in your family? . . . What does your lodge look like? . . . Where is your sleeping place in the lodge?

Now imagine a dream, and in the dream you become aware that it is time for you to leave your lodge and make your solo journey away from your home to find your Guardian Spirit. . . . Imagine leaving and walking for a long, long time . . . away from your home into the unknown countryside. . . . What do you see? . . . What is the weather like? . . . What do you hear? . . . What do you smell? . . . After walking for a long, long time, you become aware that you are ready to begin your Vision Quest. To do this, you must find a safe and protected space. You look around . . . you search until you find a safe or sheltered area. . . . If you can't find one, you now make one out of stones, rocks, branches, and trees!

You get settled in this safe place; you wait and you watch. What do you see? What do you hear? . . . You may drift off into a light sleep! Soon you begin dreaming or imagining. . . . You're seeking a vision of your Guardian Spirit. Who comes to you? What is he, she, or it like? Continue dreaming for a while. . . . Picture the animal, person, or thing closely. Notice the details. . . . What noise does it make? What size and shape is it? What color is it? . . . Picture yourself and your Guardian Spirit. What is it doing? . . . What are you doing? How could this animal, creature, or thing help you? . . . What actions or words does it have for you? . . . See if it leads you anywhere or shows or gives you anything. . . . Do you have any questions of it? . . . Let yourself ask. . . . Let him or her answer. . . .

Now it is time to say goodbye to your Guardian Spirit. Let him or her drift off, disappear, or fade away. You are left alone in your safe and protected space. How do you feel? . . . What do you think about? . . . Now clean up your camp area, say goodbye, and start walking back to your tribe. . . . As you walk think about your experience and your Guardian Spirit. . . . Now you are approaching your village and your lodge. Your friends and relatives cluster around you. How do you feel? What do you tell them? . . . You notice you are a bit tired, so you say you must go and rest. You go to your sleeping area and put your head down on your arms. . . . Slowly you become aware that the dream is over and you are in this classroom now, in X School [i.e., name of your school]. You push down with your head on your arms, slowly you open your eyes, and when you are ready lift your head and look around the room, seeing the teacher and the other students. . . . Now I'd like you to draw your Guardian Spirit and a scene from your inner journey. Later we will write stories based on the experience.

Results

Most students thoroughly enjoyed this guided imagery activity and were eager to present their stories and pictures. Several examples are now given. One unique way of starting the experience was described by a girl who imagined falling out of a tree and getting knocked unconscious. She woke up in a forest (fig. 16.1) and followed a path where she then fell asleep and dreamt about her Guardian Spirit:

> I was at my house and I was lonely, so I went out to play and I climbed a tree. But I fell out of the tree and got knocked out. When I woke up I found myself in a forest. There was a cave, some trees, and a nice bright sun, some berry trees, mountains, and a path. I wondered where the path led to but it was getting dark so I laid down my bedroll, ate some berries, and then I fell asleep. It was quiet until all of a sudden I hear a growl. I opened one eye to see what it was. A bear! I felt scared and remembered how good the berries tasted for my last meal. All of a sudden I saw a snake, my Guardian Spirit! He hissed and bit the bear. The next day I went on the path and found it led back home. What an adventure! I felt glad to be back home, but I wondered where I had been.

Another significant idea came from a student who ended his story by training his eagle Guardian Spirit to sit on his shoulder and to give him advice (fig. 16.2). When interviewed, this student said his Guardian Spirit gave him courage and a confident feeling when he was faced with difficult or trying situations.

A similar theme from another student was as follows:

> My Guardian Spirit is an eagle, and it is going to save me from a bear that is about to attack me. The eagle is on my hand right now but later it would be flying overhead. It would swoop down and attack the bear. Finally when my Guardian Spirit was finished fighting off the bear I decided to put him in my backsack, so that he would be near by to protect me.

Another creative idea was from a boy who dreamed that his Guardian Spirit was a rain cloud (fig. 16.3). The cloud protected him from a dangerous hawk by throwing a thunderbolt at it.

> My Guardian Spirit is a storm cloud. It scared away a hawk by throwing a thunderbolt at it. The storm cloud started to pour so I went under a tree. By the time it stopped I was drenched. Then I woke up and went back to my tribe to tell my story. Afterward they called me "Storm."

Another unusual Guardian Spirit was a leprechaun who, with magic, made a bow and arrow appear so that Samantha could kill a lion that was attacking her. One boy used a turtle as his Guardian Spirit. When he was in danger he would crawl into the spaces in the turtle shell, and the turtle would close the spaces and submerge itself in the pond (fig. 16.4) to avoid being in jeopardy.

> I was walking in a field and it was getting dark so I found a spot beside a pond and soon I was asleep. Ten minutes later I heard a rustling noise. I woke up and a tiger was there. Just then a turtle came over and said "Come here." So I went over to it. When I got there he inflated his shell and said: "Get in." When I got in all the openings closed. The tiger was about to pounce on us. We slid into the pond and we were safe. The next day when I got out and the shell went back to normal, I asked the turtle how he could talk and he said: "Doesn't everyone?" Then he said: "I'm your Guardian Spirit and I will protect you forever."

FIG. 16.1   My guardian spirit: A snake

'Spirit

FIG. 16.2   An eagle

FIG. 16.3   A rain cloud

FIG. 16.4   The turtle

The most common Guardian Spirit, which appeared in more than half the assignments, was a bird (i.e., eagle, hawk, raven, or thunderbird). This may be due to the fact that many of the legends that were read in class contained these figures. It may also be that, because birds can fly, they are symbols of spirit power and therefore can offer greater protection. Mentioned in three or fewer stories were wolves, ghosts, snakes, and bigfoot. A common bird example (fig. 16.5) is as follows:

> My Helper is a raven. I was being chased and was trapped in the corner of a tree. I was terrified and frightened but then I remembered my raven. I called for his voice and he came down just in time because the attacker threw a wooden spear, and my raven caught it in his beak. My raven flew up on to a wooden platform stuck on a tree. I thanked the raven for saving my life. Then I tied the guy to a tree and left him there. Then I left the village and went back home. I always remembered the raven, and when I needed help I'd call him and he would always be there. Never again will my raven leave me because he is now my helper.

In most cases, the Guardian Spirit served the function of protection from attack by wild animals. This next student (fig. 16.6) also brought back a part of the Guardian Spirit ("the feathers") to remind him of his helper:

> It was time for me to find my Guardian Spirit. I had to venture outside my village to find it. First I had to pack my things and leave. I walked for a long time but made no contact. I fell asleep while I was walking and I had a dream. In my dream a bear was chasing me. Then I heard a screech. It was a hawk. It frightened the bear and then landed on my shoulder. Suddenly I woke up and saw the sun in my eyes. Then I saw some hawk feathers. I picked them up and ran back to the village. By then I was hungry so I ate some berries. Then I saw the bear. I jumped into the brush and the hawk came back and scratched the bear's neck so the bear ran away. I felt safe in the village because I had the feathers of a hawk, my Guardian Spirit.

This activity had a profound effect on most of the students and enriched their experience of the didactic material presented on North-

FIG. 16.5　A raven

FIG. 16.6　A hawk

west Coast and Plains Indians. There was obviously a lot of pleasure experienced in the imagery activity, and the students enjoyed drawing and writing afterward. One child got stuck in imaginary "mud" and could not complete this drawing or writing activity. The teacher took him back to the mud in his imagination, helped him get "unstuck," and then the student was able to begin and complete both his drawing and writing task. Many students commented how surprised they were to see a Guardian Spirit appear (fig. 16.7) and to feel that they really had their own Guardian Spirit inside of themselves that they could call upon in their own lives when they needed to.

Summary

Puberty, and the two years following its onset, is frequently a time of turmoil, as the conscious mind of the young adolescent struggles to deal with all of the emotions and images activated by hormonal changes. Often these changes result in a fascination with the inner world of dreams and symbols and with themes of death and re-birth. Adolescents' rock music, rock videos, songs, posters, and art work are replete with images of death and re-birth.

FIG. 16.7   Big bird

A central archetypal drive during this phase of development is that of separation from family of origin. One function of separation is to attain one's own unique identity. This is painful for parents and teachers as students reject advice and affection and form new and stronger bonds with their peers. As one teenager said recently: "I have no choice. I must leave home. I want to prove I can live away from home with my friends. I know I can do it."

Guided imagery activities, such as the one described above, are particularly relevant at this stage of development, as they provide a safe and protected way of entering the inner world and of encountering one's own imagery (emotions) and symbolism. This is important, as students are striving to find not only their outer but also their separate inner identity—one that is not contaminated by parent or teacher demands or expectations. This search is what Jung (1964) called the "process of individuation" and reaches down to both the animal and vegetative layers of the human psyche.

As adolescents prepare to enter the adult world, it is helpful for them to find a sense of their own inner security and protection and to carry this feeling into the world. These imagery activities gave the students something tangible to hold on to—"I felt safe . . . because I had the feathers of a hawk, my Guardian Spirit"—and also helped them feel part of the world of nature. By "nature" we mean, not only the world around us, but the natural world of our biological, spiritual, and psychological existence. Much of contemporary education, because of its heavy reliance on rationality and cognition, fails to help students experience and understand these other aspects of life.

In this activity the students' images (i.e., guardian spirits) gave form and shape to particular emotions and feelings that are relevant to them at this stage of life. Many of these feeling-toned symbols (animals or birds) open the students up to such emotions as strength and courage (i.e., the snake and hawk) and the experience of being protected (i.e., the turtle and the rain cloud) as well as belief in their own knowledge or wisdom ("My eagle sits on my shoulder and gives me good advice"). These inner experiences, when coupled with drawings and writing activities, can have a profoundly beneficial influence on the lives of students and help them become anchored in the richness that lies within.

References

Adams, J., and Hopson, B., eds. (1977). *Transition: Understanding and managing personal change.* Montclair, NJ: Allenhald and Osmund.

Allan, J. (1978). Serial storytelling: A therapeutic approach with a young adolescent. *Canadian Counsellor* 12: 132/37.

Allan, J. (1981). Resolution of scapegoating through classroom discussions. *Elementary School Guidance and Counseling* 16: 121/32.

Allan, J. (1982). Preparation for mainstreaming: Use of problem-solving and classroom discussion formats. *Elementary School Guidance and Counseling* 16: 193/201.

Allan, J. (1983). Scapegoating: Help for the whole class. *Elementary School Guidance and Counseling* 18: 147/51.

Allan, J. (1988). *Inscapes of the child's world: Jungian counseling in schools and clinics.* Dallas, TX: Spring Publications.

Allan, J., and Bardsley, P. (1984). *Children who move.* Toronto: University of Toronto Guidance Centre.

Allan, J., and Dyck, P. (1984). Transition: Childhood to adolescence. *Elementary School Guidance and Counseling* 18: 277/86.

Allan, J., and Dyck, P. (1985). *Transition: A developmental curriculum for "growing-up."* Vancouver, BC: Faculty of Education, University of British Columbia.

Allan, J., and McKean, J. (1984). Transition: Counseling interventions in junior high schools. *School Counselor* 32: 43/48.

Allan, J., and Nairne, J. (1981). Racial prejudice in the classroom: A developmental counselling approach. *Canadian Counsellor* 15: 162/67.

Allan, J., and Nairne, J. (1989). *Class discussions for teachers and counselors in the elementary school.* Toronto, ON: OISE Press, Guidance Centre, University of Toronto.

Allan, J., and Sproule, G. (1985). *Mainstreaming: Readings and activities for counselor and teachers.* Toronto, ON: OISE Press, Guidance Centre, University of Toronto.

Barber, J., and Allan, J. (1989). *Managing common classroom problems: An ecological approach.* Toronto, ON: OISE Press, Guidance Centre, University of Toronto.

Bent, A. (1976). Orientation and the transfer student. *Clearing House* 49: 350/52.

Bernstein, B., and Splete, H. (1981). A survey of consultation as part of counselor education programs. *Personnel and Guidance Journal* 59: 470/72.

Bertoia, J., and Allan, J. (1988a). School management of the bereaved child. *Elementary School Guidance and Counseling* 23: 30/38.

Bertoia, J., and Allan, J. (1988b). Counseling seriously ill children: Use of spontaneous drawings. *Elementary School Guidance and Counseling* 22: 206/21.

Bettelheim, B. (1975). *The uses of enchantment: The meaning and importance of fairy tales.* New York: Vintage Books.

Borba, M., and Borba, C. (1982). *Self-esteem: A classroom affair.* Minneapolis, MN: Winston Press.

Brammer, L., and Abrego, P. (1981). Intervention strategies for coping with transitions. *Counseling Psychologist* 9 (2): 19/36.

Brandell, J. (1988). Storytelling in child psychotherapy. In *Innovative interventions in child and adolescent therapy,* ed. C. Schaefer, pp. 9/42. New York: John Wiley & Sons.

Breckenridge, E. (1976). Improving school climate. *Phi Delta Kappan* 58: 314/18.

Buttery, J. (1980). Journal writing: A developmental counselling program for grade seven. Master's thesis, Simon Fraser University, Burnaby, BC.

Buttery, J., and Allan, J. (1981). Journal writing as a developmental guidance method. *Canadian Counsellor* 15: 134/38.

Canfield, J., and Wells, H. (1976). *100 ways to enhance self-concept in the classroom.* Englewood Cliffs, NJ: Prentice-Hall.

Carroll, J. (1972). The written word is not dead. *Media and Method* 9: 61/63.

Childress, N. (1982). Orientation to middle school: A guidance play. *Elementary School Guidance and Counseling* 17: 89/93.

Cooper, J. C. (1978). *An illustrated encyclopedia of traditional symbols.* London: Thames and Hudson.

Cottingham, H. (1973). Psychological education, the guidance function, and the school counselor. *School Counselor* 20: 240/345.

Crabbes, M. (1973). Someone to tell my troubles to. *School Counselor* 20: 389/91.

Dinkmeyer, D. (1971). A developmental model for counseling-consulting. *Elementary School Guidance and Counseling* 6: 81/85.

Dinkmeyer, D., and Losancy, L. (1980). *Encouragement book.* Englewood Cliffs, NJ: Prentice-Hall.

Edinger, E. (1973). *Ego and archetype.* Baltimore, MD: Penguin Books.

Egan, G. (1981). *The skilled helper.* Belmont, CA: Wadsworth.

Felker, D. (1974). *Building positive self-concepts.* Minneapolis, MN: Burges.

Fordham, M. (1957). *New developments in analytical psychology.* London: Routledge and Kegan Paul.

Freed, M., and Freed, M. (1980). *Transitions: Focus rituals in eight cultures.* New York: Norton & Co.

Friedman, J. (1976). Introduction to a special project on pre-orientation of sixth grade students to seventh grade and junior high school. *Elementary School Guidance and Counseling* 11: 152/55.

Furth, G. (1987, January). *House/Tree/Person, Senoi dreamwork workshop.* Vancouver, BC.

Furth, G. (1987, August). *Fairy tales: Impromptu drawings-psychodrama.* Paper presented at Interpretations to Impromptu Drawings, No. II. Tarrytown: New York.

Furth, G. (1988). *The secret world of drawings: Healing through art.* Boston: Sigo Press.

Garfield, P. (1984). *Your child's dreams: Understanding your child better through the world of dreams.* New York: Ballantine Books.

Garrison, C. (1986). *The dream eater.* New York: Aladdin Books.

Gazda, G., and Brooks, D. (1980). A comprehensive approach to developmental instruction. *Journal for Specialists in Group Work* 5: 120/26.

Good, T., and Brophy, J. (1978). *Looking in classrooms.* 2d ed. New York: Harper & Row.

Grimm Brothers. (1944). *The Complete Grimm's Fairy Tales.* New York: Pantheon Books.

Hipple, M. L. (1985). Journal writing in kindergarten. *Language Arts* 62 (3): 255/61.

Jung, C. G. (1961). *Memories, dreams, reflections.* New York: Random House.

Jung, C. G., ed. (1964). *Man and his symbols.* New York: Doubleday.

Jung, C. G. (1966). *The practice of psychotherapy.* Trans. R. F. C. Hull. New York: Pantheon Books.

Jung, C. G. (1969). Stages of life. In *The collected works. Structure and dynamics of the psyche.* Princeton, NJ: Princeton University Press.

Jung, C. G. (1970). *Four archetypes: Mother, rebirth, spirit, trickster.* Trans. R. F. C. Hull. Princeton, NJ: Princeton University Press.

Kahnweiler, W. (1979). The school counselor as a consultant: A historical review. *Personnel and Guidance Journal* 57: 374/80.

Kalff, D. (1980). *Sandplay.* Boston: Sigo Press.

Keats, E. (1974). *Dreams.* New York: Macmillan.

Kincher, J. (1988). *Dreams can help: A journal guide to understanding your dreams and making them work for you.* Minneapolis, MN: Free Spirit Publishing.

Kraus, R. (1972). *Leo, the late bloomer.* London: Puffin.

Krell, R. (1987). Divorce: Recognizing the effects on children. *Diagnosis* 4: 12.

Krementz, J. (1984). *How it feels when parents divorce.* New York: Alfred A. Knopf.

Lawson, D. (1987). Using therapeutic stories in the counseling process. *Elementary School Guidance and Counseling* 22: 134/142.

Lincoln, B. (1981). *Emerging from the chrysalis: Studies in women's initiation.* Cambridge, MA: Harvard University Press.

Mad Scientist Dissect-An-Alien™ (1986). Hawthorne, CA 90250: © Mattel Inc.

Martin, R. (1980). *Teaching through encouragement.* Englewood Cliffs, NJ: Prentice-Hall.

Morris, G. B. (1978). The middle school and the child. A paper prepared for the Saskatchewan Joint Committee on the Middle School Years. University of Saskatchewan, Saskatoon.

Neumann, E. (1955). *The great mother*. Trans. R. Manheim. Princeton, NJ: Princeton University Press.

Niehardt, J. (1972). *Black Elk speaks*. New York: Pocket Books.

Nisbet, J., and Entwistle, N. B., eds. (1969). *Transition to secondary education*. Edinburgh: University of London Press.

Noller, R., Parnes, S., and Biondi, A. (1976). *Creative action book*. New York: Scribners.

Offer, D. (1969). *The psychological world of the teenager*. New York: Basic Books.

Orlick, T. (1976). *Cooperative sports and games book*. Toronto: Random House.

Piaget, J. (1948). *The moral judgment of the child*. New York: Free Press.

Podemski, R., and Childers, J. (1980). The counselor as change agent: An organizational analysis. *School Counselor* 27: 33/39.

Progoff, I. (1975). *Attending a journal workshop*. New York: Dialogue House.

Purkey, W. (1978). *Inviting school success: A self-concept approach to teaching and learning*. Belmont, CA: Wadsworth.

Randolph, N., and Howe, W. (1966). *Self-enhancing education*. Palo Alto, CA: Stanford Press.

Riordan, R., and Matheny, K. (1972). Dear diary: Logs in group counseling. *Personnel and Guidance Journal* 50: 379/82.

Rogers, C. R., ed. (1967). *The therapeutic relationship and its impact*. Madison, WI: University of Wisconsin Press.

Salerno, N., and Vanderburgh, R. (1980). *Shaman's daughter*. New York: Dell.

Samuels, A., Shorter, B., and Plaut, F. (1986). *A critical dictionary of Jungian analysis*. London: Routledge and Kegan Paul.

Scarfe, N. (1963). Play in education. *Texas Quarterly* 6: 114/20.

Schmuck, R., and Schmuck, P. (1979). *Group processes in the classroom*. 3rd ed. Dubuque, IA: W. C. Brown.

Schniedewind, N. (1978). Human interaction in the classroom. *Contemporary Education* 49: 215/19.

Schoolcraft, H. (1851). *History, conditions and prospects of the Indian tribes of the United States*. Philadelphia: Lippincott, Grambo and Co.

Schuncke, G., and Bloom, J. (1979). Cooperation as a goal and a tool in the classroom. *Clearing House* 53: 117/22.

Scollay, C. (1980). Arnhem land aboriginals cling to dreamtime. *National Geographic Magazine* 158: 644/63.

Sharp, E. (1978). *Nkwala*. Toronto: McClelland and Stewart.

Simon, S. (1973). *I am lovable and capable: A modern allegory on the classical put-down* [filmstrip]. Niles, IL: Argus Communications.

Stinson, K. (1984). *Mom and Dad don't live together anymore*. Toronto: Annick Press Ltd.

Tanner, J. M. (1970). Physical growth. In *Carmichael's manual of child psychology*, ed. P. H. Mussen. Vol. 1. New York: Wiley.

Tedder, S., Scherman, A., and Wantz, R. (1987). Effectiveness of a support group for children of divorce. *Elementary School Guidance and Counseling* 22: 102/09.

Thompson, C., and Rudolph, L. (1983). *Counseling children.* Monterey, CA: Brooks/Cole Publishing Company.

Turner, V. (1967). *Forest of symbols.* Ithaca: Cornell University Press.

Vacha, E., McDonald, W., Coburn, J., and Black, H. (1979). *Improving classroom social climate.* New York: Holt, Rinehart and Winston.

Van Gennep, A. (1960). *Rites of passage.* London: University of Chicago Press.

Von Franz, M.-L. (1982). *An introduction to the interpretation of fairy tales.* Dallas, TX: Spring Publications.

Waldo, A. (1980). *Sacajawea.* New York: Avon.

Zieman, M. W. (1973). *The first Americans: How people learned to live in North America.* Toronto: McClelland and Stewart.

Zolotow, C. (1963). *The quarreling book.* New York: Harper & Row.

Books about Childhood and Families

Inscapes of the Child's World
Jungian Counseling in Schools and Clinics   JOHN ALLAN

The fruit of over twenty years of clinical work with children—"normal" ones as well as those abused and terminally ill—this award-winning book describes different ways to use art. Rooted in Jung's theory of the regenerative ability of psyche, Allan's approach is pragmatic and sensitive. The drawings, paintings, and writings by children open a profound dimension of their suffering and strength. (235 pp.)

The Cult of Childhood   GEORGE BOAS

Could our fascination with our early years and the issues of child abuse, abortion, and family therapy mean that we are caught in a myth of ideal purity and innocence? Innocence, rather than the true nature of children, may be a fond fantasy about them. By examining the *idea* of childhood, Boas exposes the buried assumptions that continue to influence nearly everything we do and say about children. (120 pp.)

Rosegarden and Labyrinth   SEONAID M. ROBERTSON

A classic work in art education by one of the field's most thoughtful practitioners. With care and precision Seonaid Robertson explores the relationship between art and psyche. Focusing on the drawings of children and adolescents, she views these first products of the imagination against the background of artistic and cultural history. Illustrations, index. (xxix, 216 pp.)

Broodmales   NOR HALL, WARREN R. DAWSON

Men becoming women? In the folk customs of couvade, a man takes on the events of a woman's body—pregnancy, labor, nursing—so that her experience becomes his. Rather bizarre than perverse or deluded, these behaviors reveal a natural symbolic process, which Hall's essay explains psychologically. Dawson's classic cross-cultural study gathers evidence for what often still occurs today in men's private experiences. (173 pp.)

Fathers and Mothers   BLY, HILLMAN, JUNG ET AL.

Twelve chapters break old habits of thinking about family. Robert Bly and James Hillman on the agonies of father-son love; Ursula K. Le Guin's Persephonic prose poem; Marion Woodman on changes in the mother image during analysis; the stepmother; the mothering of desire. The classic essay by Erich Neumann on matriarchal moon consciousness and C. G. Jung's original 1938 "The Mother Archetype." (259 pp.)

SPRING PUBLICATIONS, INC.   P.O. BOX 222069   DALLAS, TEXAS 75222